IMAGES of America

MARION ART CENTER

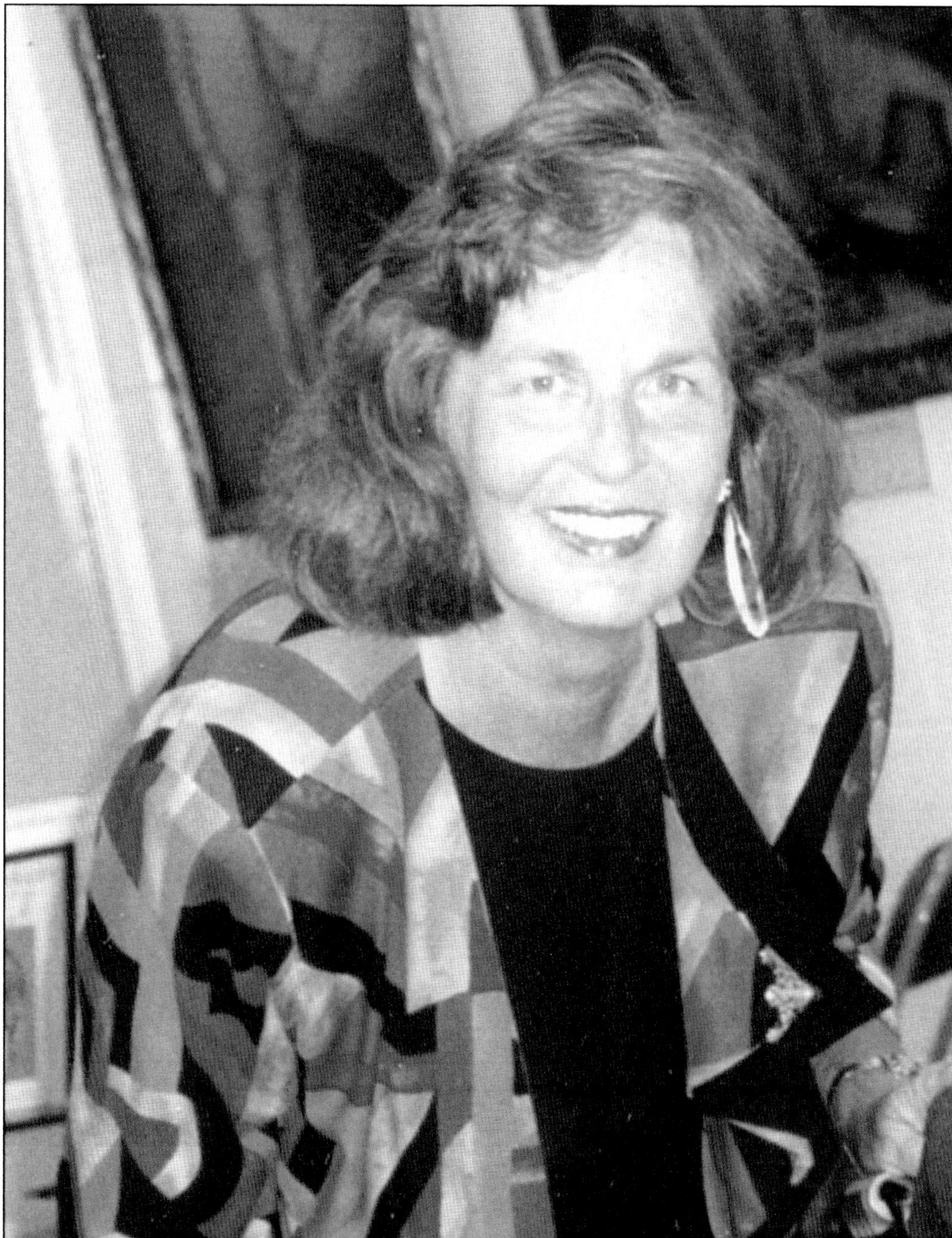

Wendy Bidstrup has been the executive director of the Marion Art Center since 1985.

On the cover: Please see page 9. (Photograph by Hollywood Studio, Alfred R. Gonsalves, New Bedford, Massachusetts; courtesy of the Marion Art Center.)

IMAGES
of America

MARION ART CENTER

Judith Westlund Rosbe

ARCADIA
PUBLISHING

ISBN 978-0-7385-4981-1

Published by Arcadia Publishing
Charleston SC, Chicago IL, Portsmouth NH, San Francisco CA

Printed in the United States of America

Library of Congress Catalog Card Number: 2006938419

For all general information contact Arcadia Publishing at:
Telephone 843-853-2070
Fax 843-853-0044
E-mail sales@arcadiapublishing.com
For customer service and orders:
Toll-Free 1-888-313-2665

Visit us on the Internet at www.arcadiapublishing.com

For my grandson William James Vrattos, born June 29, 2004.

CONTENTS

ACKNOWLEDGMENTS

Most of the images in this book are from the Marion Art Center's files. Six years after the art center was founded in August 1957, Wendy Bidstrup moved to Marion. She had recently graduated from Wells College with a major in art history, married Larry Bidstrup, and came to Marion in the fall of 1963 when Larry accepted a teaching position at Tabor Academy in its history department. Because of her interests in art and the theater, she joined the art center and became an active volunteer. She has played many roles as a volunteer; longtime member of the board of directors, Exhibition Committee, and Theater Committee; president; the founder of Art Camp in 1985; composer of the "Art Camp Alma Mater;" director of 17 plays; producer of most theatrical productions; occasional performer and lecturer; and curator of the permanent collection of the portraits by Cecil Clark Davis. I would not have been able to write this book without Wendy's assistance. She diligently kept files of all the theater productions, art gallery shows and the other various activities at the art center.

Early organizers of the art center also assisted me with their recollections: Aileen and Hilliard "Hilly" Lubin (who now live in Maine), Betty Prewitt Dyer (who now lives in California), and Katy Babbitt (who still lives in Marion). Landis Major photographed many of the Cecil Clark Davis portraits for me, and my neighbor Gary Grainger provided me with technical assistance when I thought that I had accidentally deleted all of the photographs that I had scanned into my computer. He rushed over and miraculously found them all somewhere. I am also grateful for many others who assisted me with this project to record the first 50 years of the Marion Art Center. The center is a very important part of our community, and this book celebrates its first 50 years from 1957 to 2007.

—Judith Westlund Rosbe
Member of the Board of Directors, Marion Art Center

INTRODUCTION

The Marion Art Center was officially incorporated in August 1957. Prior to that time, two endeavors were undertaken by Marion townspeople that officially joined to form the Marion Art Center. One group was the Hornblowers, which consisted of young members of St. Gabriel's Episcopal Church in Marion. The Reverend John J. Albert was very interested in the theater and formed a group of actors to put on plays in the summer as a fund-raiser for the church. They were held at the Music Hall, a building donated to the town of Marion by Elizabeth Taber, an early town benefactor. Katy and Ted Babbit Jr. and Hilliard "Hilly" Lubin were early actors with the Hornblowers, who put on *You Can't Take It with You*, *Arsenic and Old Lace*, *Ten Little Indians*, and *My Three Angels* to benefit St. Gabriel's Church.

Meanwhile, friends Betty Prewitt and Aileen Lubin (wife of Hilly Lubin), acknowledged that Marion was a wonderful place to bring up children, but that artistic activities were missing. They decided to put on an art show in the summer of 1956 and secured permission to use an empty lot across from St. Gabriel's Church for it. They called it the Clothes Line Exhibit, and there was so much interest that they were encouraged to proceed with more art shows.

The local Universalist church and rectory next door, located on the corner of Main and Pleasant Streets and built in 1830, had remained empty for many years after membership dwindled and the church was closed. Andrew and Dorothy Patterson of Marion decided to purchase the property, which included the church and rectory, so that the foreman of their plant could live in the rectory. The Prewitts, Lubins, and Babbitts spent an evening together and decided to approach the Pattersons and offer to fix up the church if they could rent it for $1 a year in order to form an art center to put on plays and hold art exhibits. The Pattersons agreed, and thus began the Marion Art Center in 1957.

Volunteer work crews fixed up, cleaned, and painted the church. The volunteers approached many local hardware stores and asked for donations of paint. They mixed all the paint into a large barrel and the resulting color was a gray that they called "hardware gray." Ted Babbitt Jr.'s family company donated a furnace for the building. Everyone pitched in, including young children, to help make the building work as an art center for the town.

Officers and directors were elected in August 1957. Parker Converse, Hilliard Lubin, and Dr. James Lincoln were elected for a term of one year. Betty Prewitt, Patsy Francis, and George Carrington were elected for a term of two years. Thelma Sequeira, Aileen Lubin, and Jane Beaton were elected for three years. The officers elected were president, Aileen Lubin; vice president, Betty Prewitt; treasurer, Dorothy Patterson; and secretary, Priscilla Chandler.

The first major production put on by the Marion Art Center's theater group was Arthur Miller's *View from the Bridge*, directed by Hilliard Lubin. It was such a success that the actors were asked to bring it to a summer theater in Little Compton, Rhode Island, for a week's run. The art center theater group also served as a training ground for amateur actors, actresses, behind-the-scenes workers, and directors. They decided to put on a minimum of three plays per year of different types: drama, comedy, and avant-garde. They also added musicals, melodramas, and one-act plays. In the early years, plays by Noel Coward, George Bernard Shaw, Anton Chekhov, Arthur Miller, Tennessee Williams, Peter Shaffer, Samuel Beckett, and Edward Albee were produced, providing variety to many groups of theatergoers. During the early years of the art center, it also offered a wide variety of arts and crafts classes for the benefit of both adults and children.

In 1964, a newly appointed board of directors decided that the building was in need of major repairs. As a result, a drive got under way to raise $10,000 to purchase the building (with a mortgage) and to make necessary building improvements. To the delight of everyone, the $10,000 was raised in a single year. New members were added to the rolls and the new Cecil Clark Davis Gallery was opened on August 13, 1964.

Cecil Clark Davis was Marion's most prominent artist. Her family, the John Marshall Clarks, lived in Chicago and spent the summers in Marion. Cecil was born in Chicago in 1877. Her father was a successful businessman and was a partner with Alexander Graham Bell. He was also collector for the Port of Chicago during the 1893 World's Columbian Exposition. Cecil was a teenager at that time and must have seen the great "white city" being built and decorated by the top architects and artists in America. The sculptor, Augustus St. Gaudens once exclaimed, "Do you realize that this is the greatest assembling of artists since the Renaissance!"

In 1898, the Clark family stopped staying at the grand old Sippican Hotel in Marion and purchased "the house in the lane" (now called Water Street), a large, rambling 23-room cottage on 10 acres of waterfront land. The Davises from Philadelphia were their summer neighbors. Richard Harding Davis, the famous war reporter, novelist, and playwright at the beginning of the 20th century, attended dances at the casino across from the Sippican Hotel and noticed the beautiful Cecil Clark, whose mother played the piano for the dances. Richard was 35 years old and Cecil was 21. Richard was very handsome and was the most sought after man in America. Booth Tarkington wrote, "His stalwart good looks were as familiar to us as were those of our own football captain; we know the face of the President of the United States, but we infinitely preferred Davis's. . . . When we went to the Waldorf to see the world at lunch in its new magnificence, and Richard Harding Davis came into the Palm Room, then, oh then, our day was radiant! Of all the great people of every continent, this was the one we most desired to see."

Cecil epitomized the American girl: she was beautiful, independent, athletic, talented, bold, and adventurous. She resembled the heroines in some of Davis's novels: "She was tall, slim with brave, boyish eyes; someone who could understand what you were trying to say before you said it. She nurtures a man's finer instincts, but does not arouse his feverish ardor. She is, in short, his best and noblest friend."

Their wedding at St. Gabriel's chapel on May 4, 1899, was an international event. Ethyl Barrymore was maid of honor. Charles Dana Gibson was a groomsman. The Gibsons were lifelong friends and Davis was often the model for the perfect escort for the "Gibson girl." Cecil and Richard traveled all over the world. They lived in London and Paris and when Richard was assigned to cover the Boer War in Africa, Cecil went with him. Thus began the pattern of their life together, traveling wherever his assignments took him—to South Africa, England, Spain, and Russia for the coronations of Edward VII, Alfonso XII, and Nicholas II, then on to Japan to report on another war. They rented houses with studio space for Cecil. In London, she became friendly with John Singer Sargent and wrote in her diary about these meetings. Richard wrote to his mother, "Imagine the nerve of Cecil calling the world famous portrait painter to ask for advice!"

After 13 years of marriage, in which it was rumored that they lived only as brother and sister, Richard asked for a divorce and married 19-year-old Bessie McCoy, the "Yama Yama Girl," in 1912. After that, Cecil devoted herself to her painting and to her large number of dogs. She died at the age of 78 in 1955. The Marion Art Center is proud to own many of Cecil's paintings in its permanent collection.

—Judith Westlund Rosbe

One

THEATER

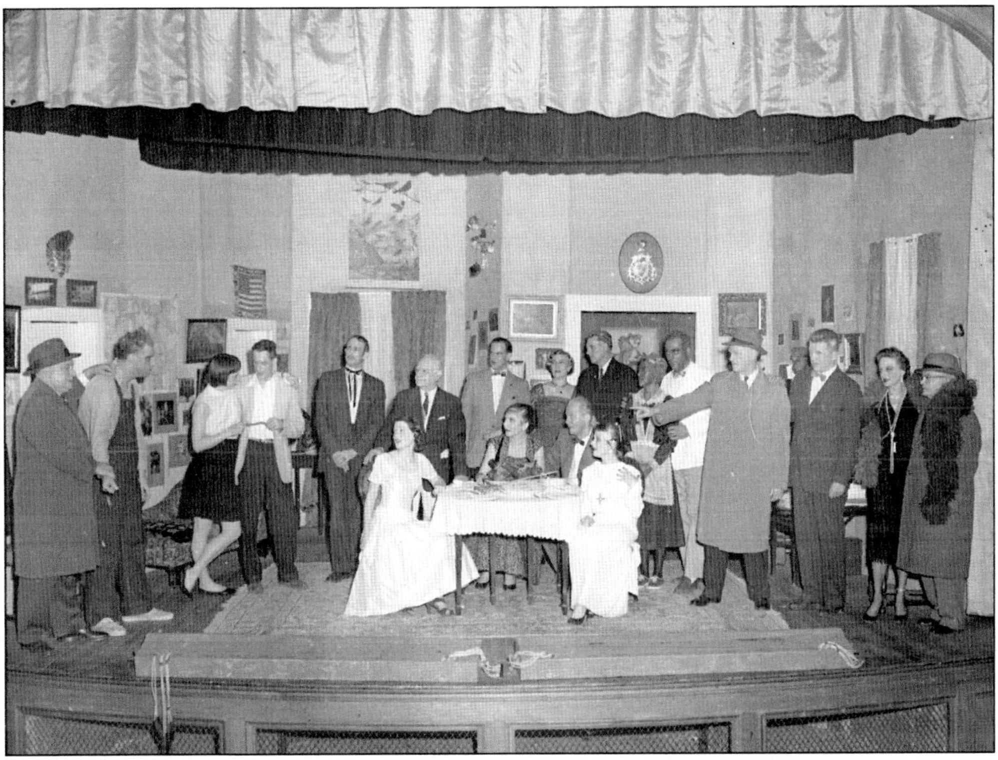

Members of St. Gabriel's Episcopal Church formed a group called the Hornblowers to put on plays as a fund-raiser for the church. Rev. John J. Albert directed the play put on at the Music Hall in Marion, *You Can't Take It with You*, in 1955. Shown from left to right are (first row) Katheryn Babbitt, Marilyn Heikoff, Frantz Warner, and Minna Andres; (second row) Al Query, Peter Freedman, Sue Roche, Ted Babbitt Jr., Hilliard Lubin, Rev. Lawrence Somers, James Babbitt, Audrey Goodwin, Brooks Hawkins, Mary Betty Albert, Robert Snyder, Dr. Ray Baxter, Warren Ide, Alys Nowell, and Dr. James Arne.

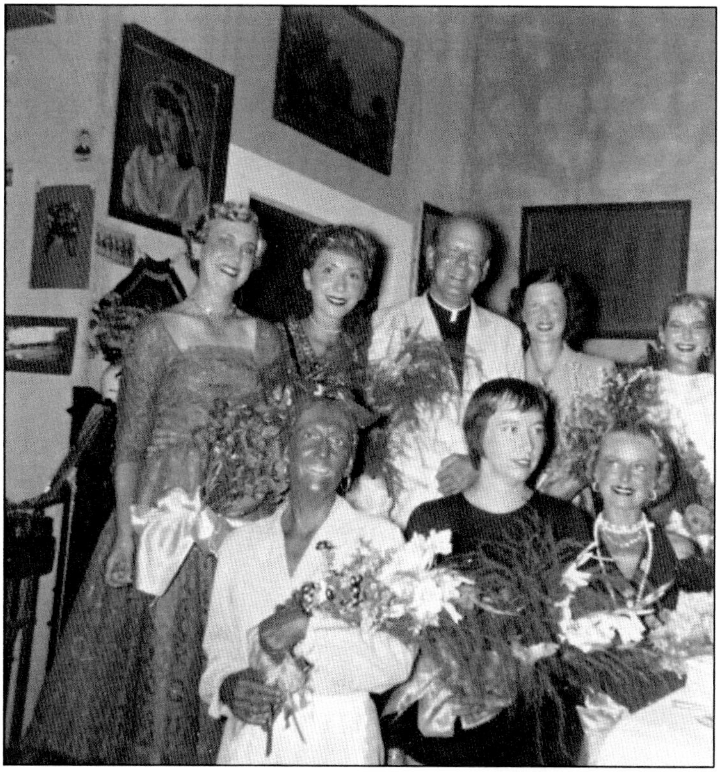

The ladies in the cast of *You Can't Take It with You* pose with Rev. John J. Albert. The Hornblowers group included the Lubins and Babbitts, who were instrumental in founding the Marion Art Center in 1957. The comedic play by George S. Kaufman and Moss Hart opened in New York on December 14, 1936, and won a Pulitzer prize.

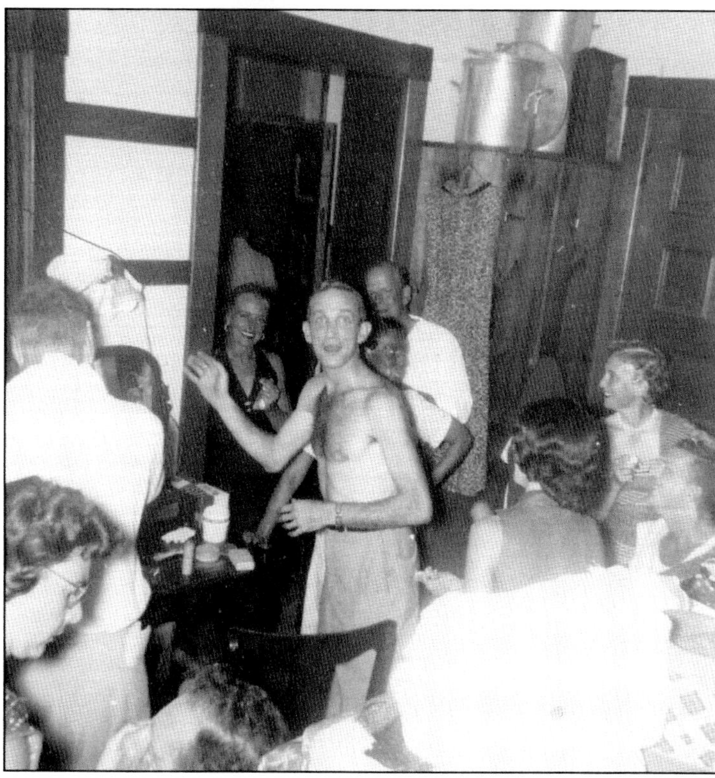

This snapshot was taken back stage of *You Can't Take It with You.* Hilly Lubin is the man without a shirt on.

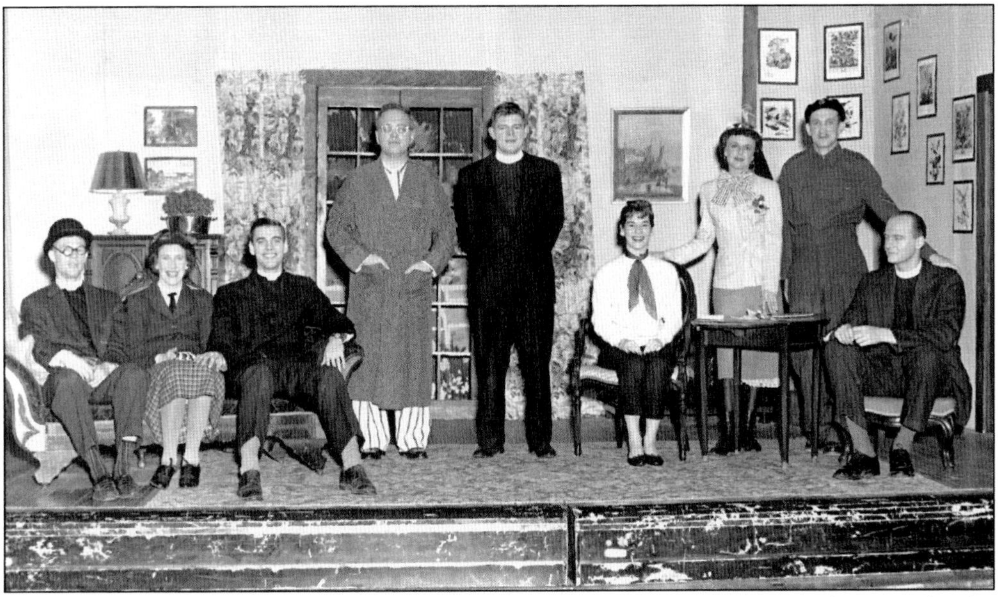

Another early production of the Hornblowers was the stage farce *See How They Run*, by the British playwright Philip King. This popular British comedy was written in 1945 about the comings and goings of clerics in an English vicarage during World War II, one of whom was an escaped Nazi prisoner-of-war in disguise. The cast, from left to right, includes Ted Babbitt Jr., Peggy Dyer, Winthrop Baylies, Don Durfee, John Albert, Alys Nowell, Moma Andres, Hilly Lubin, and Franz Warner.

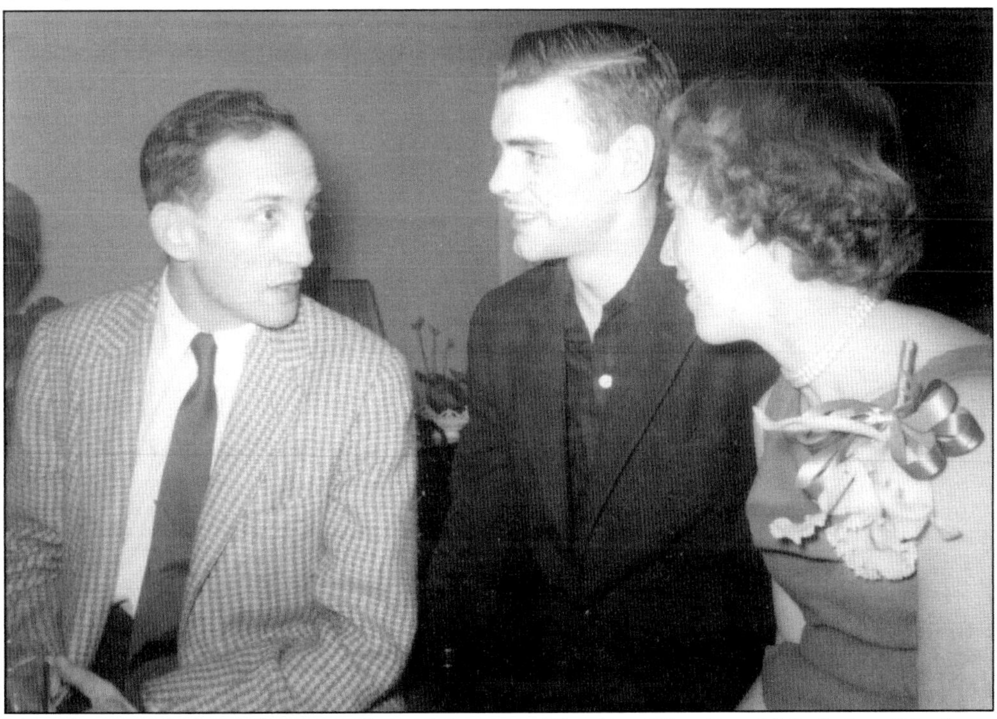

This photograph shows three members of the cast of *See How They Run*: Hilly Lubin, Winthrop Baylies, and Peggy Dyer.

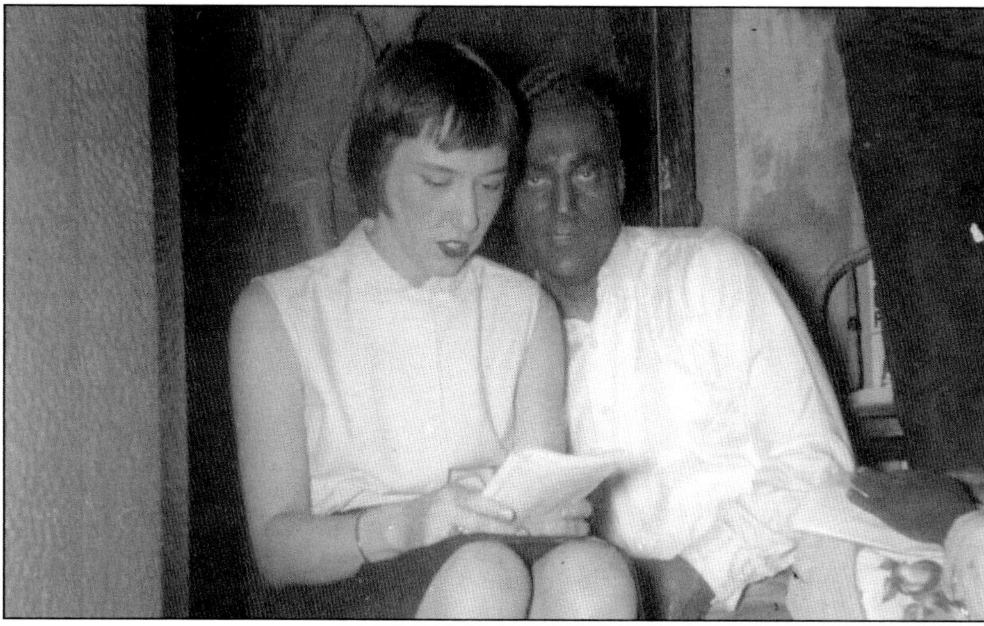

The Hornblowers also put on the play, *Arsenic and Old Lace*, a dark comedy by American playwright Joseph Kesselring, written in 1939. Two spinster aunts of the main character have taken to murdering lonely old men by poisoning them with a glass of home-made elderberry wine laced with arsenic. This photograph shows Sue Roche and Bob Snyder, two members of the cast.

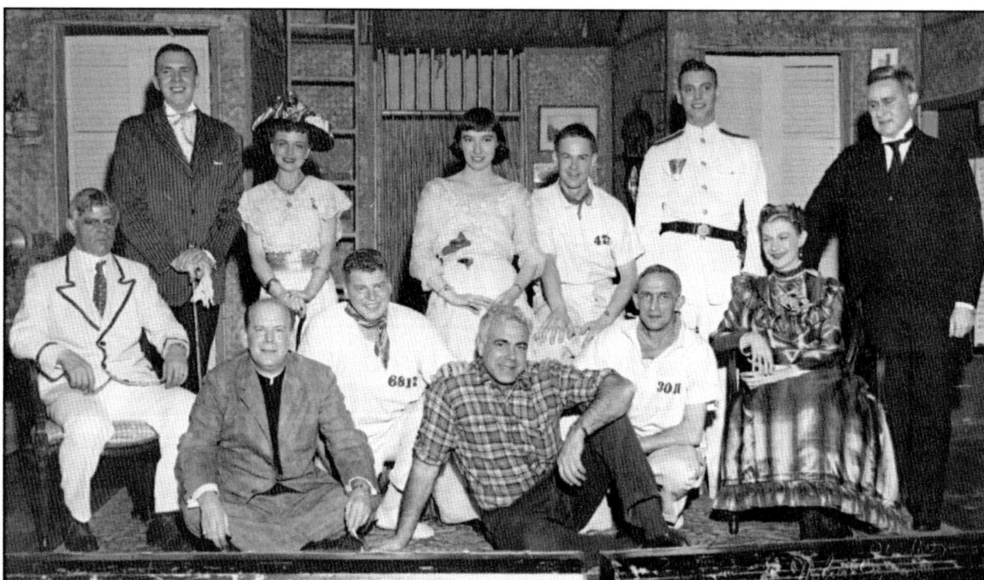

In 1957, the Hornblowers put on the play, *My Three Angels*, a comedy written by Samuel Spewack and Bella Spewack, which is set in the penal colony on Cayenne, French Guiana, in 1910. The three angels are actually convicts who assist the family who owns the general store. This photograph shows, from left to right, (first row) director Rev. John Albert and Rick Angle; (second row) Don Durfee, Dick Peters, Hilly Lubin, and Ellie Freedman; (third row) Clayton Livingston, Alys Nowell, Sue Roche, Ted Babbitt Jr., Winthrop Baylies, and Jack Somers.

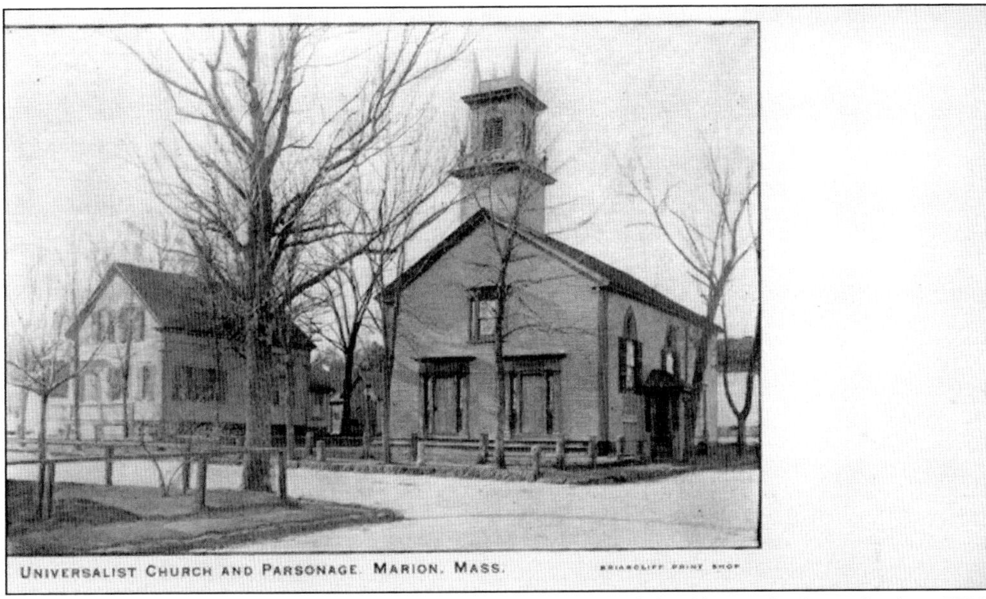

The Marion Art Center initially rented the Universalist church building, which was built in 1830, from the Pattersons who purchased the church and the rectory next door from the Universalist Church. The church and rectory had remained empty for many years. The Pattersons purchased the property so that the foreman at their plant could live in the rectory next door. The initial rent for the church building for the first year was only $1 in exchange for volunteers agreeing to fix up the building.

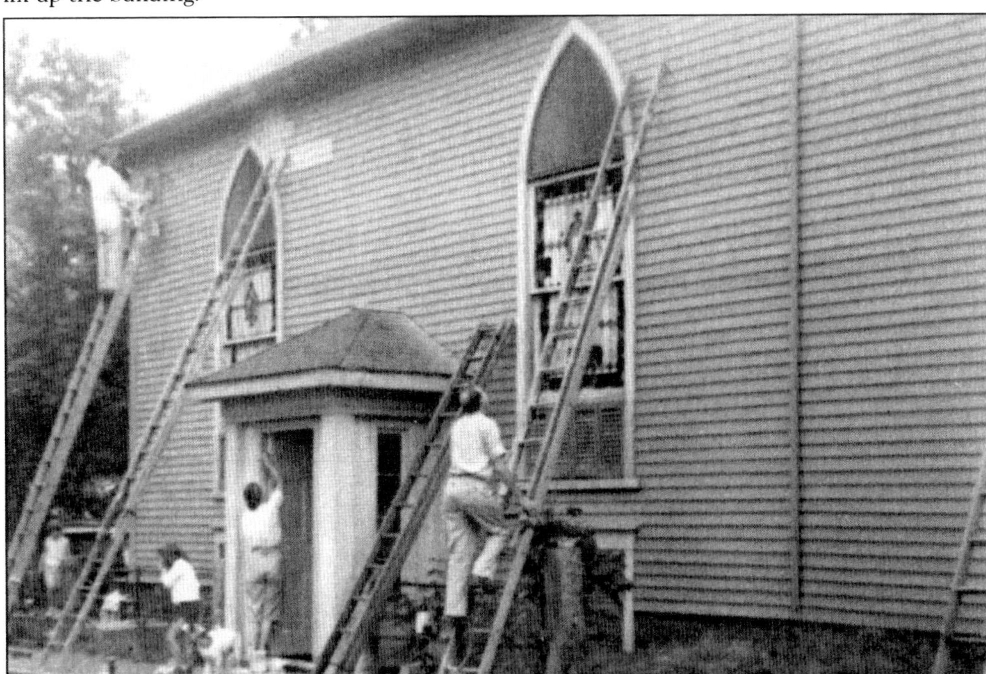

The first meeting of the Marion Art Center was held in August 1957. In September, workers volunteered to paint and fix up the building so that the art center could open on October 1, 1957. Plans included a theater, auditorium, gallery, and classrooms for both adults and children.

First Meeting Called To Plan Permanent Marion Art Center

Officers To Be Elected

The first meeting of a permanent art center for Marion, will be held in the Universalist Church Building, corner of Main and Pleasant Sts., Sunday evening at 7:30. The business will include the election of officers and signing of the charter. The meeting is open to Marion residents who are interested in becoming charter members.

Use of the building has been granted for one year by Mr. and Mrs. Andrew Patterson of South St. Work necessary to adapt the building to its proposed use is to commence the second weekend in September and will be on voluntary basis. Committees w be named and projects assigned the meeting Sunday. It is hoped have the building ready for ope ing by Oct. 1.

Present plans include a litt theatre, auditorium, gallery a classrooms, to embrace adu courses in wood carving, actir technique, beginners sculpture a advanced painting, tray paintir and furniture painting, also blo printing and mosaics.

Children's courses will inclu ceramics, painting, drama wor shop and pre-school age story te ing hours.

It is the hope of the promote of this community project that t art center may be used for mus cales, for modern dancing, a other arts and crafts that t people of Marion and surroundi communities request in sufficie numbers, to warrant. Experime tal cinema programs are also co templated.

To quote Mrs. Hilliard Lubi a prime mover in this undertakin "A good working art center only practical when it is used its fullest extent, and will pro successful only through the part cipation of a majority communi residents."

This is a newspaper article in the *Wareham Courier* on August 8, 1957, announcing the first meeting of the Marion Art Center to elect its officers and to sign its charter. Aileen Lubin was quoted in the local *Wareham Courier*, "A good working art center is only practical when it is used to its fullest extent, and will prove successful only through the participation of a majority of community residents." Lubin was elected president; Dorothy Patterson, vice president; and Will Prewitt, chairman of the building committee.

This Indenture, MADE the Thirtieth day of September in the year of our Lord one thousand nine hundred and fifty-eight

Witnesseth, That We, Andrew N. Patterson and Dorothy B. Patterson, of Marion, Massachusetts, Lessors

do hereby lease, demise, and let unto Marion Art Center Inc., Lessee, of Marion, Massachusetts, the premises located on Pleasant Street corner of Main Street, Marion, Plymouth County, Massachusetts, conisting of the first floor,(closet under stairs in kitchen not included) and basement only.

It is understood and agreed that:

1. The Lessee shall pay all charges for electricity, water, fuel, and telephone (if any) used during the term of this lease.
2. The Lessee shall keep the grounds in good order and condition during the term of this lease.
3. Lessee shall be responsible for rubbish removal and keeping sidewalks around the building as well as the steps cleared of snow.
4. Lessee shall not make any major alterations to the premises (interior or exterior) without the approval of the Lessors.
5. Lessee shall carry a public liability policy during the term of this lease.
6. The Lessee shall have the privilege of renewing this lease for the same term and with the same conditions upon written notice to the Lessors on or before August 1, 1959. If the Lessors do not wish to renew this lease for the same term and with the same conditions, written notice on or before August 1, 1959 shall be given to this effect.

To hold for the term of One Year

from the First day of October nineteen hundred and fifty-eight

yielding and paying therefor the rent of Six hundred (600) dollars.

And said Lessee do promise to pay the said rent in as follows:

Fifty (50) dollars on signing this lease.
Fifty (50) dollars per month in advance beginning November 1, 1958

and to quit and deliver up the premises to the Lessors, or their attorney, peaceably and quietly, at the end of the term, in as good order and condition, reasonable use and wearing thereof, fire and other unavoidable casualties excepted, as the same now are, or may be put in to by the said Lessors, and to pay the rent as above stated, during the term, and also the rent as above stated, for such further time as the Lessee may hold the same, and not make or suffer any waste thereof; nor lease, nor underlet, nor permit any other person or persons to occupy or improve the same, or make or suffer to be made any alteration therein, but with the approbation of the Lessors thereto, in writing, having been first obtained; and that the Lessors may enter to view and make improvements, and to expel the Lessee, if they shall fail to pay the rent as aforesaid, or make or suffer any strip or waste thereof.

And provided also, that in case the premises, or any part thereof during said term, be destroyed or damaged by fire or other unavoidable casualty, so that the same shall be thereby rendered unfit for use and habitation, then, and in such case, the rent hereinbefore reserved, or a just and proportional part thereof, according to the nature and extent of the injuries sustained, shall be suspended or abated until the said premises shall have been put in proper condition for use and habitation by the said Lessor, or these presents shall thereby be determined and ended at the election of the said Lessor or their legal representatives.

In witness whereof, The said parties have hereunto interchangeably set their hands and seals the day and year first above written.

Marion Art Center, Inc.

In 1958, the Marion Art Center renewed its one-year lease of the former Universalist church from the Pattersons for another year for $50 per month.

The Marion Art Center Inc.
Box 602
Marion, Massachusetts
July 19, 1963

Mr. Andrew Patterson
Vine Street
Marion, Massachusetts

Dear Mr. Patterson:

In accordance with our phone conversation of last week, I have checked with the Officers and such Directors as were available on the matter of the rent. It would appear that Mr. Beardsley, in his contacts with you, did not properly express the sense of the vote of the Board of Directors. The position of the Board is that, while the Art Center, as tenant, has an obligation to pay its rent in a prompt manner; that the Landlord, in turn, has an obligation to maintain the premises in suitable condition for its intended uses. We do not feel that this is being done, particularly with respect to the poor condition of the roofing. We deem actions to be better than words. The Board has authorized me, as a show of good faith, to forward you the rent for the month of June 1963, which you wáll find enclosed. We trust you will reciprocate by instituting action on the roof repairs.

The Art Center stands ready and able to continue rental payments when due, however, no further payments will be made until such time as the roof is properly repaired.

We have investigated the other matter which you mentioned and have satisfied ourselves as to the situation. The Marion Police Dept. has no record of or knowledge of the allegations.

Very truly yours,

Treasurer, for the
Board of Directors,
Marion Art Center Inc.

In 1963, relations between the tenant, Marion Art Center, and the landlord, Andrew Patterson, became strained when the Marion Art Center withheld its rent until the landlord repaired the roof. In 1964, Marion Art Center members raised $10,000 and purchased the old Universalist church building from the Pattersons.

MARION ART CENTER PLAYERS

present

TOM JONES

a play based on the novel by

Henry Fielding

Director: MR. LAWRENCE LAMARRE

Richard Foreu
Wallace Keith
Shirley Peach
Katherine Sweeney
Virginia Mower
George Carns
Burt Zukerman
William Shannon
Carol Shannon
Dorothy Brown
Shirley Brown

Mary Alice Sylvia
Lawrence Brooks
Val Campbell
Robert McCabe
Richard Kelloway
Donal Durfee
Jerry Finn
Beverly Knapton
Mary Stedman
Louise Carns

— PERFORMANCES —

December 2, 3, 4, 10, 11

8:30 p.m.

For reservations call:

MRS. DAVID PALAMOUNTAIN	748-1057
MRS. LAWRENCE BROOKS	748-0959
MRS. ROBERT McCABE	993-0036

or write:

MARION ART CENTER, BOX 602, MARION MASS. 02738

In December 1965, the Marion Art Center put on the play *Tom Jones*, based on Henry Fielding's lively novel of the same name.

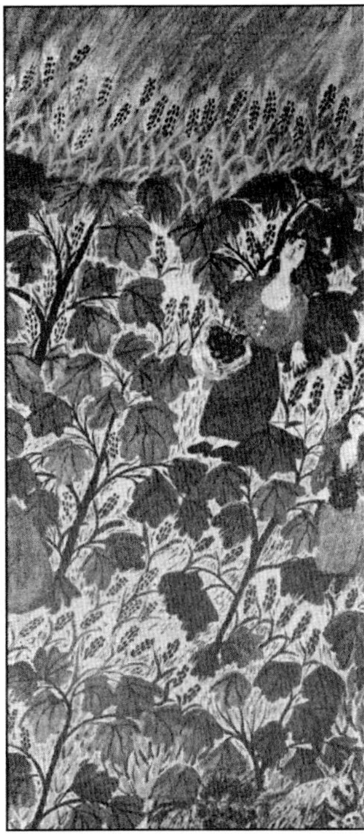

MARION ART CENTER PLAYERS

present

GiGi

A Comedy in Two Acts

by Colette

November 4, 5, 10, 11, 12

8:30 P.M.

Director: Lawrence Lamarre

with

Dagmar Unhoch
Margery Dyer
Faith Thompson
Patricia Demeo
Joan Olsen
Larry Novick
Lawrence Lamarre

For Reservations: Call Marion Art Center 748-1266
Call Mrs. Palamountain 748-1057

Tickets: Non-Members $1.75
Members $1.50

In November 1966, the Marion Art Center presented the comedy *Gigi*, by Colette, which was directed by Lawrence Lamarre.

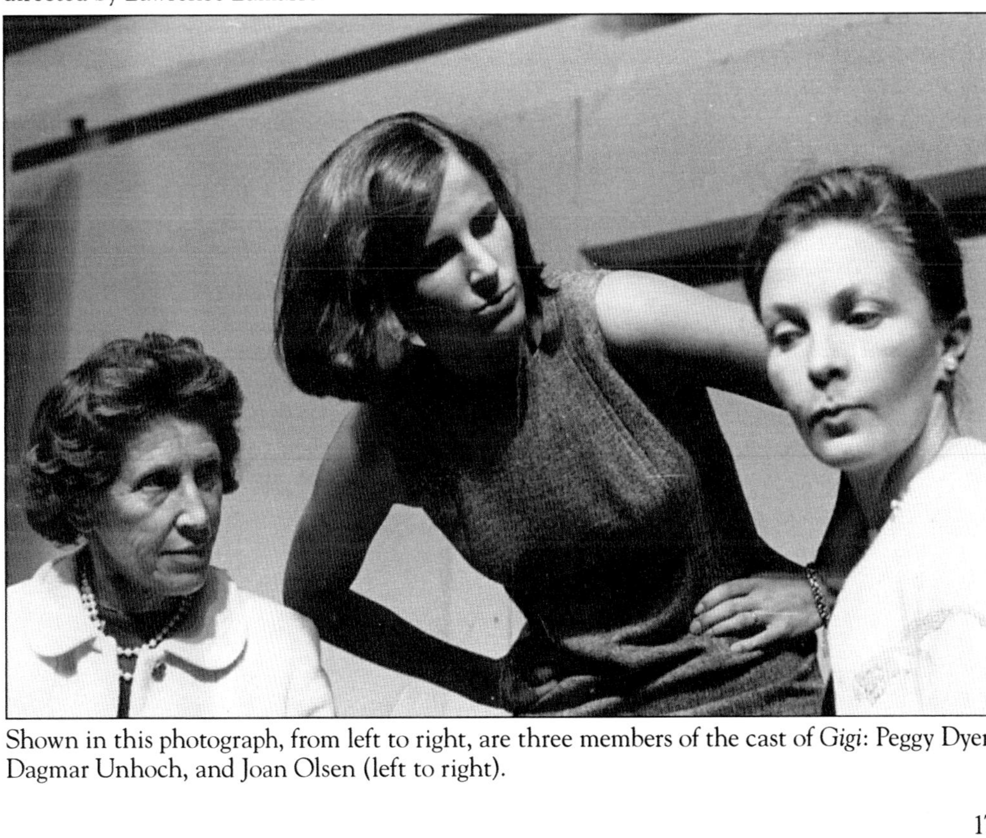

Shown in this photograph, from left to right, are three members of the cast of *Gigi*: Peggy Dyer, Dagmar Unhoch, and Joan Olsen (left to right).

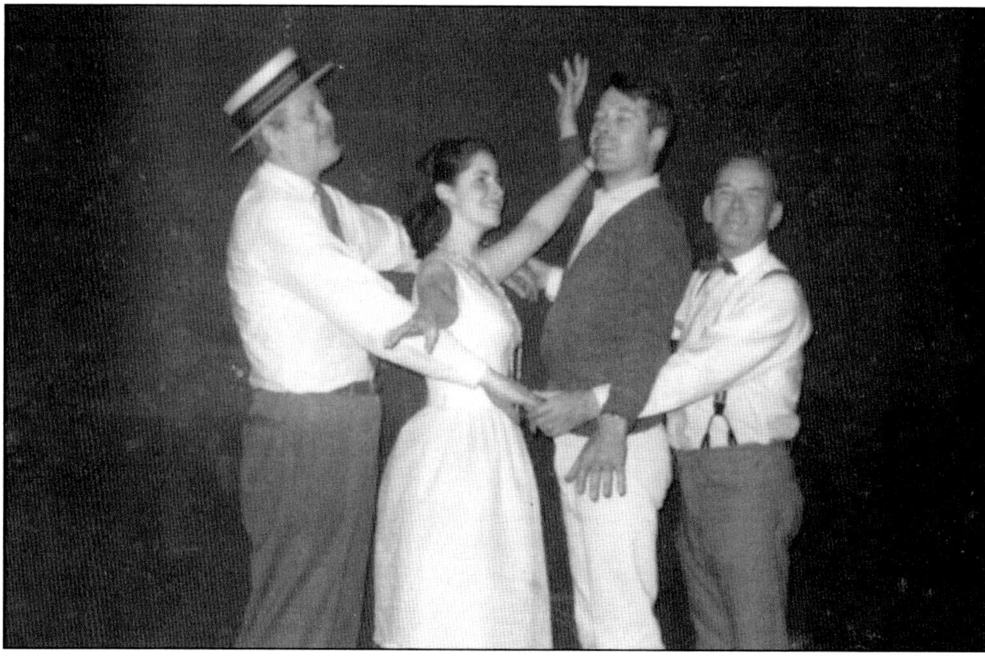

The Marion Art Center has presented the popular musical comedy *The Fantasticks*, many times. The first presentation occurred in 1967 and was directed by Dick Foren. This photograph shows, from left to right, Bill Poor, the Girl's Father; Susie Richardson, the Girl; Ed Roberts, the Boy; and George Keith, the Boy's Father.

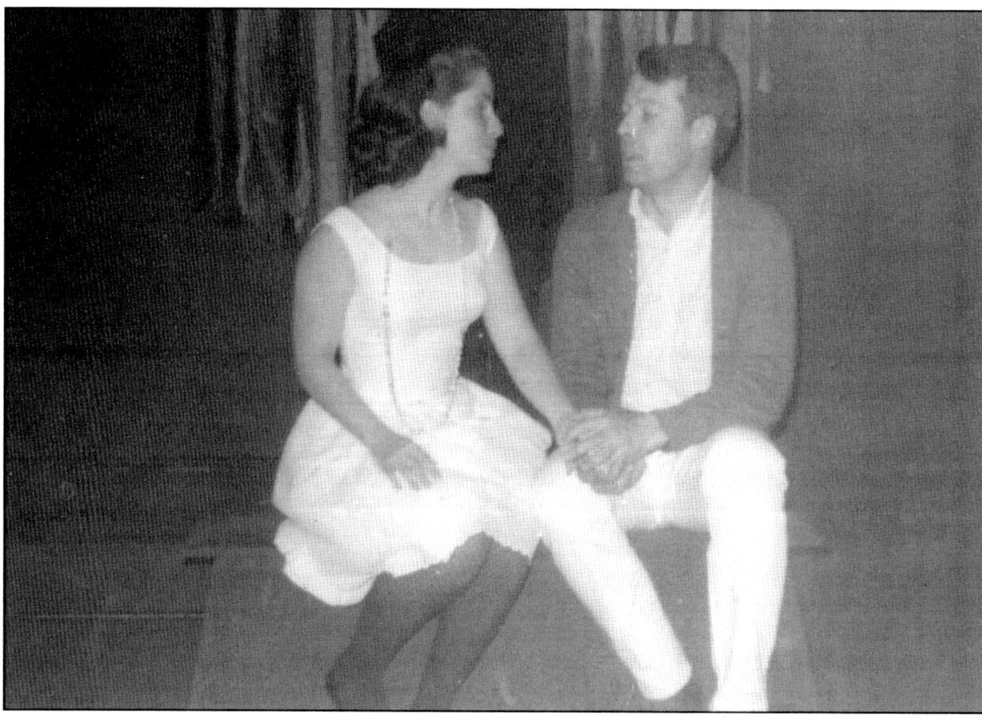

Sue Richardson, the Girl, and Ed Roberts, the Boy, hold hands in this photograph from the art center's archives.

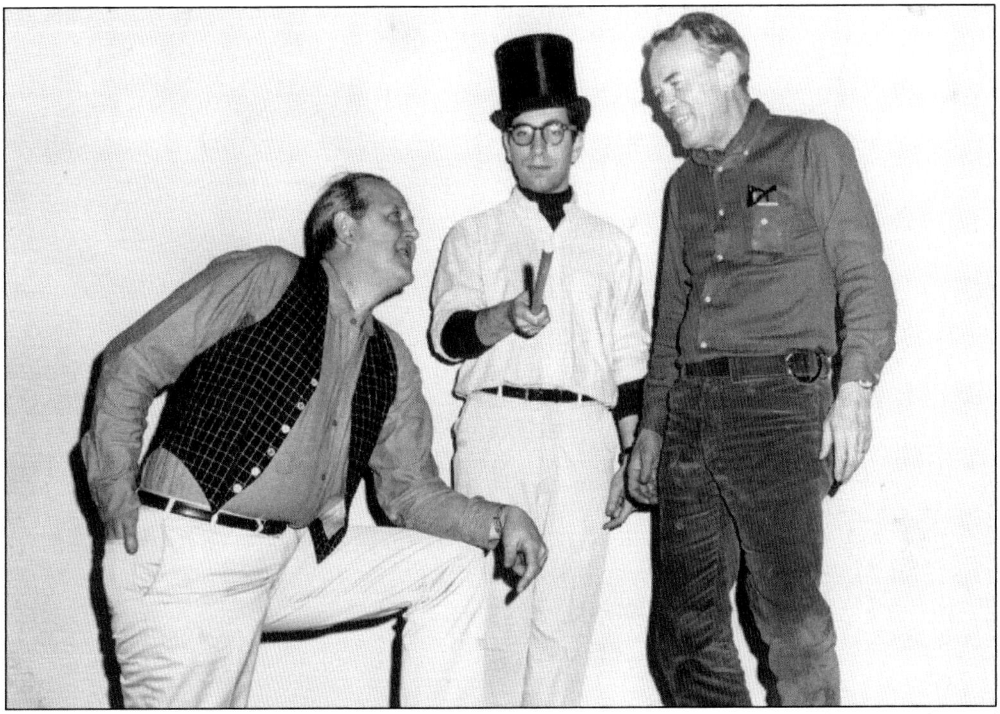

The Fantasticks was also presented again in 1968. Shown from left to right are three members of the cast: Bill Poor, Don Fried, and George Keith.

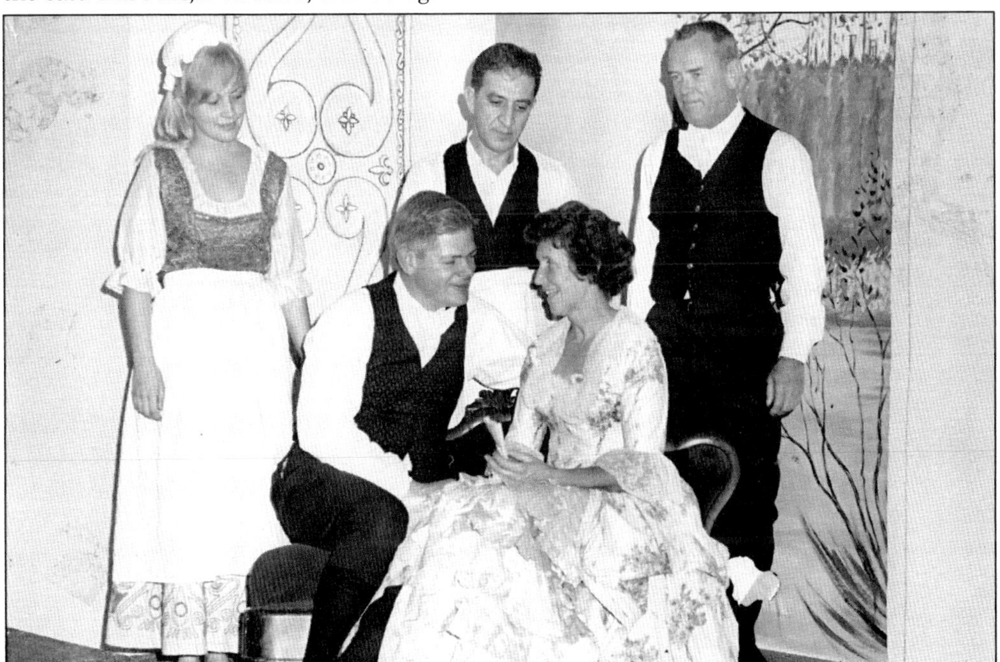

In 1967, the art center put on the 1668 ridiculous comedy of manners, *The Miser*, by the French playwright Moliere. Shown here are cast members (first row) Don Durfee and Peggy Dyer; (second row) Peggy Doran, Peter Roy, and George Keith.

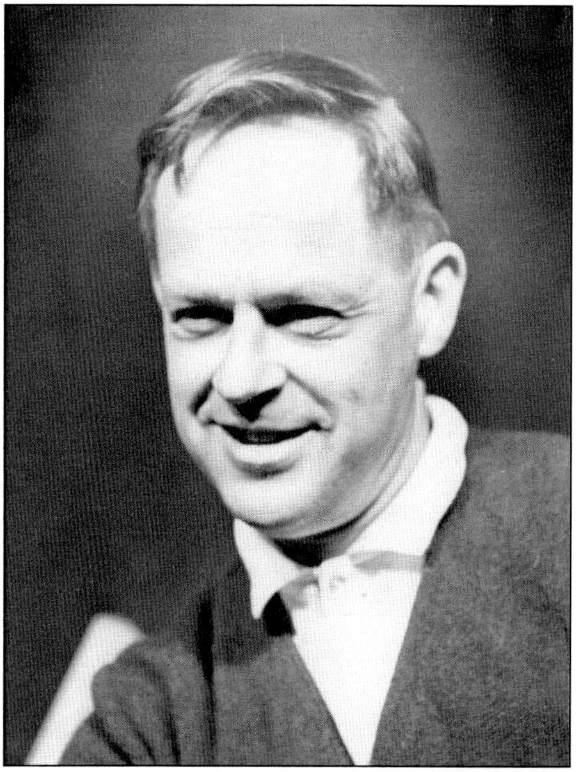

The Odd Couple was presented in 1968 at the Marion Art Center. The 1965 Broadway production by Neil Simon was directed by Mike Nichols and starred Walter Matthau and Art Carney. The plot concerns two mismatched roommates, one uptight and the other slovenly. Ted Babbitt Jr. is shown here as Oscar Madison, the slovenly recently divorced sportswriter.

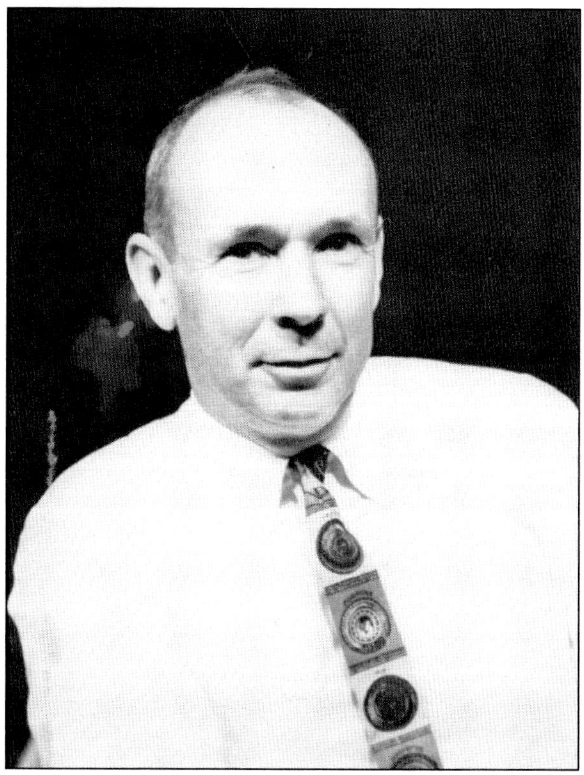

Larry Brooks played Felix Unger, a fastidious, hypochondriac news writer whose marriage was ending. The play was directed by Lawrence Lamarre.

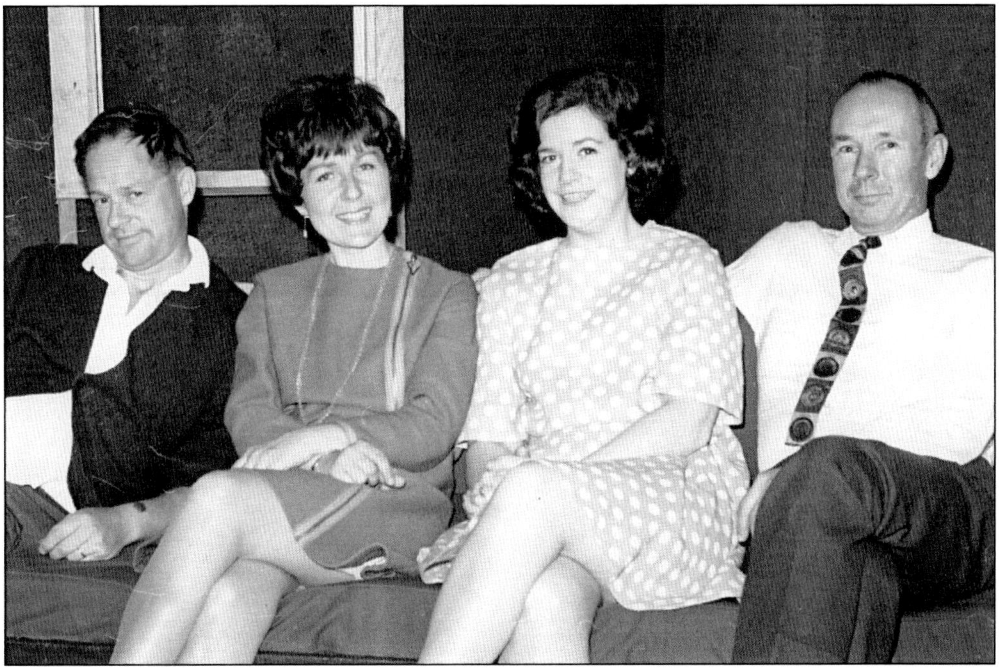

This photograph shows members of *The Odd Couple* cast. From left to right they are Ted Babbitt Jr., Joan Prescott, Gail Swain, and Larry Brooks.

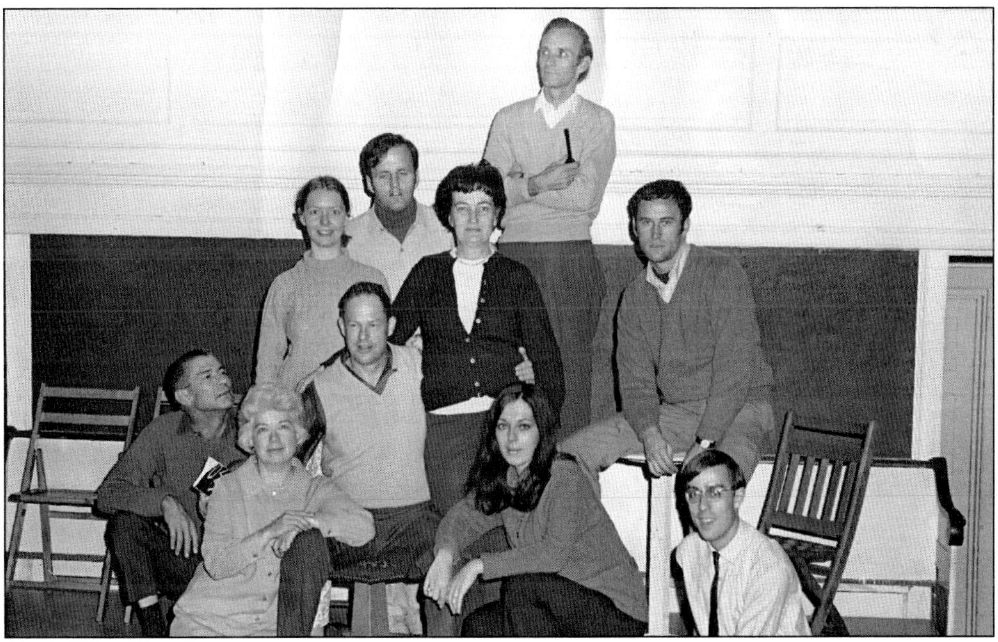

In 1970, the Marion Art Center presented *Under Milk Wood* by Dylan Thomas, which he wrote originally as a radio play first recorded in 1945. In 1954, the BBC recorded the stage play. The cast of the Marion Art Center's production includes, from left to right, (first row) Vivian Robb, Mary Tchakirides, and David Timms; (second row) Tom Meier, Ted Babbitt Jr., Kay Sweeney, and Mac Nyborg; (third row) Joyce Russe, Tim Walsh, and Jim Carr. The play was directed by Bill Tchakirides.

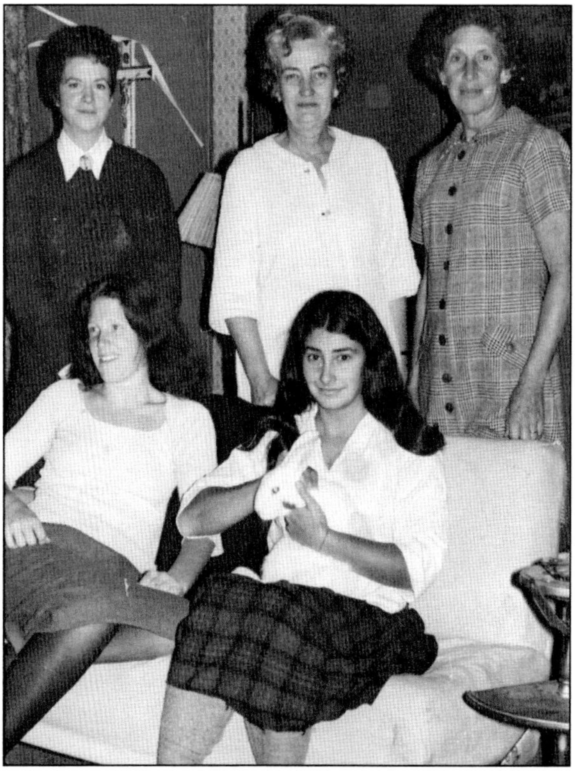

The Effect of Gamma Rays on Man-in-the-Moon Marigolds was presented by the Marion Art Center in 1973 and directed by Nancylee Gaucher. The Pulitzer prize–winning play was written by Paul Zindel and first produced in 1964. The play involved an embittered single mother whose husband had left her. Her daughter's science experiment showed that marigolds exposed to gamma rays (radiation) were sometimes killed, but sometimes they grew even more beautiful. Shown here is the cast, from left to right: (first row) C. C. Dyer and Kim Barry; (second row) Gail Swain, Kay Sweeney, and Peggy Dyer.

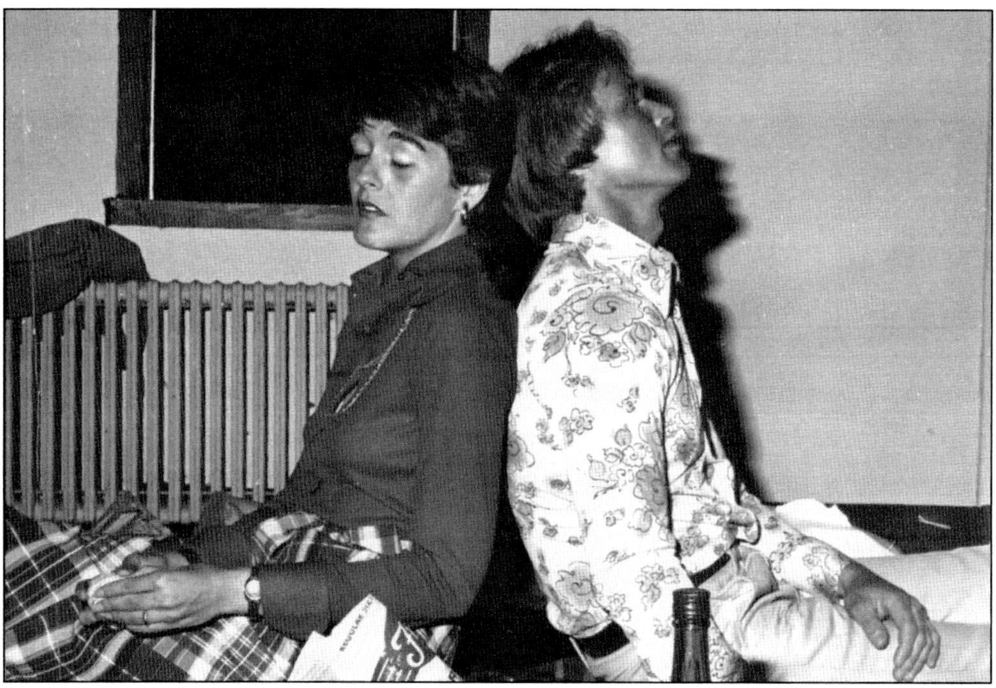

In 1977, the Marion Art Center presented the play, *6 Rms Riv Vu*, written by Bob Randall, which was first produced in 1972. The title describes a six-room apartment overlooking the Hudson River on Riverside Drive in Manhattan. Shown here are Karen Chase and Jim Bruce.

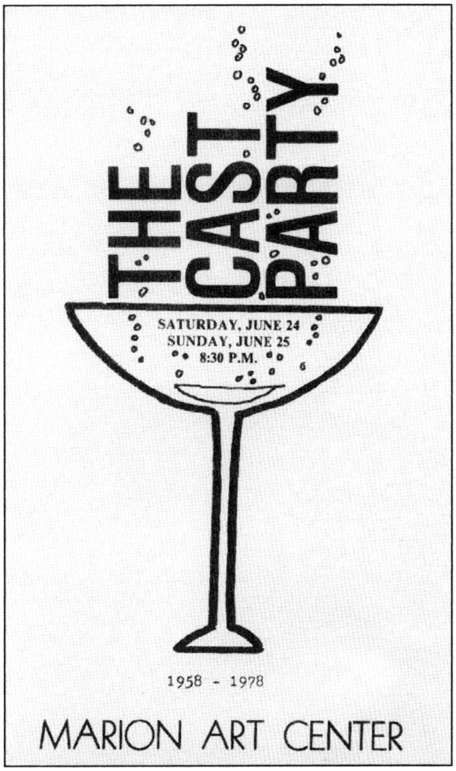

In 1978, The Marion Art Center presented "The Cast Party," an evening of short presentations from prior theater productions at the art center from 1958–1978. Original cast members came from afar to reenact scenes, and it was a wonderful reunion of most of the original casts. The evening was wildly successful. Shown here are members of the chorus of *Cabaret* (1974): Sarah Brown, Joan Roller, Wendy Bidstrup, Anna Silipo, Daphne Hubbard, Ann Martin, and Bill Bradford.

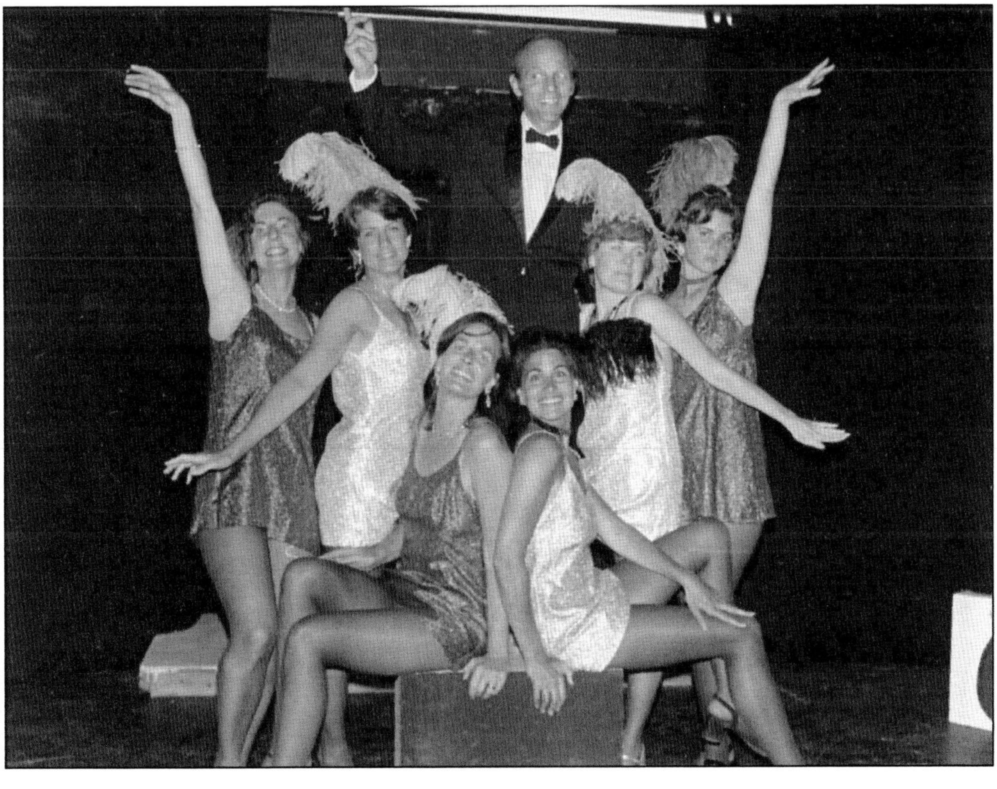

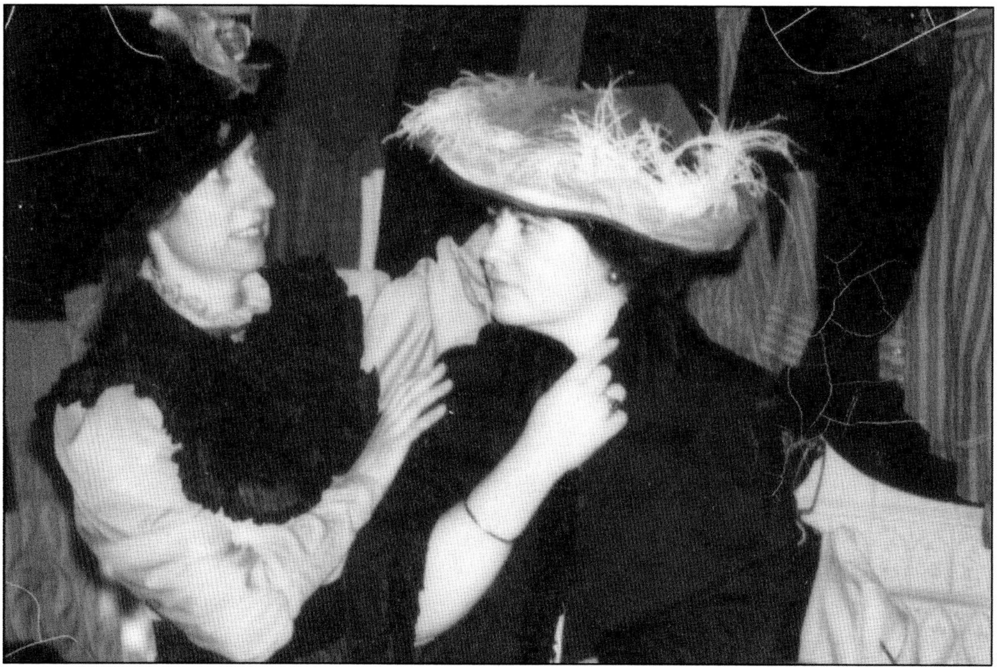

In 1978, the Marion Art Center presented *The Threepenny Opera* by Bertolt Brecht, a musical comedy written in 1928 as a socialist critique of the capitalist world. Shown here are Sarah Brown (left) and Mary Alice Sylvia.

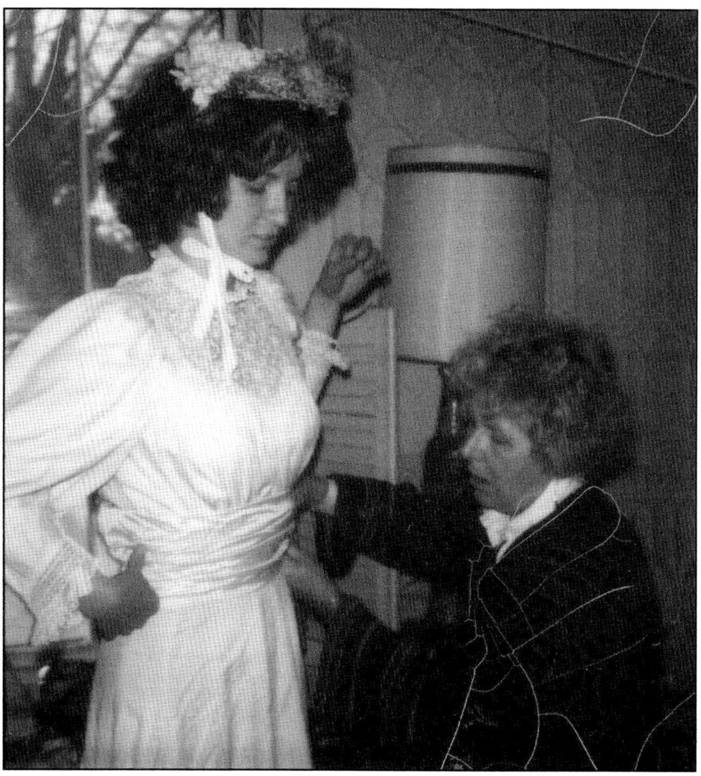

Karen Chase's costume is being fitted by Patricia Finn for the musical *The Threepenny Opera*. Pat Finn studied costume design at Yale's Drama School and worked as a professional costume designer before moving to Marion. She not only lent her expertise to many of the Marion Art Center's theater productions, she was also a major force in fund-raising efforts to renovate the building.

Play It Again, Sam by Woody Allen was also presented in 1978 at the Marion Art Center. The plot involved a recently-divorced Allan Felix, who was encouraged to go out with women again and received advice from Humphrey Bogart, which no one else could hear. The ending was a parody of *Casablanca's* famous ending. Howard Purdy played the ghost of Humphrey Bogart (Bogey). The Marion Art Center's production was directed by Karen Chase.

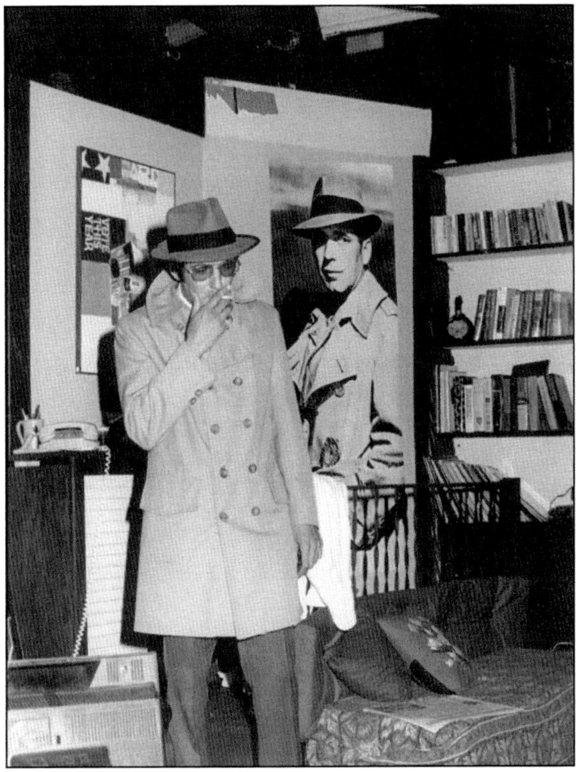

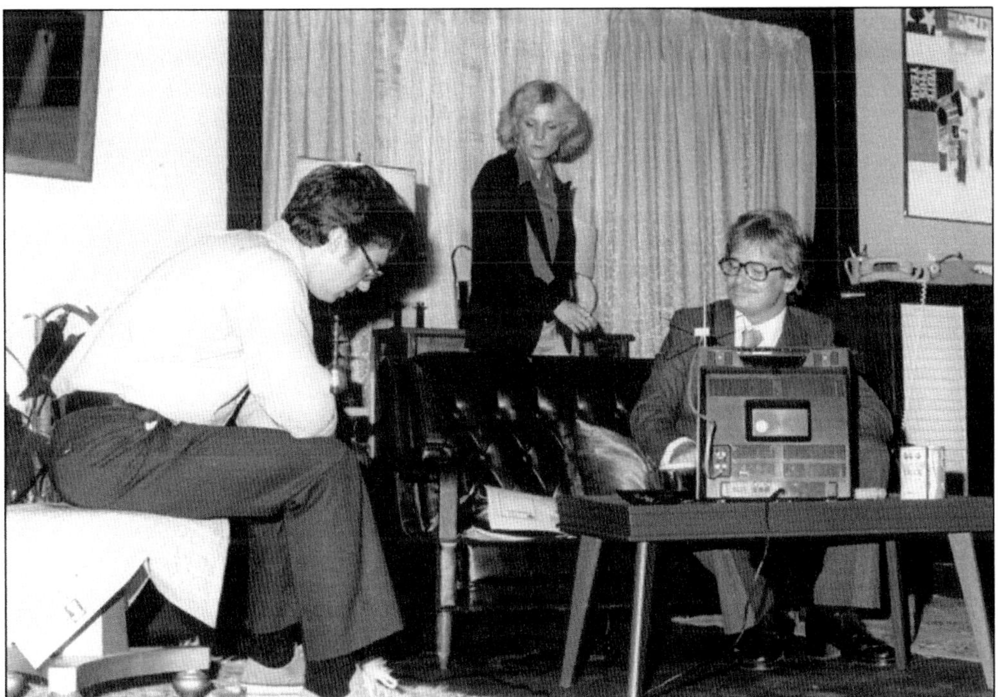

Chris Gaucher (left) was the set designer for *Play It Again, Sam*. Also shown are Laurie Applefeld, who played Vanesse, and Gregory Doench, who played Allan Felix.

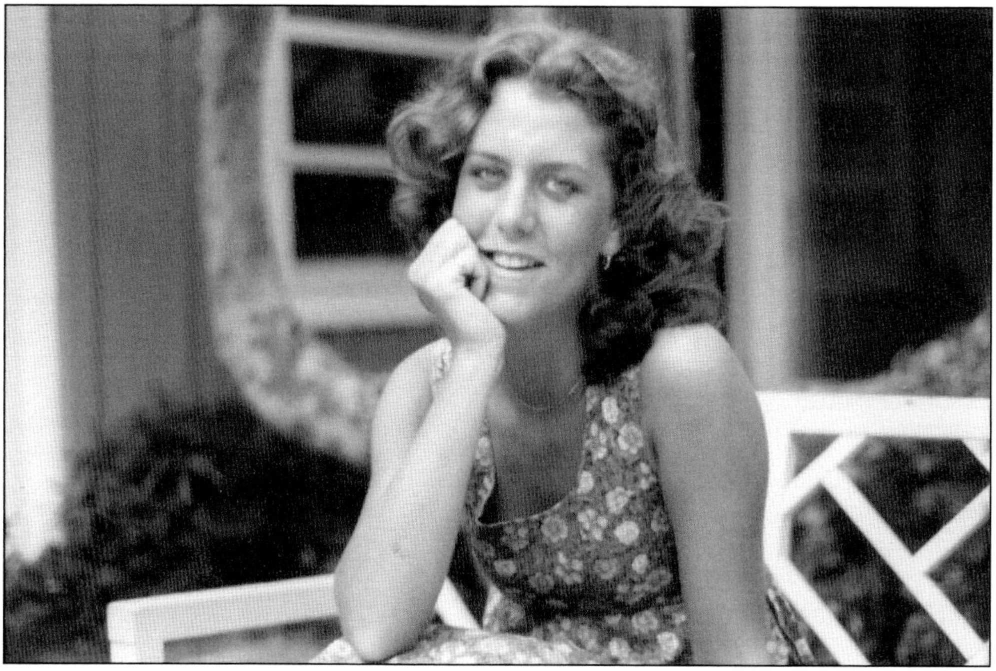

Kate Benton directed the 1979 production of *The Fantasticks* for the Marion Art Center. She was Sylvia Bigelow's granddaughter and inherited her grandmother's interests and talents in the theater.

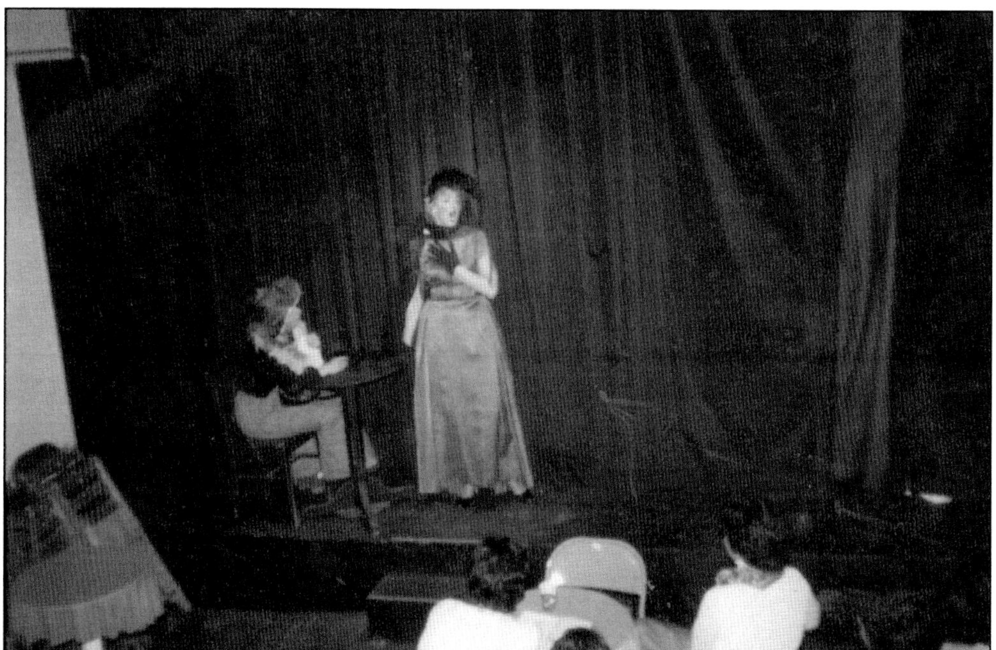

Gold in the Hills, an 1890s melodrama written by J. Frank Davis in 1930, was also presented by the Marion Art Center in 1979. Brett Thacher played John Dalton and Anne Schenck played Ida Reingold. The melodrama was directed by Wendy Bidstrup.

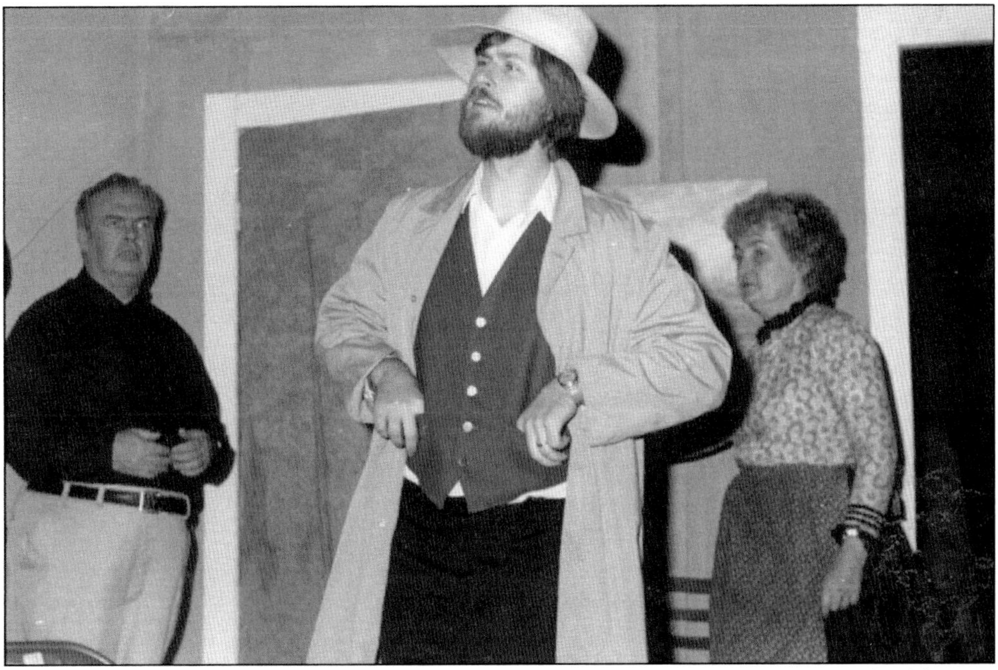

This photograph from the Marion Art Center's archives shows Vincent Worden, Ted Babbitt III, and Kay Sweeney in *Gold in the Hills*.

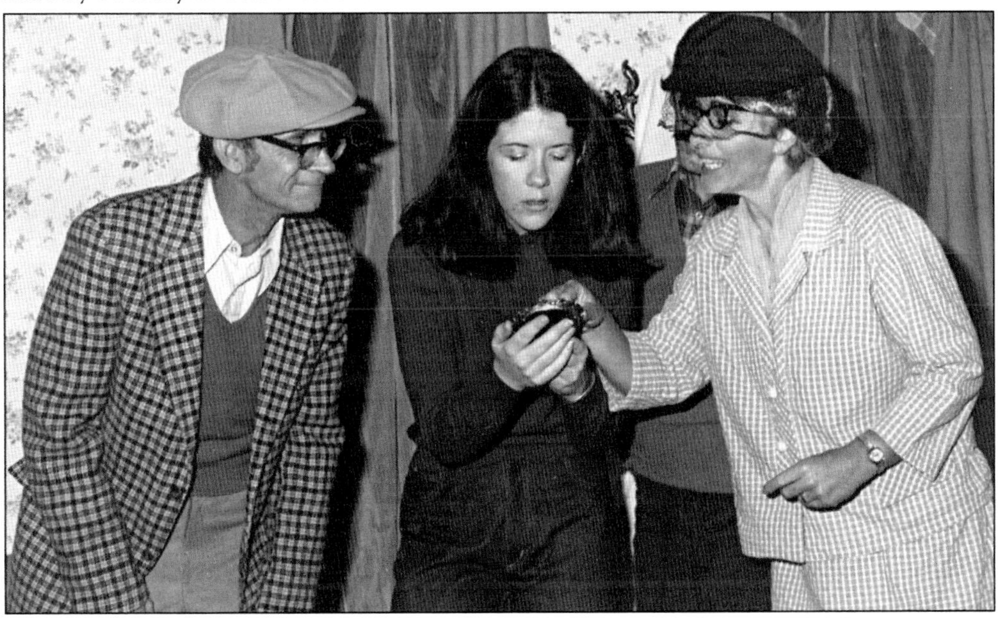

In 1980, *Veronica's Room* was presented by the Marion Art Center. The two-act play was written by Ira Levin in 1973. A young girl, Susan, was asked by an Irish couple to do a favor for them—to impersonate Veronica, who had died of tuberculosis, to please Veronica's younger sister, who was dying of cancer. This photograph shows Jim Carr, Jane Babbitt, and Faith Thompson. There was a power outage on the evening that the play was to open at the Marion Art Center. Finally, at 9:00 p.m., with the power still off, the audience arrived with flashlights and the show went on with only flashlights as the light source.

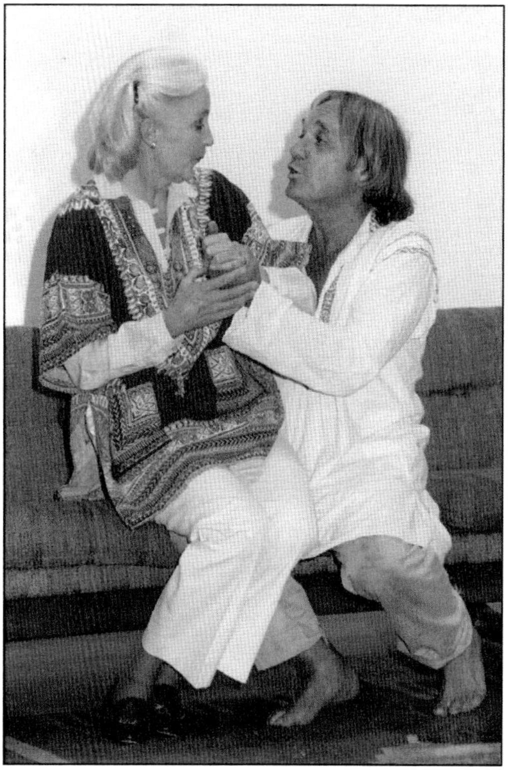

Swan An American Ballad, an original play written by Te Lo Reifel, directed by David B. Boyee, was presented in 1984 by the Marion Art Center. Shown here are Joan Olsen and Fred Lewis.

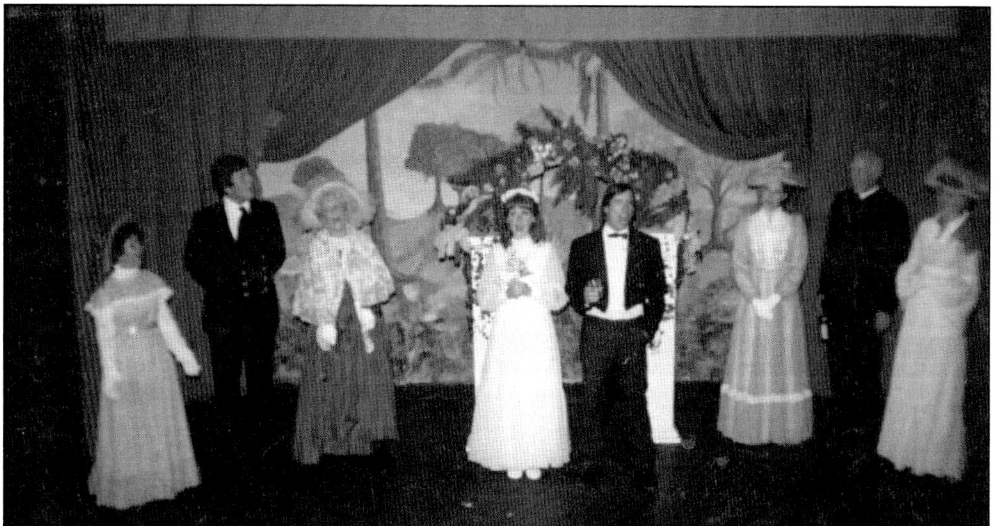

In 1982, the Marion Art Center presented *The Drunkard*, by W. H. S. Smith, a *c.* 1844 American temperance play. The cast included, from left to right, Sandra Jackson, Michael Curran, Jane Marso, Sally Jones, Edwin Barton, Susan Everett, Hamilton Brush, and Georgette Morrell.

Scenes from American Life, written by A. R. Gurney Jr., was presented by the Marion Art Center in July 1984 and directed by Anthony Farrar. This play was presented to celebrate the reopening of the theater after major renovations in 1982–1983, when the theater was closed for two years. Seated are Elayne Sama and Peggy Dyer. Standing are George Carnes and Jane Marso.

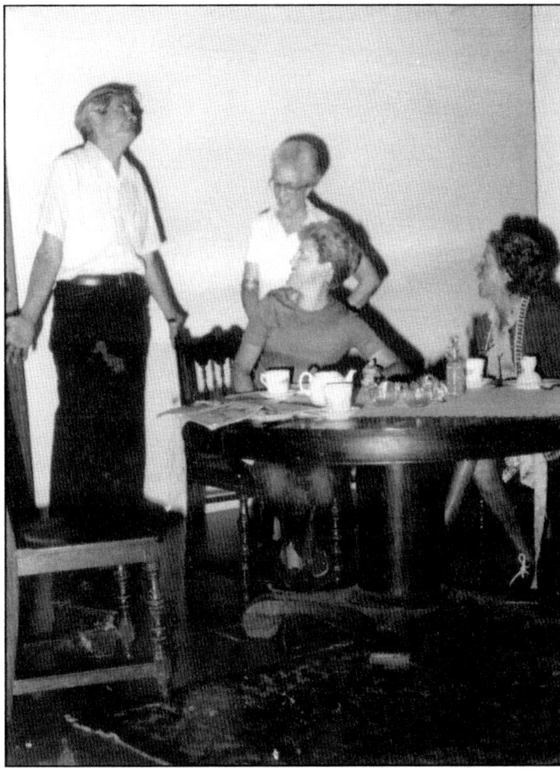

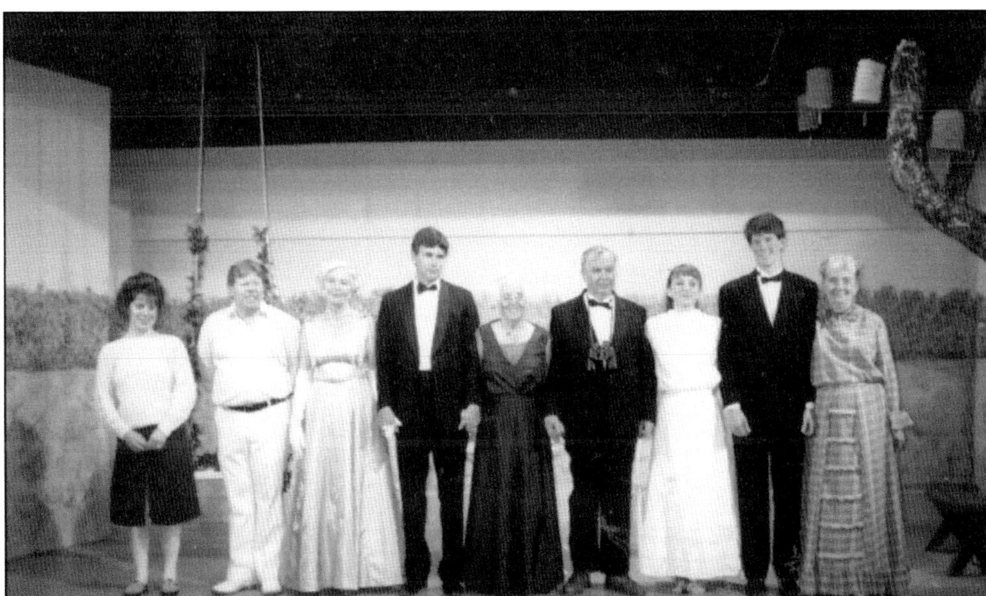

Sylvia Bigelow directed *Joy*, by John Galsworthy, in 1986. The cast included Joan Olsen, Mark Parsons, Jessica Shephardson, and others from Marion.

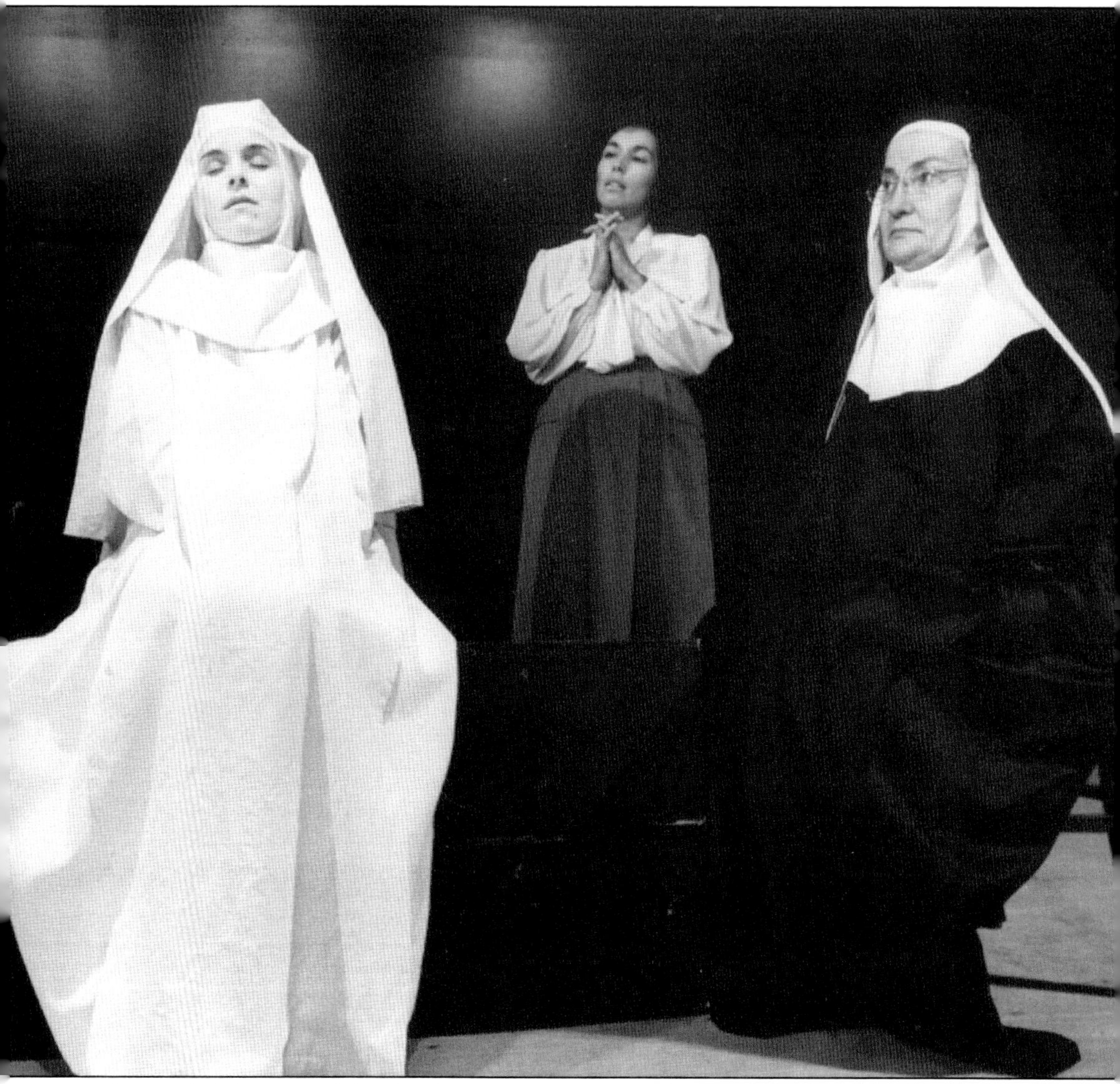

Agnes of God, directed by David Boyce, was presented in October 1987 by the Marion Art Center. This moving play by John Pielmeier told the story of a novice nun who was accused of murdering her newborn baby. An investigation and trial ensue. This photograph shows actors Sheryl Miller, Sandee Freitas, and Kay Sweeney.

In 1990, the Marion Art Center presented *The Real Inspector Hound* written by Tom Stoppard in 1962 as a parody of the typical Agatha Christie parlor mystery. This photograph shows Brian Scott, Kay Sweeney, and Kate O'Malley. The play was directed by Wendy Bidstrup.

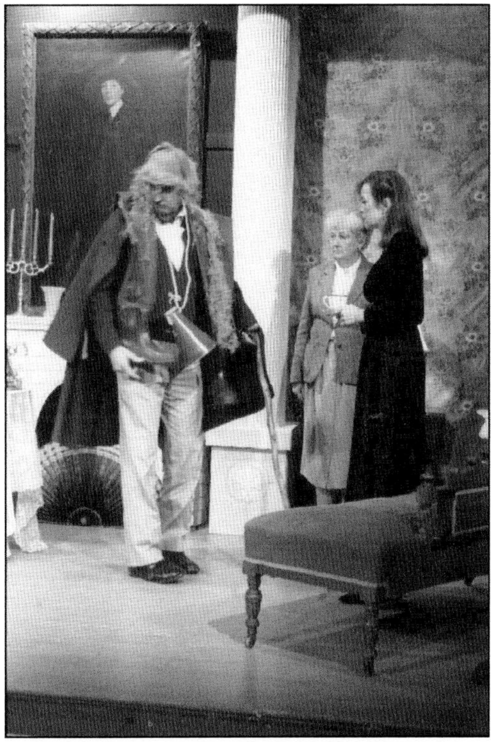

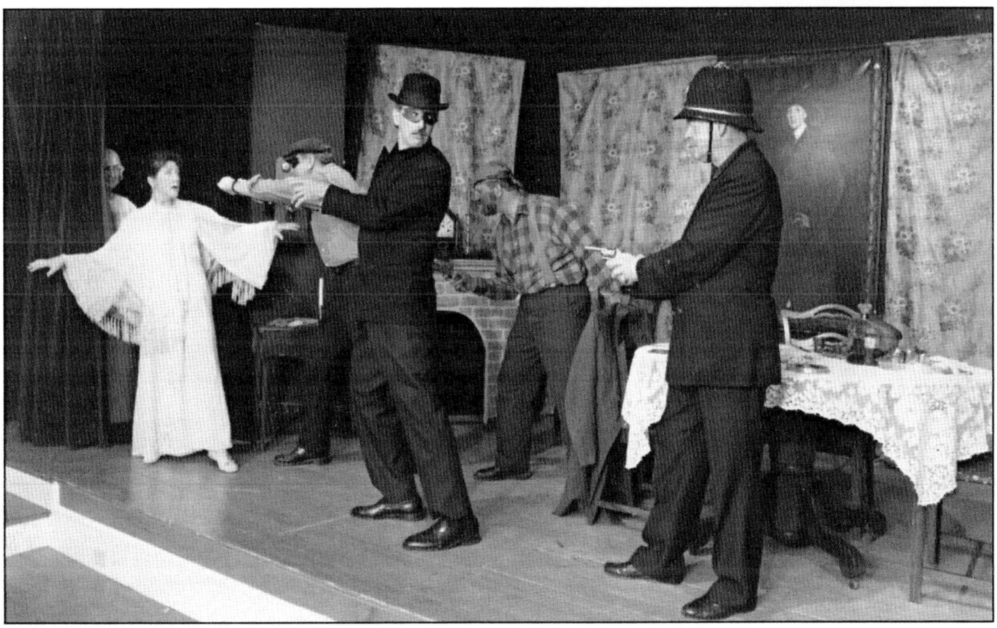

Miss Civilization, a comedy written by Richard Harding Davis (a Marion summer resident at the beginning of the 20th century and married to Marion summer resident, artist Cecil Clark Davis), was presented by the Marion Art Center in 1991 and directed by Wendy Bidstrup. This photograph shows Jane Babbitt, Brian Scott, Peter Brown, and Ted Babbitt Jr. *Miss Civilization* was first produced in Marion in 1905, with a cast of New York actors. It was very popular and was translated into several languages.

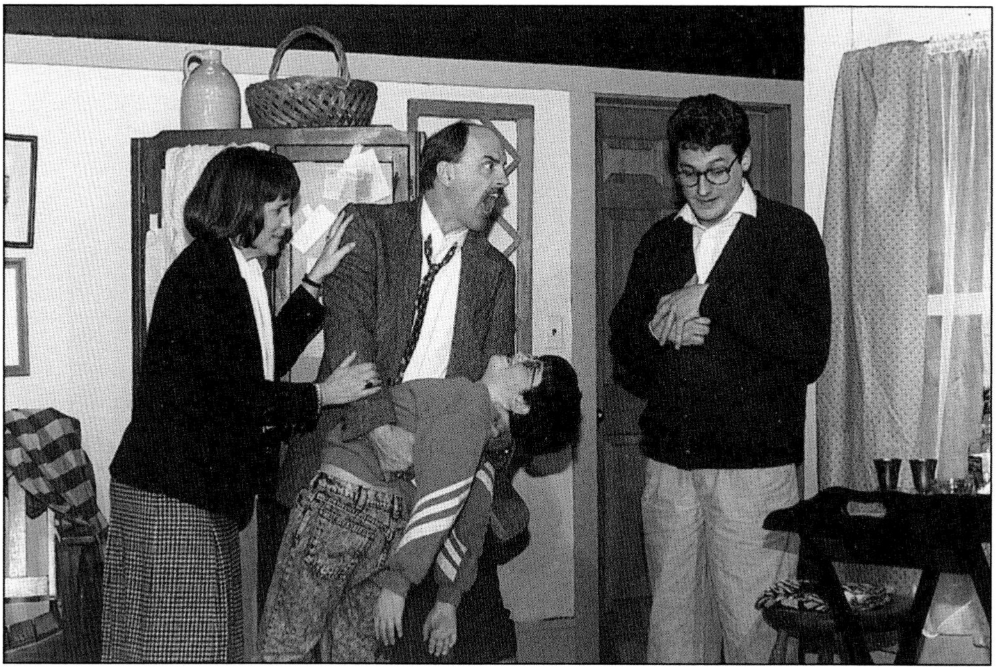

In 1991, the Marion Art Center presented the goofy, hilarious farce *The Nerd*, by Larry Shue and directed by Wendy Bidstrup and Chris LeBlanc. The cast includes, from left to right, Judith Coykendall, Brian Scott, Chris LeBlanc, and Nick Pizzolato (in front being held up).

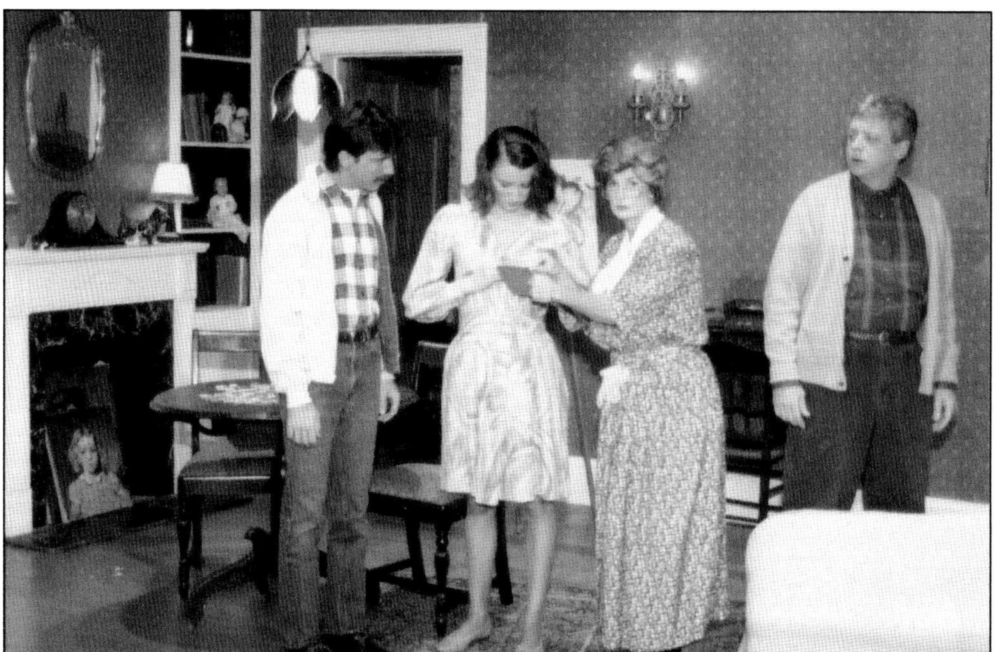

In 1992, the Marion Art Center presented *Veronica's Room* for the second time. Shown in this photograph are actors, from left to right, Charlie Murphy, Jessica Shepardson, Anne Schenck, and Donn Tyler.

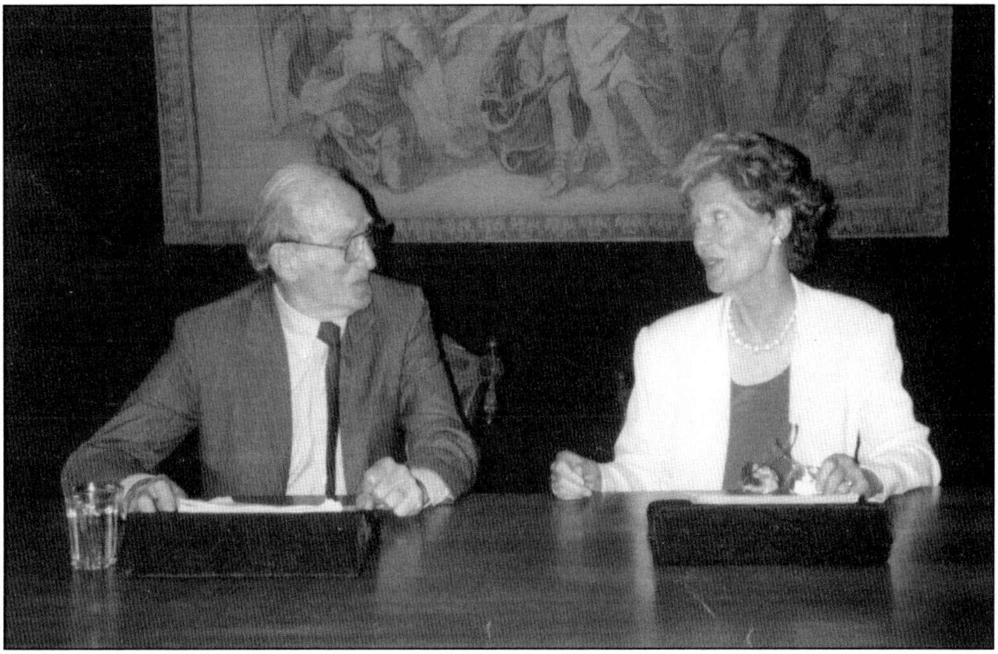

Love Letters, by A. R. Gurney, was presented in 1993 by three sets of actors on three separate evenings. The play presents a couple who read their emotional love letters to each other over a 50-year span. This photograph shows original Hornblower actors Hilly Lubin and Katy Babbitt reading their love letters.

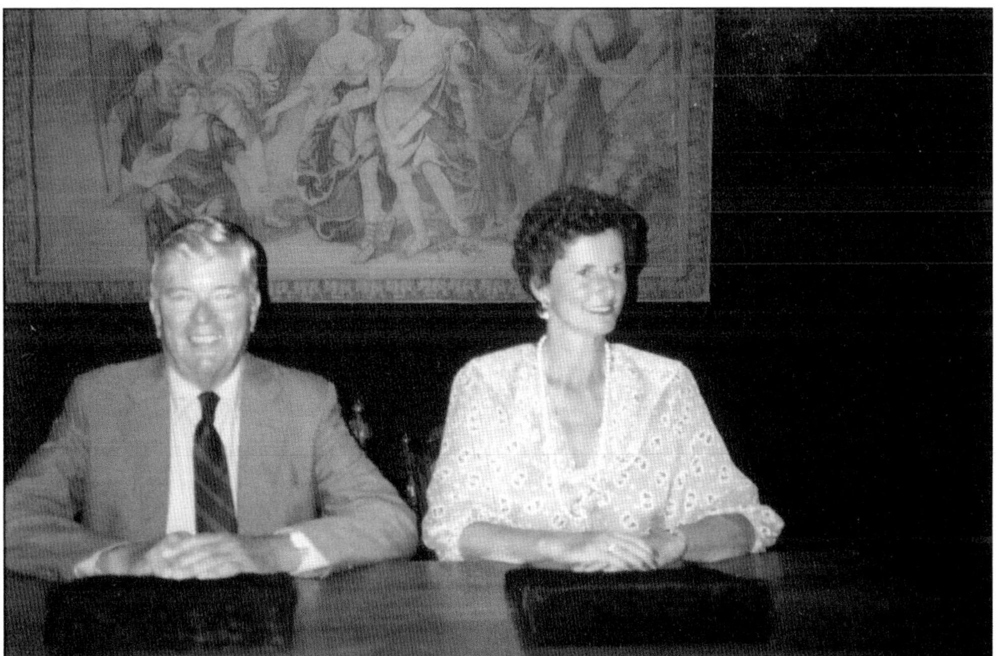

Dick Webb and Dagmar Unhoch also performed A. R. Gurney's *Love Letters* in 1993. Not shown are actors Geraldo Rivera and C. C. Dyer, who also performed on one of the three evenings of the play.

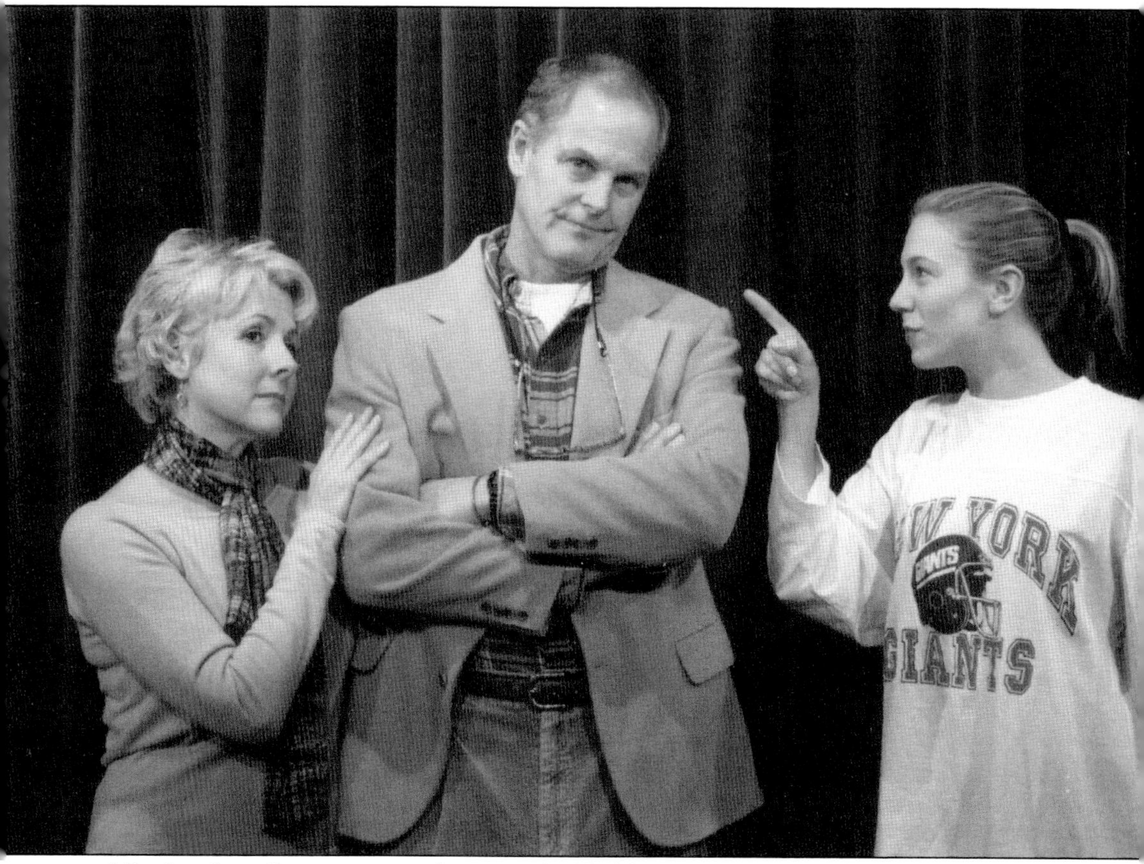

I Ought to be in Pictures, a comedy written by Neil Simon, was presented in January 2004 by the Marion Art Center. A struggling screen-writer found his 19-year-old daughter at his Hollywood doorstop after he deserted his family many years before. She moved in and interfered with her father's lifestyle and his relationship with his girlfriend. Bruce Lackey directed Cynthia Latham, Jay Gould, and Jennifer Golarz.

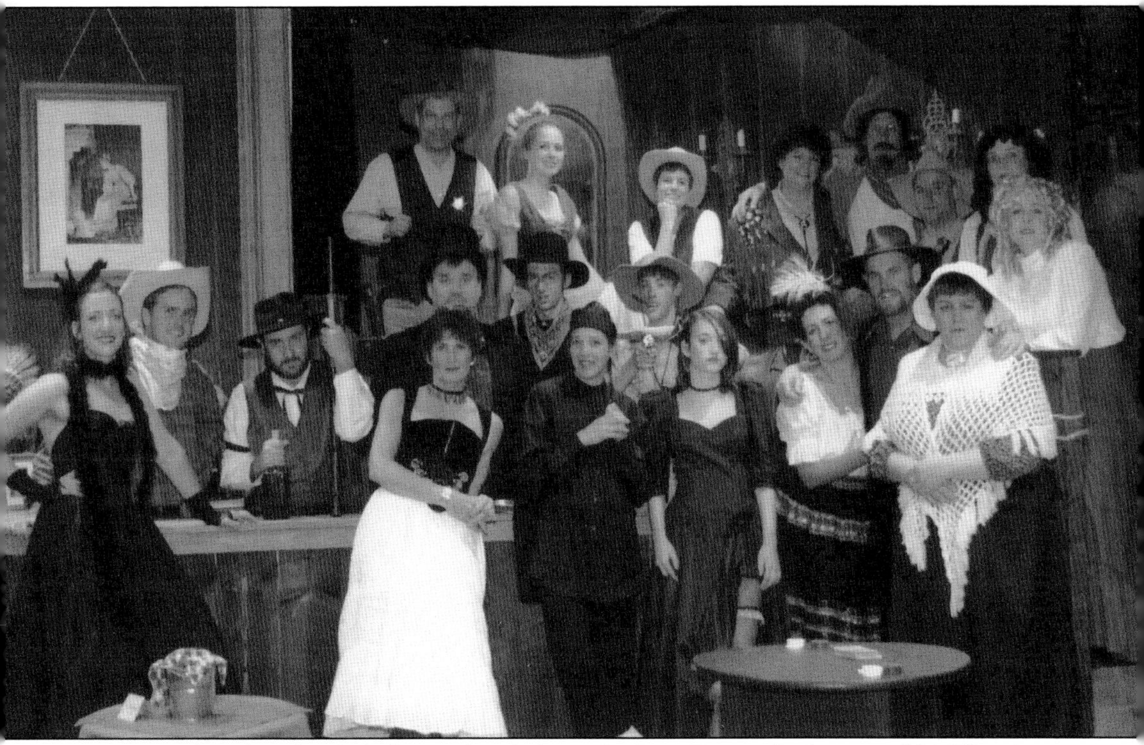

In 2005, *Deadwood Dick*, a light-hearted melodrama by Tom Taggert had a cast of 24. The play was directed by Susan Gould and Michelle Kelley. This photograph includes the following actors: (first row) Nancy Sparklin, Susan Gould, Nancy Havel, Jackie Scholz, Ruth Olson, Jay Gould, and Sheila Furtado; (second row) Bruce Cobb, Mark Letaurneau, Norris Brown, Matt Gould, and Jack Walsh; (third row) Peter Havel, Kirsten Thuestad, Michele Kelley, Deborah Bokelkamp, Carl Lamoreau, Colin Geil, Suzy Taylor, and Cynthia Latham.

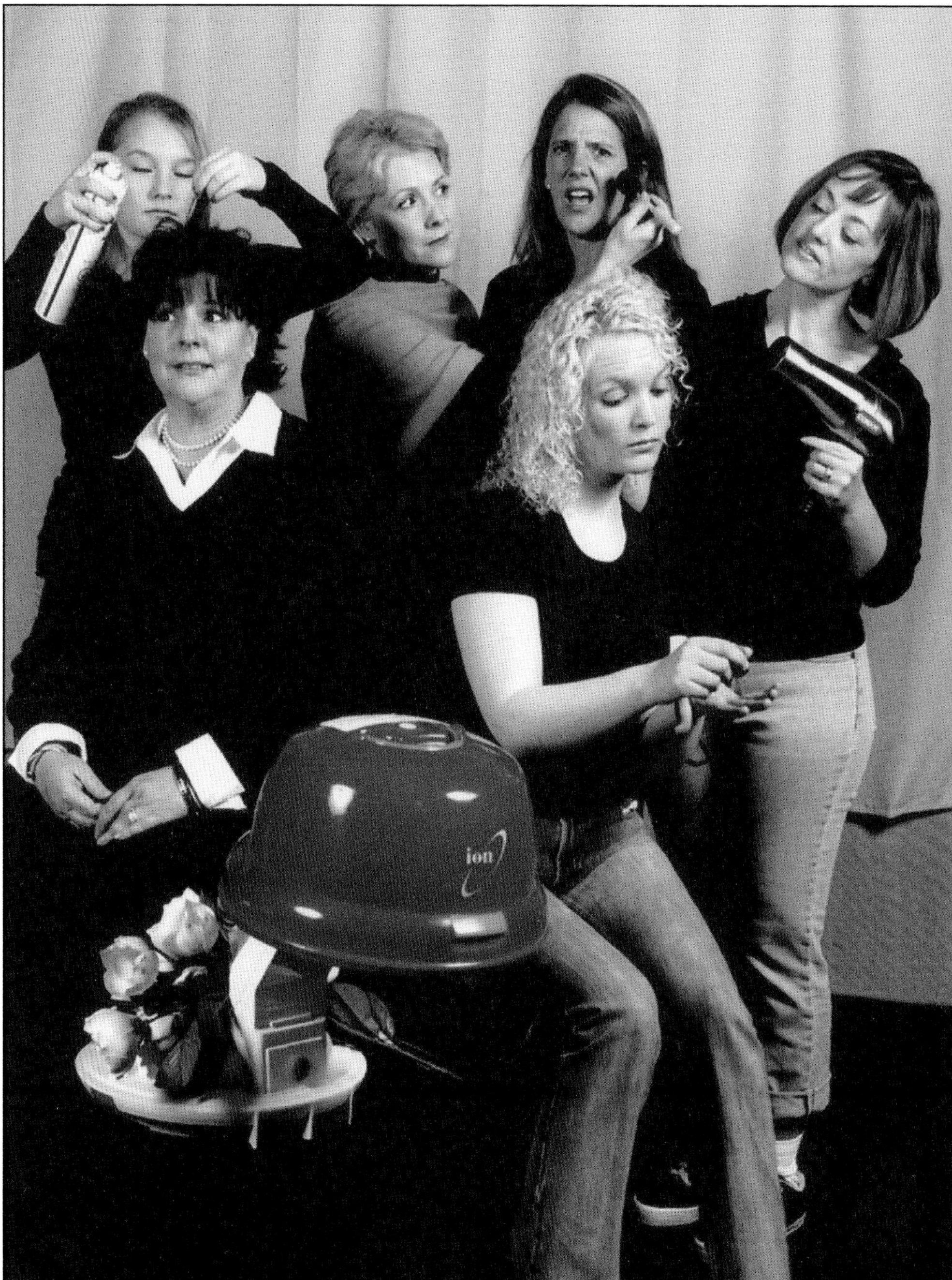

The 2006 production of *Steel Magnolias* by Robert Harling was the season's hit at the Marion Art Center. The comedy-drama reveals the bond among a group of southern women in Louisiana. The 1987 off-Broadway play was based on the author's experience with the death of his sister. The actors in this photograph include, from left to right, (first row) Deb Bokelkamp and Shannon Farrel; (second row) Caralyne Fondulis, Cynthia Latham, Nancy Havel, and Denise Giblin.

Two

Art Gallery

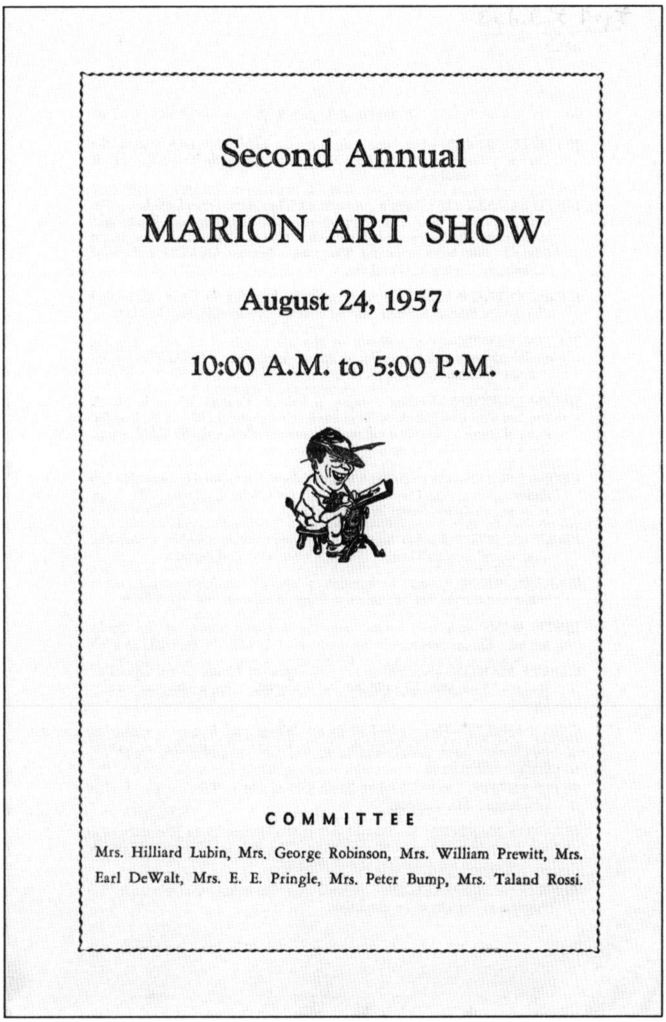

Second Annual

MARION ART SHOW

August 24, 1957

10:00 A.M. to 5:00 P.M.

COMMITTEE

Mrs. Hilliard Lubin, Mrs. George Robinson, Mrs. William Prewitt, Mrs. Earl DeWalt, Mrs. E. E. Pringle, Mrs. Peter Bump, Mrs. Taland Rossi.

The Second Annual Marion Art Show was held shortly after the Marion Art Center was incorporated. The pamphlet welcomed those who had come to the second clothesline exhibit and announced the formation of a permanent Marion Art Center in the old Universalist church. Announcements were made inviting volunteer work crews to fix up the building. Membership fees were established at $1 per person and $2 per family.

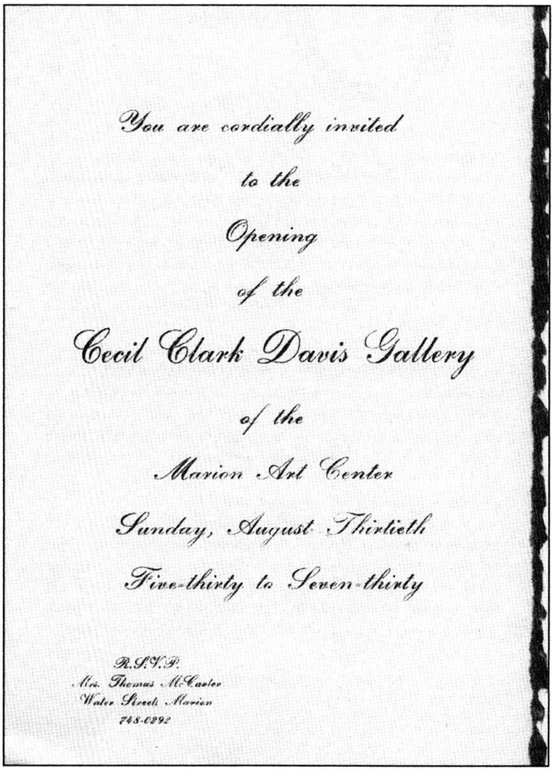

You are cordially invited
to the
Opening
of the
Cecil Clark Davis Gallery
of the
Marion Art Center
Sunday, August Thirtieth
Five-thirty to Seven-thirty

R.S.V.P.
Mrs. Thomas McCarter
Water Street, Marion
748-0292

On August 30, 1964, the Cecil Clark Davis Gallery was officially opened after major renovations were done. One hundred invitations were sent out and approximately 100 people attended. Sixteen portraits painted by Cecil Clark Davis were on loan from Tabor Academy, Mrs. Paul Burdett, June Converse, Patsy Francis, the Woman's Club, and Rosie Cutler. Three portraits were donated to the Marion Art Center—two painted by Cecil Clark Davis given by Mary Clark Silver Smith and her sister, Mrs. Usher P. Coolidge, and one given by Frederica Poett, which was a portrait of Cecil Clark Davis painted by her teacher, Ellen Emmet Rand.

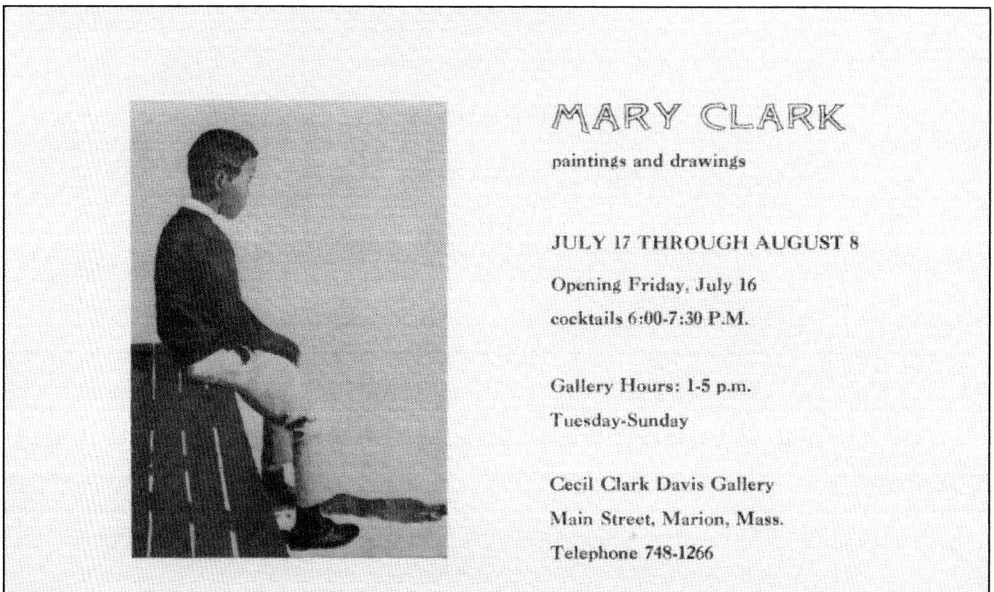

MARY CLARK
paintings and drawings

JULY 17 THROUGH AUGUST 8
Opening Friday, July 16
cocktails 6:00-7:30 P.M.

Gallery Hours: 1-5 p.m.
Tuesday-Sunday

Cecil Clark Davis Gallery
Main Street, Marion, Mass.
Telephone 748-1266

On January 10, 1965, Mary H. Clark exhibited her oil paintings, pencil sketches, watercolors, and sculpture at the Cecil Clark Davis Gallery in the Marion Art Center. Clark was born in Providence, Rhode Island, and her formal training consisted of occasional classes at the De Cordova Museum in Lincoln, Massachusetts. She was married to Van Allen Clark and lived on Ram Island with her six children and assorted livestock.

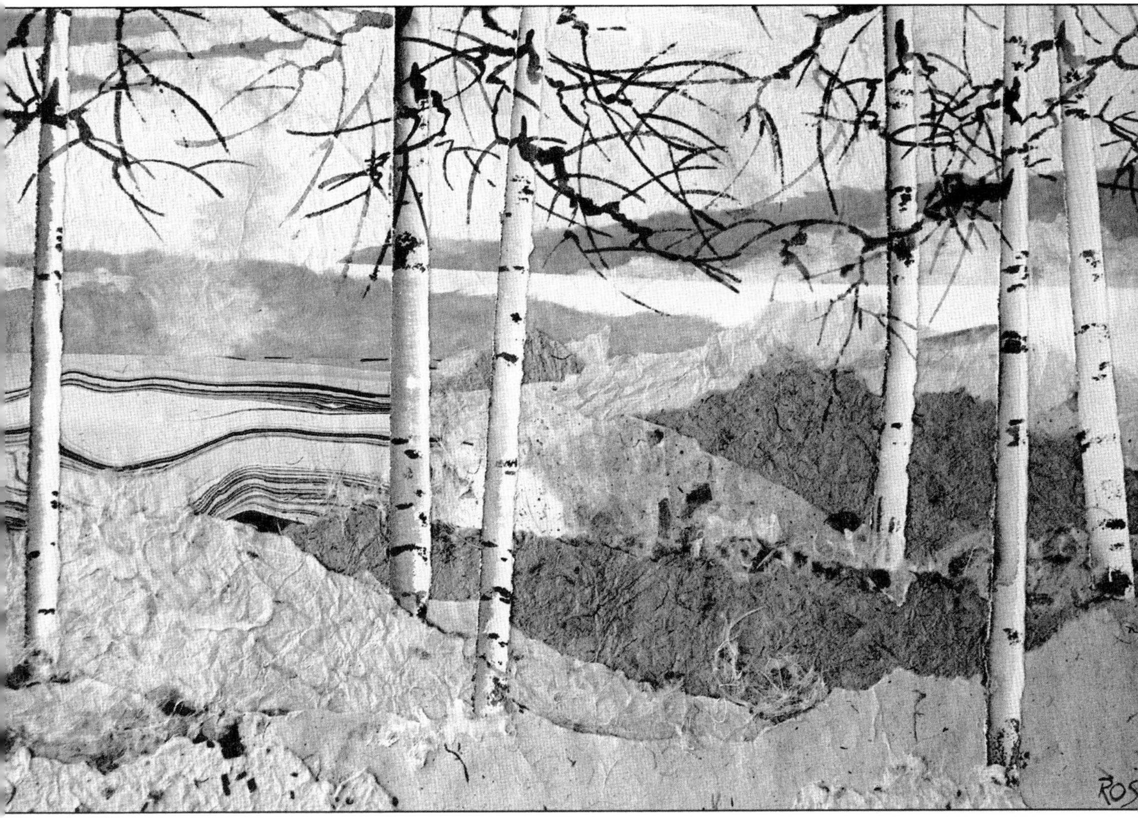

Mary Ross, a longtime resident of Marion, has shown her work at the Marion Art Center since the 1960s. She studied art at Massachusetts College of Art, Boston University, and Boston Museum of Fine Arts and has had many shows all over New England. Her work is in the permanent collections of Harvard Law School, Bank of Boston, Harvard Trust, and many other collections. She began her artistic career as a painter, but her recent work focuses on collages. They are delicate, airy, and utilize varied colored and textured handmade Japanese papers. Watercolor and acrylic are used to enhance and create an unusual effect. Shown here is one of her collages.

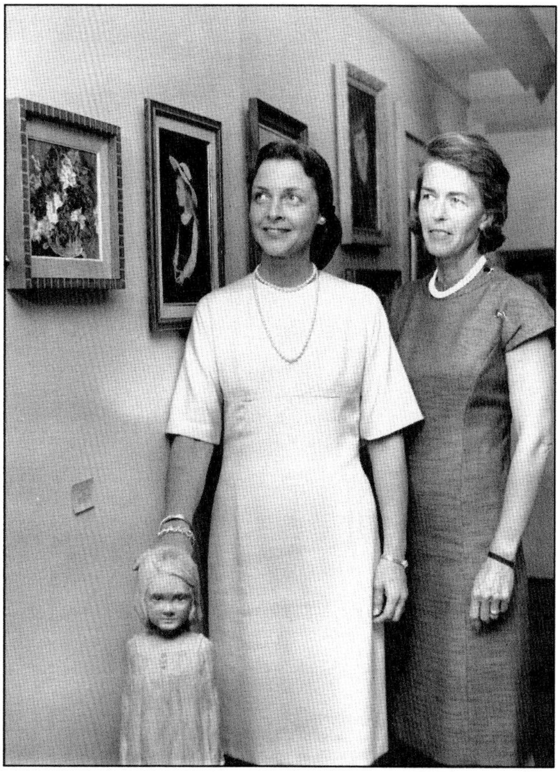

In 1966, Elizabeth Peabody Miller, painter and sculptor, showed her work at the Marion Art Center. The bronze figure under Miller's right hand was titled *Little Friend* and was modeled after the artist's own children. The artist was the daughter-in-law of Jill and John W. Miller, longtime summer residents of Marion. Elizabeth was born in Chicago and attended the Art Institute of Chicago, the Art Student's League in New York City, and the Pennsylvania Academy of Fine Arts in Philadelphia. On the right stands Violet Eaton, president of the center and founder of the Cecil Clark Davis Gallery.

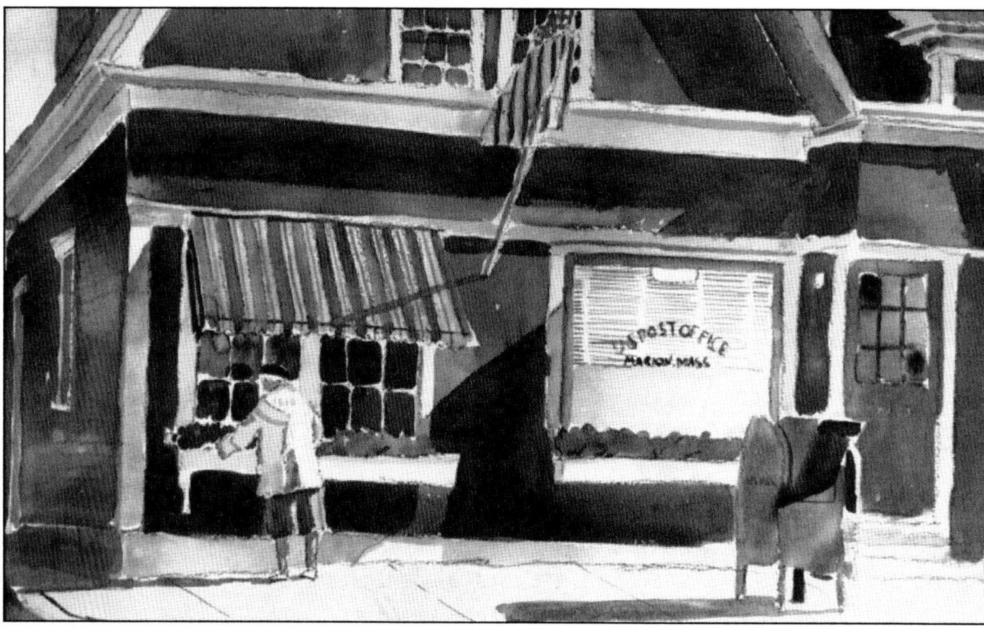

Norman Fortier became an avid amateur, self-taught marine photographer as a young man. He served as a U.S. Navy photographer during World War II. After the war he setup his own commercial photography studio in the New Bedford area. In 1966, he exhibited his watercolors and marine photographs at the Cecil Clark Davis Gallery. This watercolor depicts the Marion Post Office.

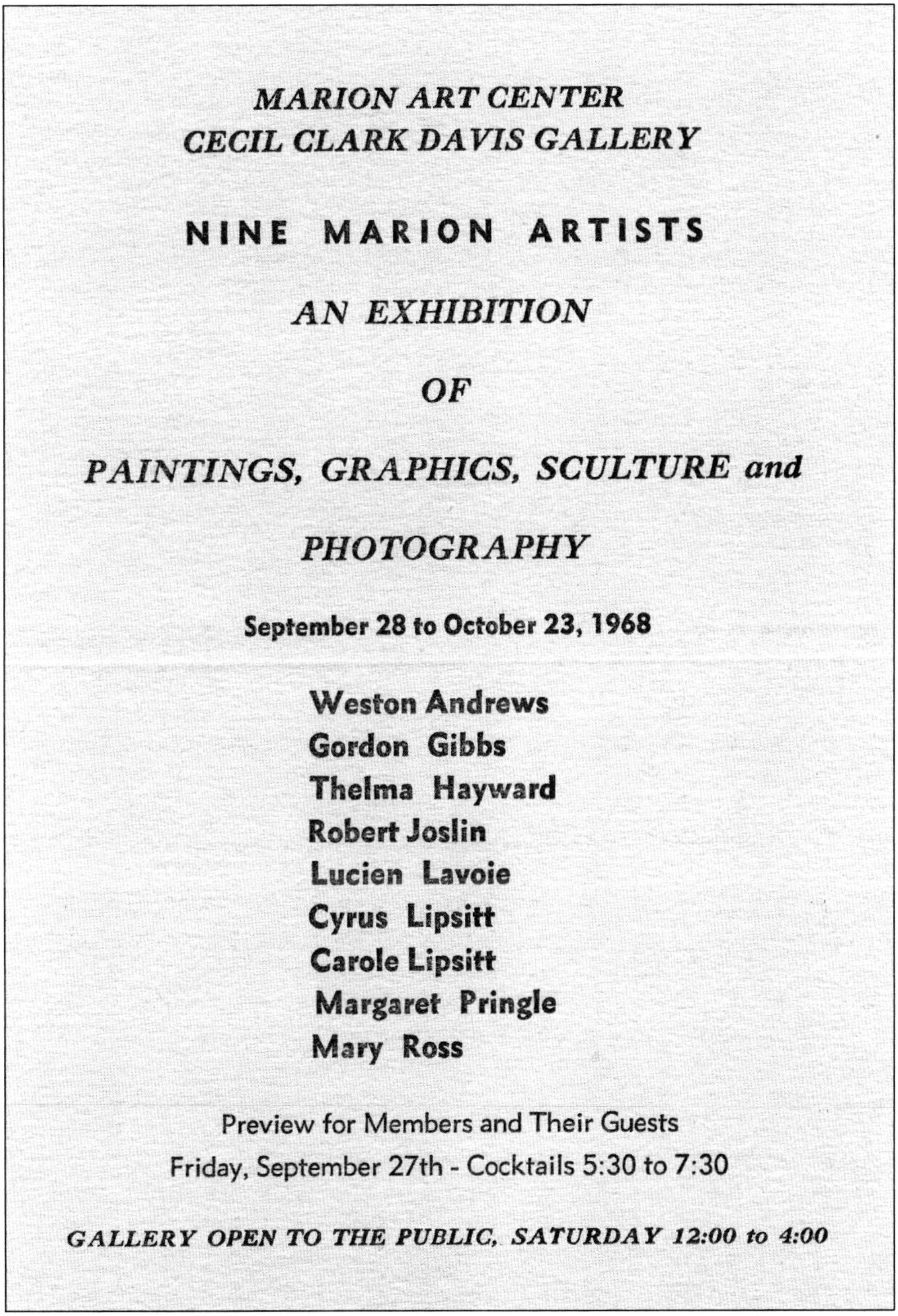
MARION ART CENTER
CECIL CLARK DAVIS GALLERY

NINE MARION ARTISTS

AN EXHIBITION

OF

PAINTINGS, GRAPHICS, SCULTURE and

PHOTOGRAPHY

September 28 to October 23, 1968

Weston Andrews
Gordon Gibbs
Thelma Hayward
Robert Joslin
Lucien Lavoie
Cyrus Lipsitt
Carole Lipsitt
Margaret Pringle
Mary Ross

Preview for Members and Their Guests
Friday, September 27th - Cocktails 5:30 to 7:30

GALLERY OPEN TO THE PUBLIC, SATURDAY 12:00 to 4:00

In 1968, nine Marion artists exhibited their work consisting of paintings, graphics, sculpture, and photography in the Cecil Clark Davis Gallery.

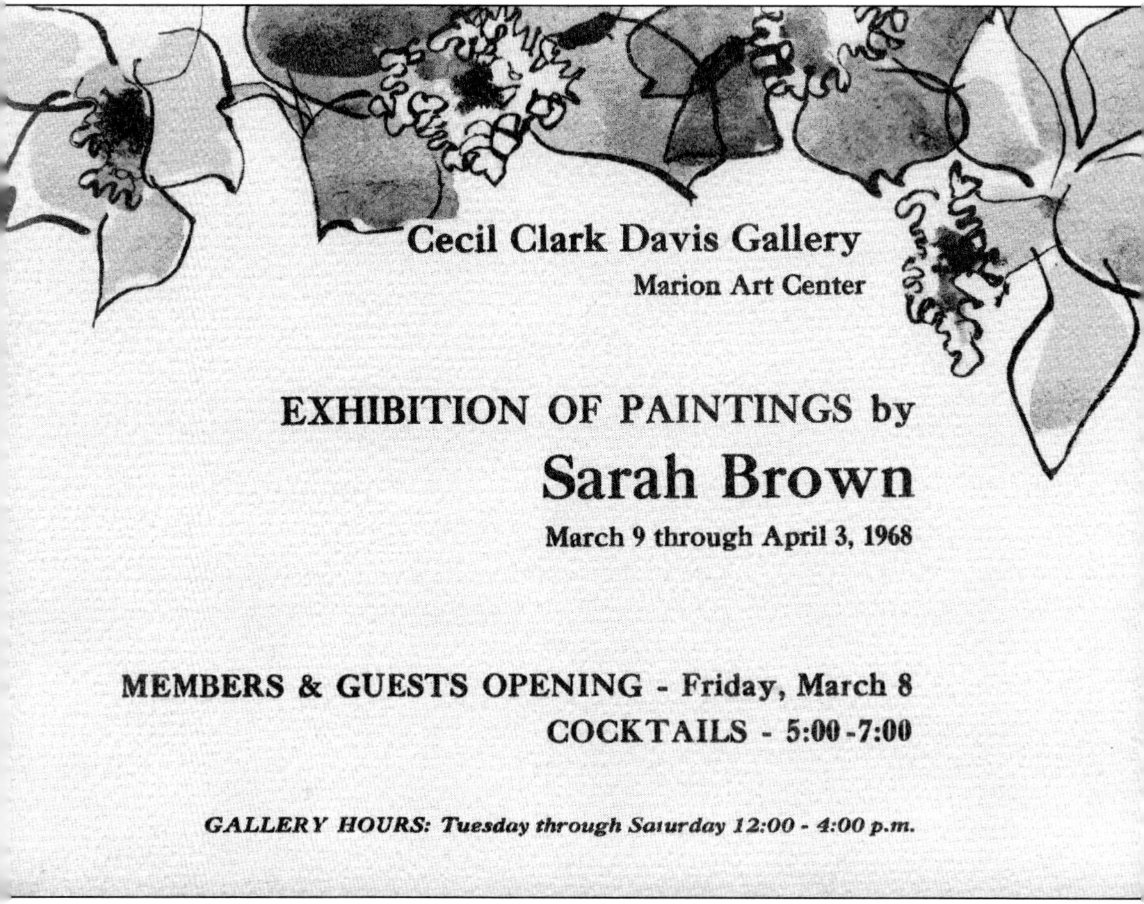

Sarah Brown studied art at De Pauw University and then went to art and music school in France at Fontainebleau. She was a fashion illustrator for the Outlet Company, Peerless, Ann and Hope, and Silverstein department stores for many years. She has been involved with art her whole life and taught painting classes at the Marion Art Center for many years. This announcement for an exhibition of her paintings was for her first show at the Marion Art Center in 1968.

In 1975, Brown exhibited watercolors at the Marion Art Center. She was on the board of directors of the art center for many years and was president of the board for two years. She also participated in musicals with the theater group.

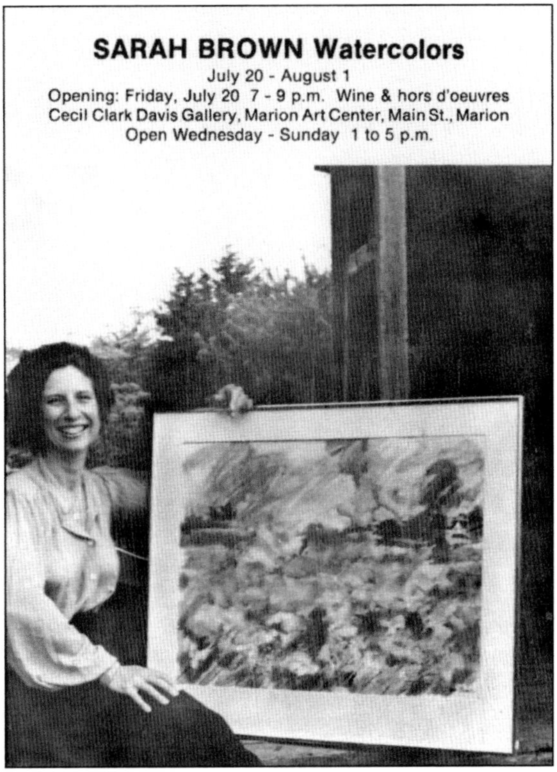

marion art center

p.o. box 602
marion, mass. 02738

The logo of the Marion Art Center was designed by Brown in 1974. For over 30 years, the snail shell has adorned all communication by the center.

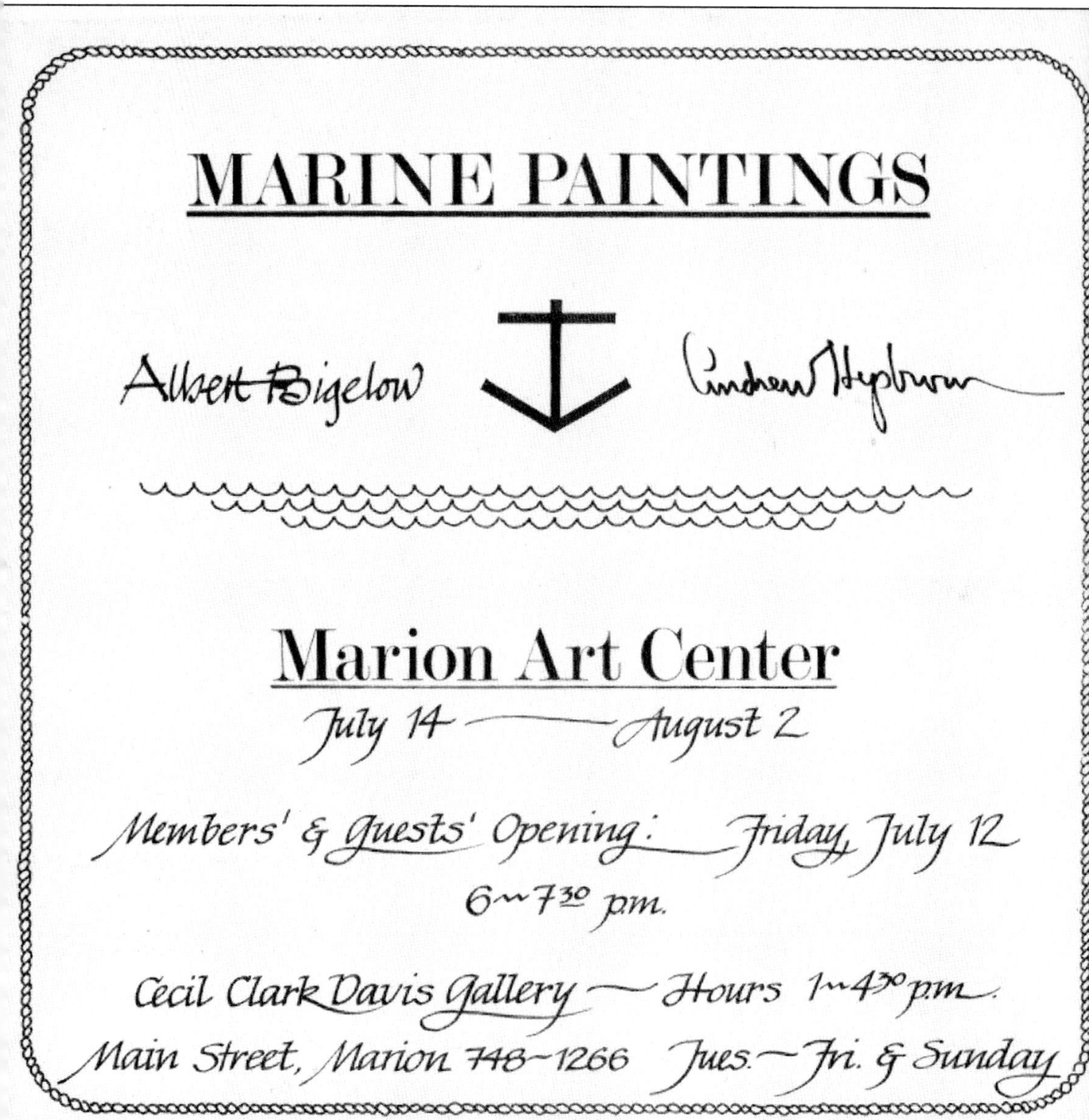

In 1974, the Marion Art Center exhibited the marine paintings of two Marion residents, Albert Bigelow and Andrew Hepburn. Since Marion is a seashore town, many of its residents collect marine art.

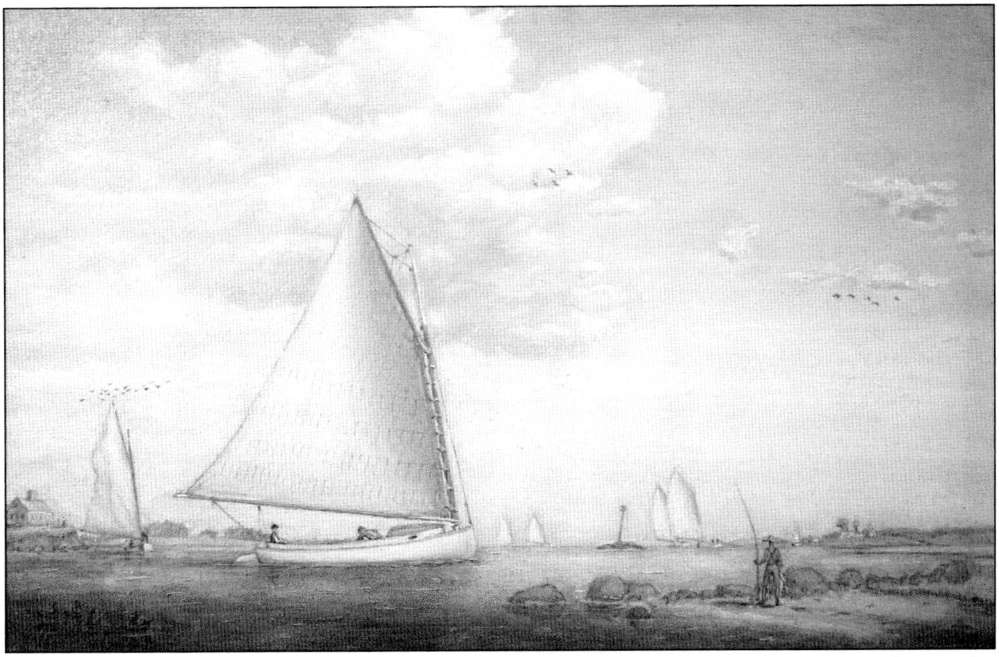

Bigelow's marine paintings are collected by many Marion residents. His work is also in the permanent collection of the Mystic Maritime Museum in Mystic, Connecticut. This painting is from the Cooney collection.

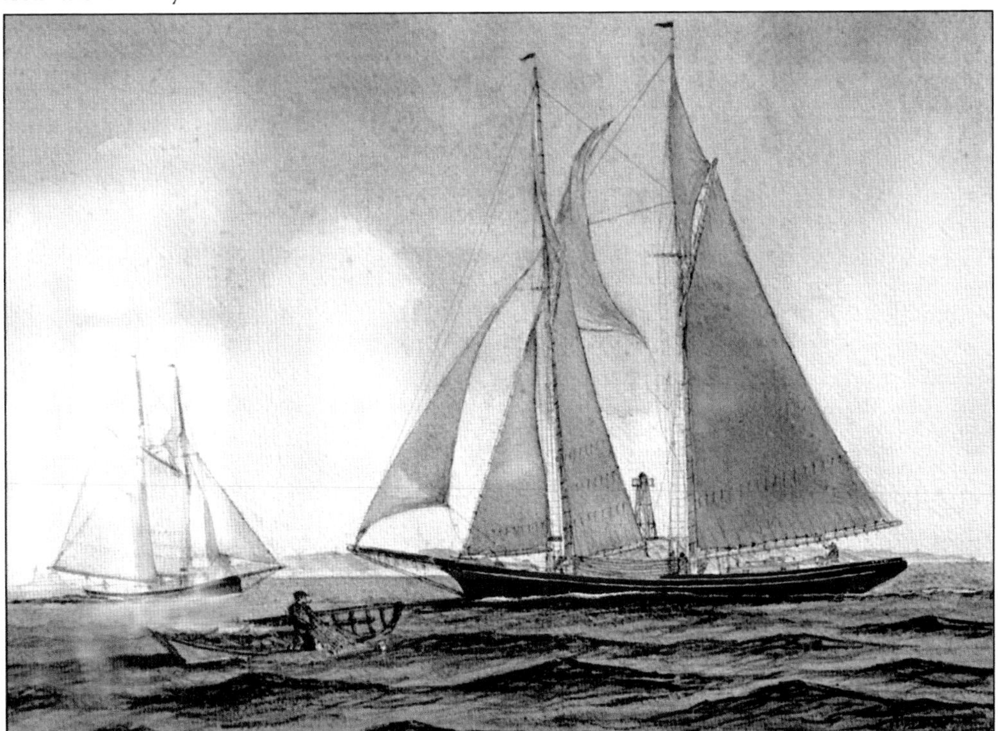

Hepburn's nautical paintings are also collected by Marion residents. This painting is from the Putnam collection.

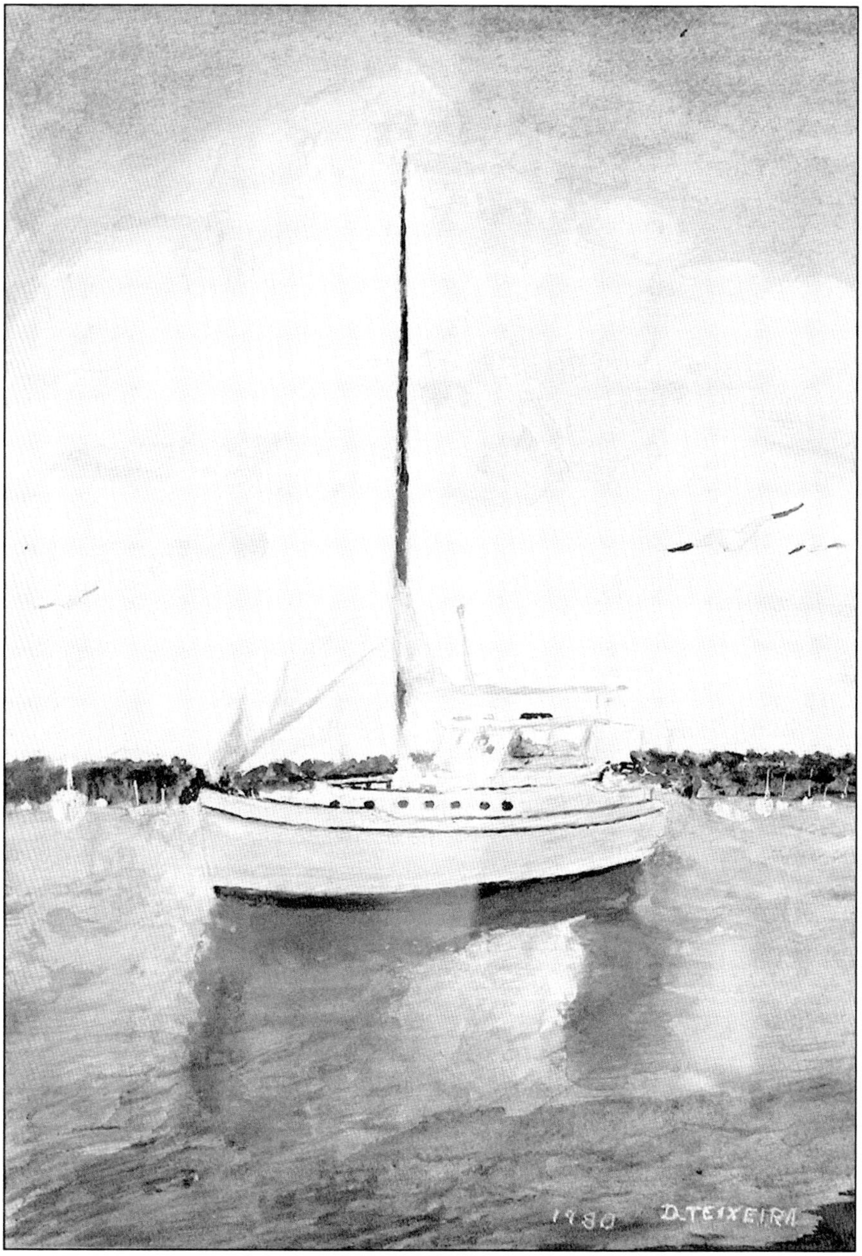

Domingo Teixeira was a local artist who worked for the Miller/Durkee family in Marion for 52 years and in Jill Miller's Overflow Antiques shop. He was born in Marion, and his ancestors came from the Cape Verdean Islands. He was a self-taught artist who began painting in his 60s and had his first show at the Marion Art Center in 1986 when he was 69. He exhibited both his paintings and his carved decoy ducks. This painting is of Jill Durkee's motorsailer, which was designed by John Hand. When Jill Miller went to Maine to purchase antiques, she would drive a big station wagon to Maine and Teixeira would sail their boat to Maine. Then he would drive the station wagon filled with antiques to Marion and the Millers would cruise on their boat in Maine. Then he would drive the station wagon back to Maine for another load and sail the boat back while Jill Miller drove the station wagon loaded with antiques back to Marion.

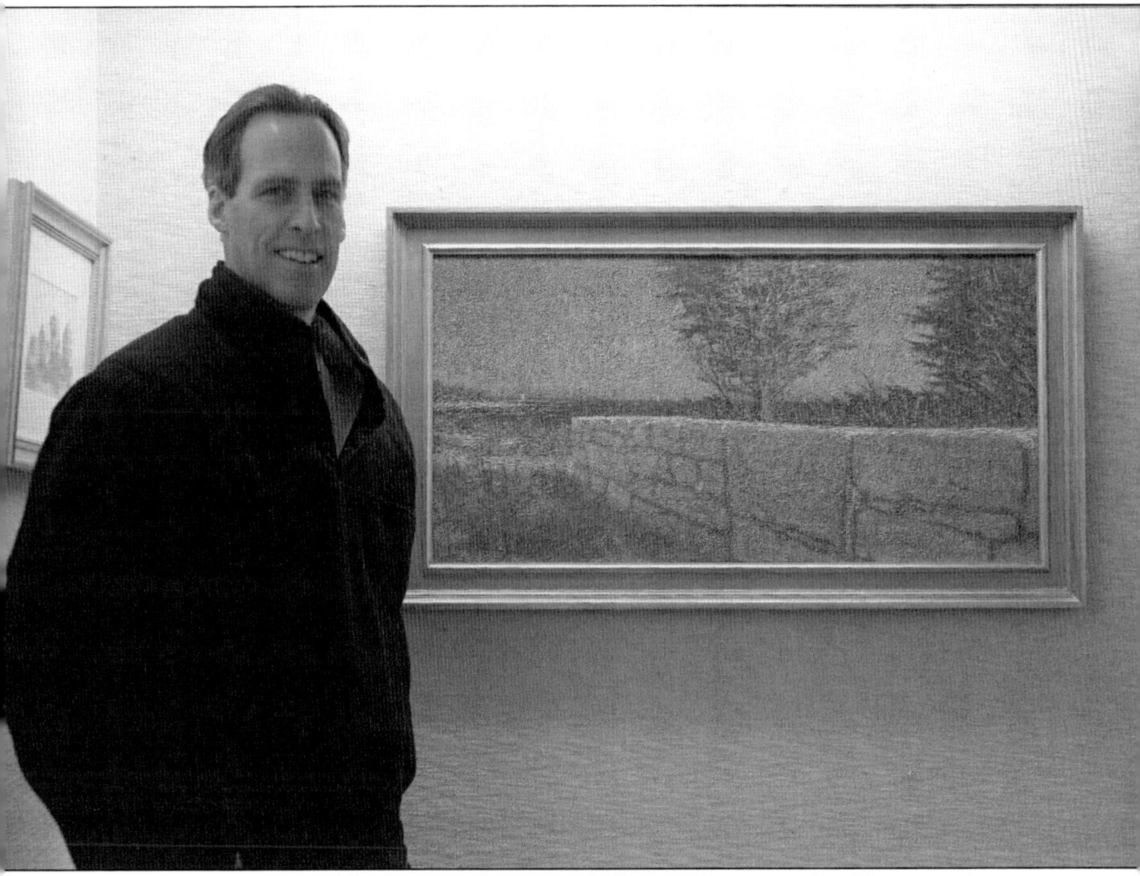

Peter Stone studied art and biology at Claremont College and works in his Marion studio as a full-time artist and writer. Early on, he decided that he wanted three elements in his paintings—en plein air, texture, and luminosity. He wanders all over the world with his easel and has spent over a decade painting and exploring Atlantic Canada, primarily Labrador. His remote landscapes reflect the spiritual response to what he sees. He has developed a unique style of Tonal-Realism in oils with a sophisticated glazing technique. Since 1983, he has presented more than 40 solo shows and numerous group exhibitions at galleries and museums in the United States, Canada, and England, including Art Expo New York; the Royal Academy of Art, London; and the De Cordova Museum.

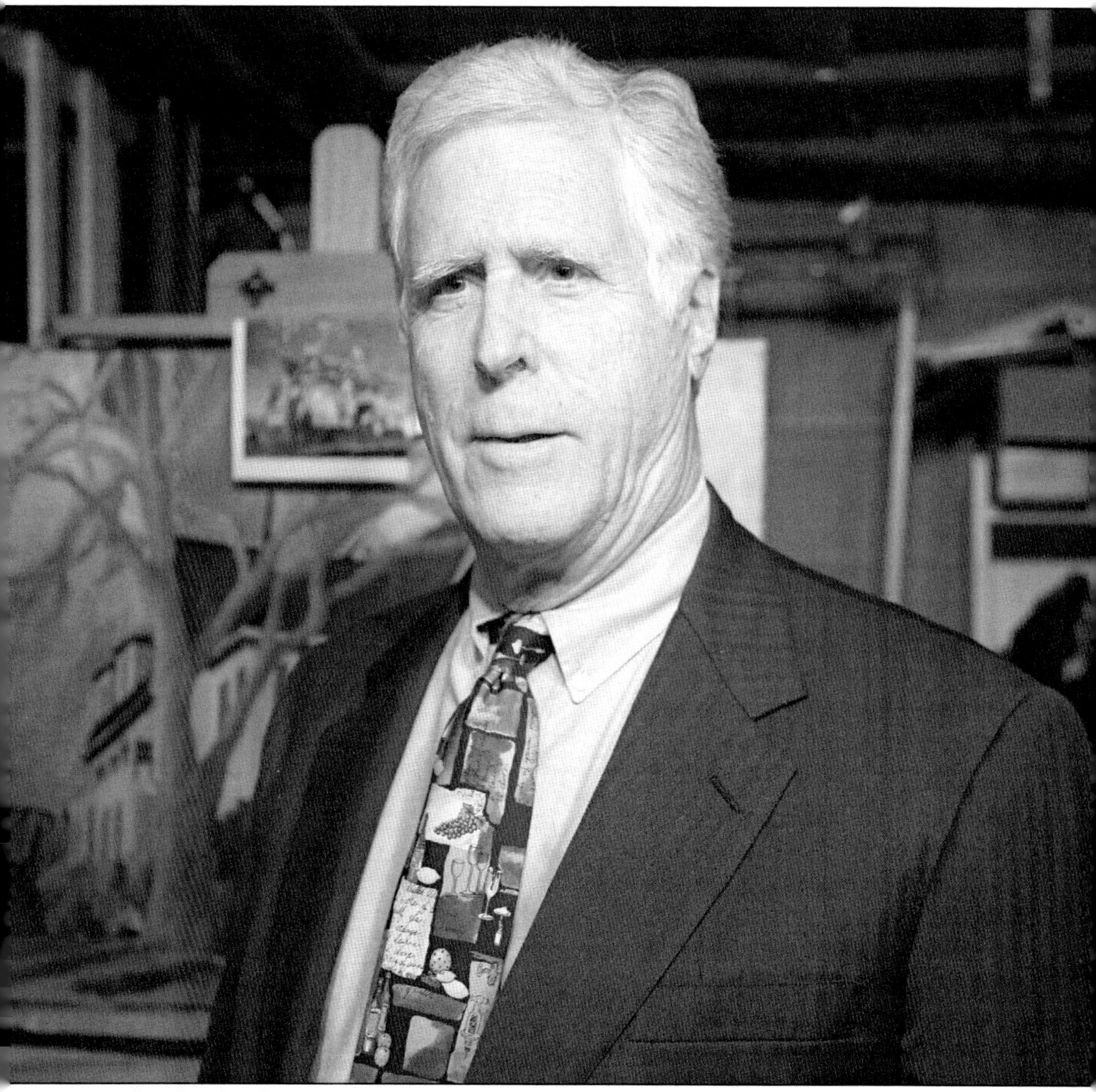

Jack Wheatley drew cartoons as a youngster and watched his mother do ornamental painting. He painted as a hobby while attending Dartmouth College and Northwestern University Law School. While practicing law and during the years he served as a judge, he continued to paint and to take evening classes at the Massachusetts College of Art, the Boston Museum of Fine Arts, the Design School at Harvard, and the Rhode Island School of Design. Upon his retirement he has devoted himself to art and attempts to capture the realities of light and color around him. His work has been shown at the Marion Art Center.

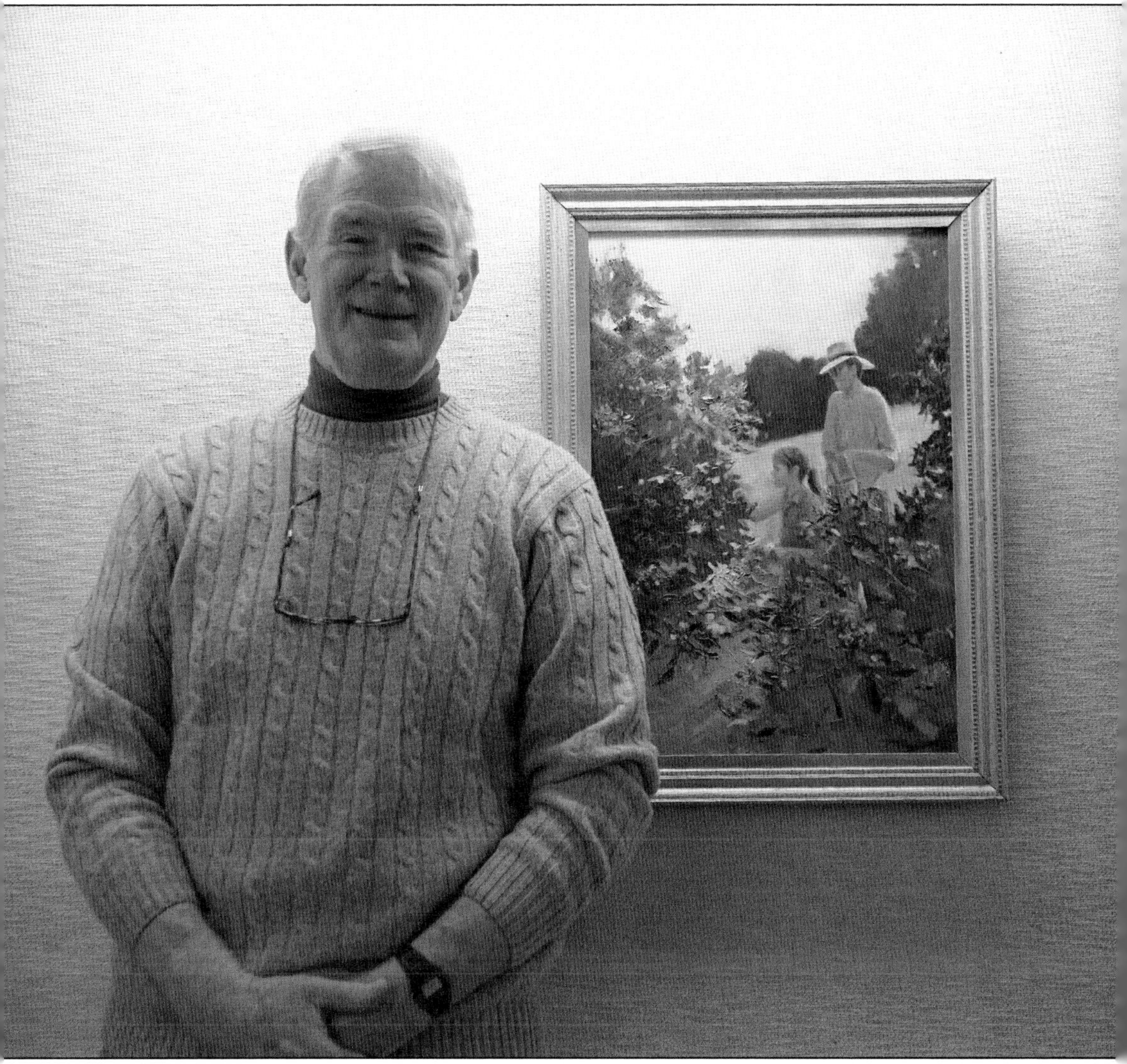

Charlie Parsons grew up being exposed to painters—in fact his mother was a professional painter, as is his sister. While at Bucknell University he majored in premed studies, but took art electives when he wanted to boost his grade point average. When he retired as an orthopedic surgeon, he devoted his retirement to his painting, both in watercolors and oils. Charlie has had many exhibitions nationally and internationally, including Japan. He has shown his work at the Artist's Association of Nantucket, the Providence Art Club, the Artists' Society of Bermuda, the Copley Society, and many other venues. Whenever Parsons shows his work at the Marion Art Center, members vie to purchase his lyrical depictions of local Marion scenes.

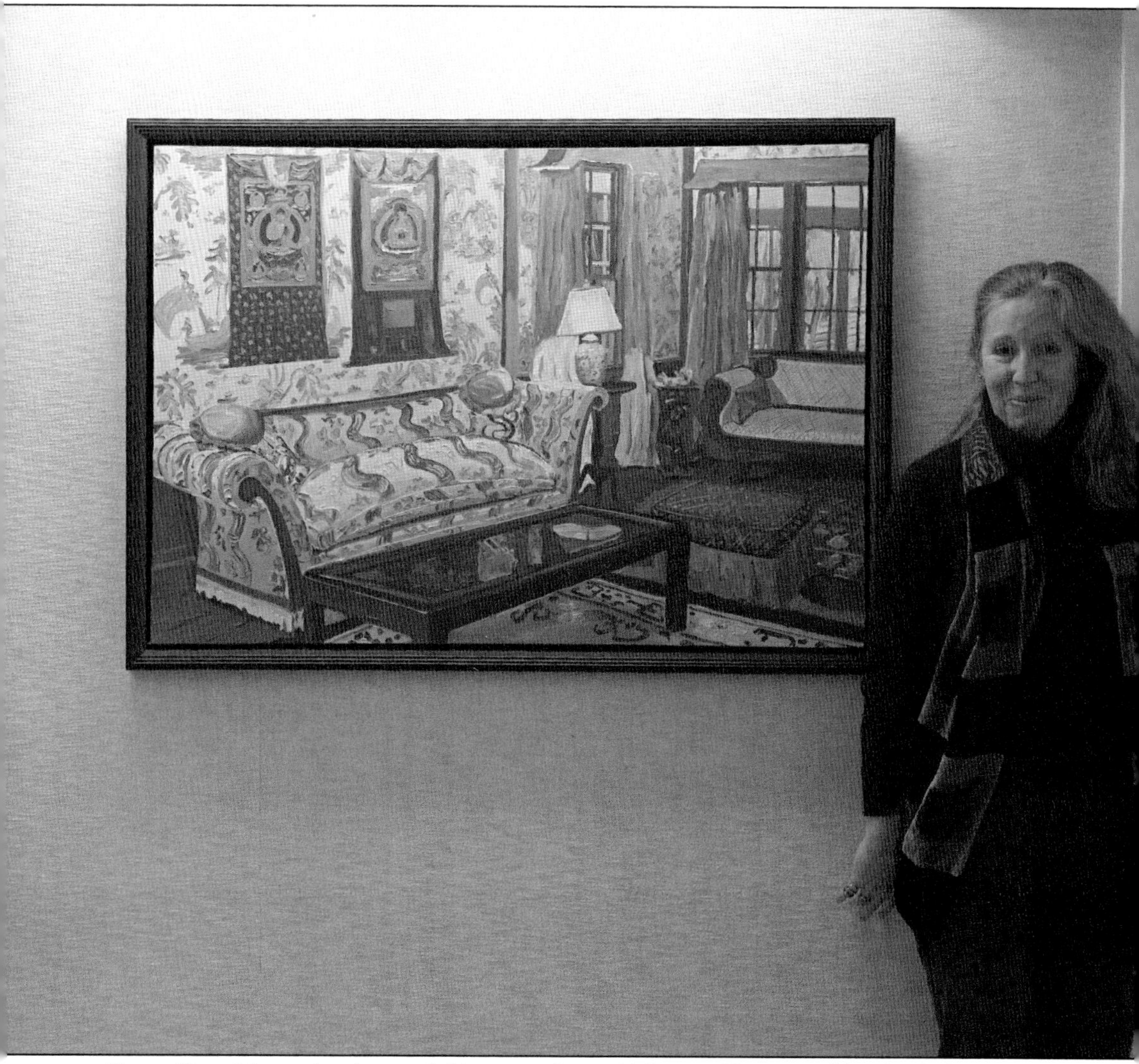

Nancy Dyer Mitton has been a lifelong resident of Marion. She earned her bachelor of fine arts in painting from the Massachusetts College of Art in Boston. Her paintings have been in gallery exhibitions in New York, Chicago, Boston, Baltimore, and throughout the East Coast and at the Museum of Rochefort-en-Terre in Brittany, France, where she was awarded an artist residency by the Maryland Institute of Baltimore in 1995. She is a member of the Artists Fellowship and the National Arts Club in New York City. Mitton's paintings are included in the permanent collections of the National Arts Club in New York City; *Readers Digest* in Pleasantville, New York; Fidelity Company in Boston, and in private collections in France, Switzerland, Canada, and throughout the United States. She is also the author of *A Romantic Art Colony: Marion Massachusetts*.

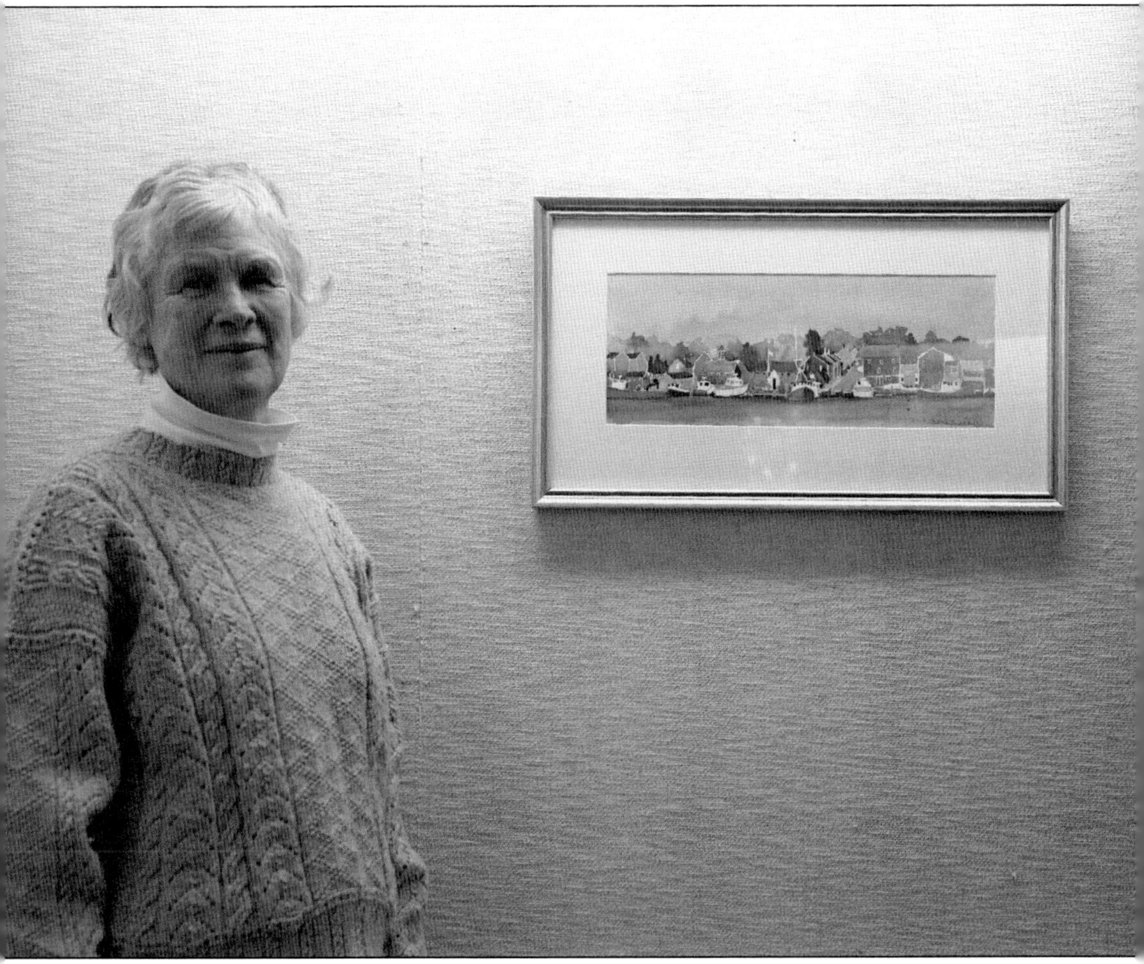

Sharlie Sudduth first came to Marion when she was 12 and summered with her family in the "Big House" on the harbor. She has been coming to Marion ever since and now lives here permanently. In her late 50s she started with a beginning watercolor class at the Rhode Island School of Design and has been avidly painting ever since. She recently published a book of her watercolor paintings titled *My Marion*. In it she stated, "I start with a feeling of beauty about the places I am in and just enjoy the process of drawing and finding my way into what I think I want to paint. Often I discover something more as I go along doing the painting. I settle in, feeling the sun and the wind, often losing a sense of time and myself as if in a meditation. I always like to be in my paintings rather than paint from pictures, so in the winter I paint in my car. I like my paintings to tell stories and reflect the feelings of the places I paint."

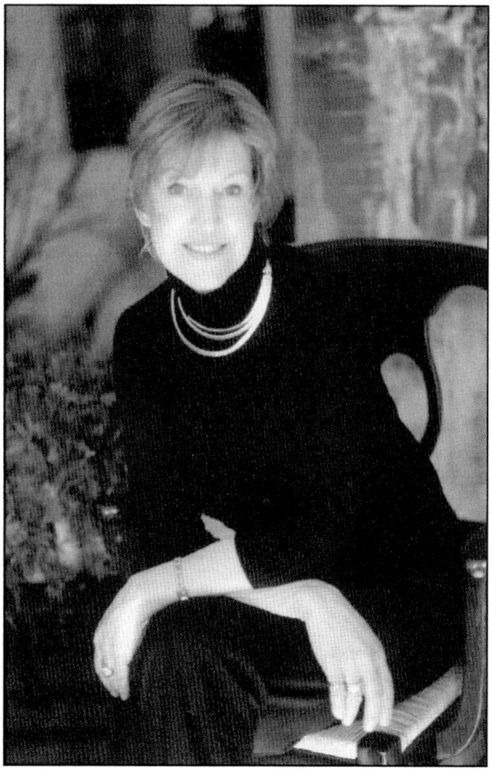

New York City's garment industry is where Joan De Rugeris started her commercial art career. Working for leading textile converters, she designed prints for ready to wear and home furnishing. After receiving her degree from the State University of New York, Fashion Institute of Technology, De Rugeris's paintings were widely exhibited throughout the mid-Atlantic states and New England. Her work utilizes pattern and design elements through the use of mixed medium, acrylics, and oils. Within her portfolio, landscapes, global architecture, human spirituality, and generations of rebirth evolve from an amalgamation of color and pattern.

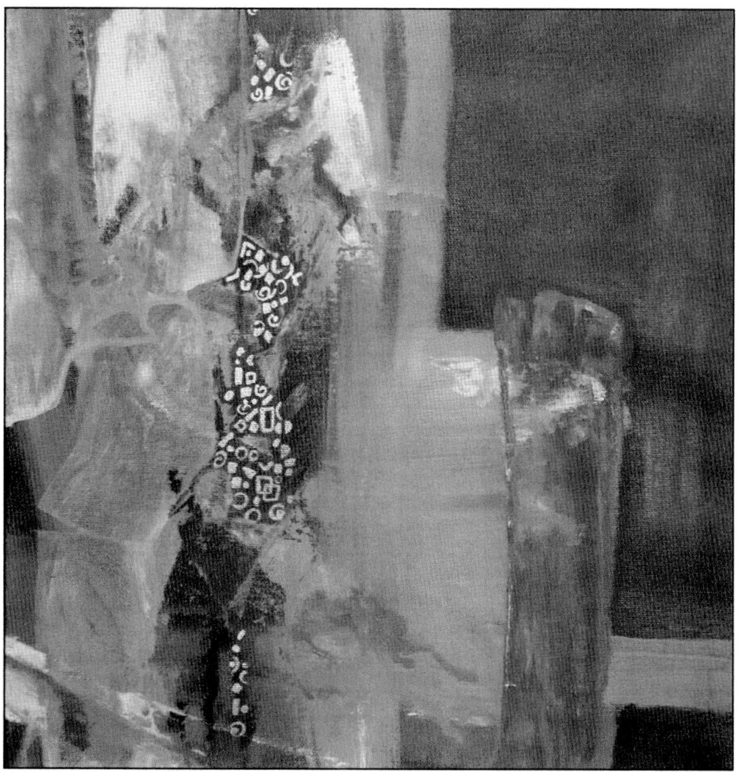

De Rugeris's work has been widely exhibited in New England. A native of Long Island, New York, she has been a resident of Marion since 1986, where she maintains her studio.

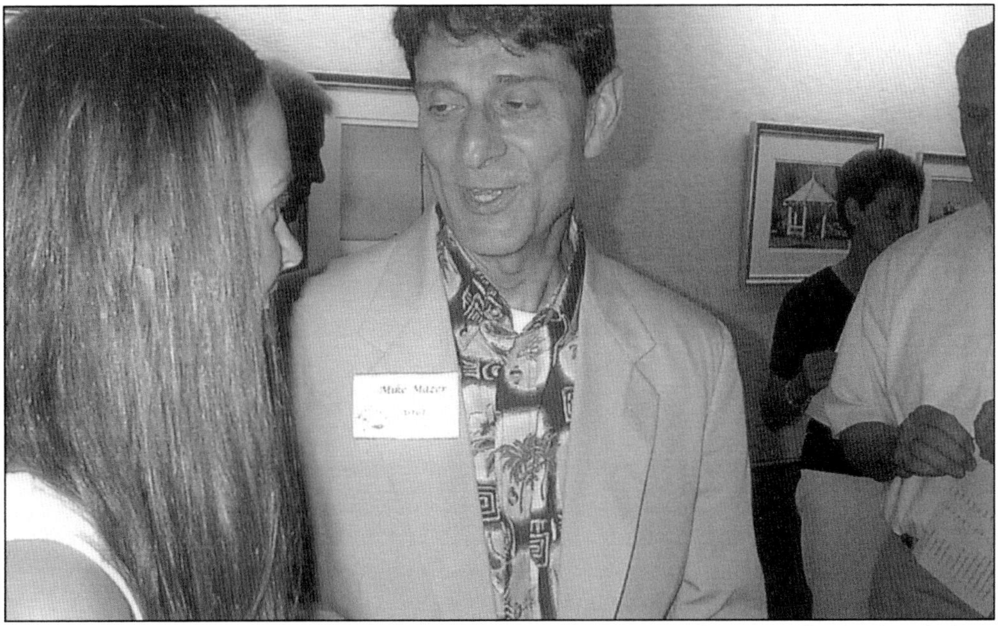

Since retiring in 1998 from a very fulfilling 36-year career as simultaneous chiefs of cardiology and nephrology at several Greater Boston area hospitals, Mike Mazer's representational land and seascape works have been juried into more that 160 national and international exhibitions while being the recipient of 44 awards including best of show and first place. He also belongs to more than 21 national art societies.

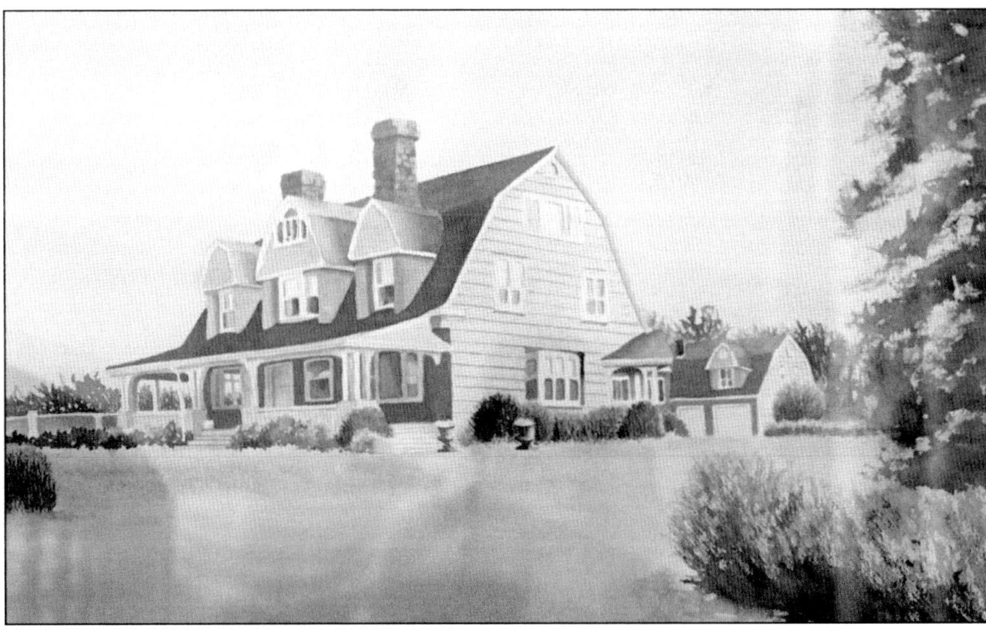

This painting of a home located at 46 Water Street in Marion was exhibited at Mazer's show at the Marion Art Center and purchased by the owners of the home at the show. Examples of his work can be seen in the publications of the American Society of Marine Artists *Contemporary American Marine Art* 12th and 13th National Exhibitions, as well as their Web site. His work is in many public, private, and corporate collections throughout the United States.

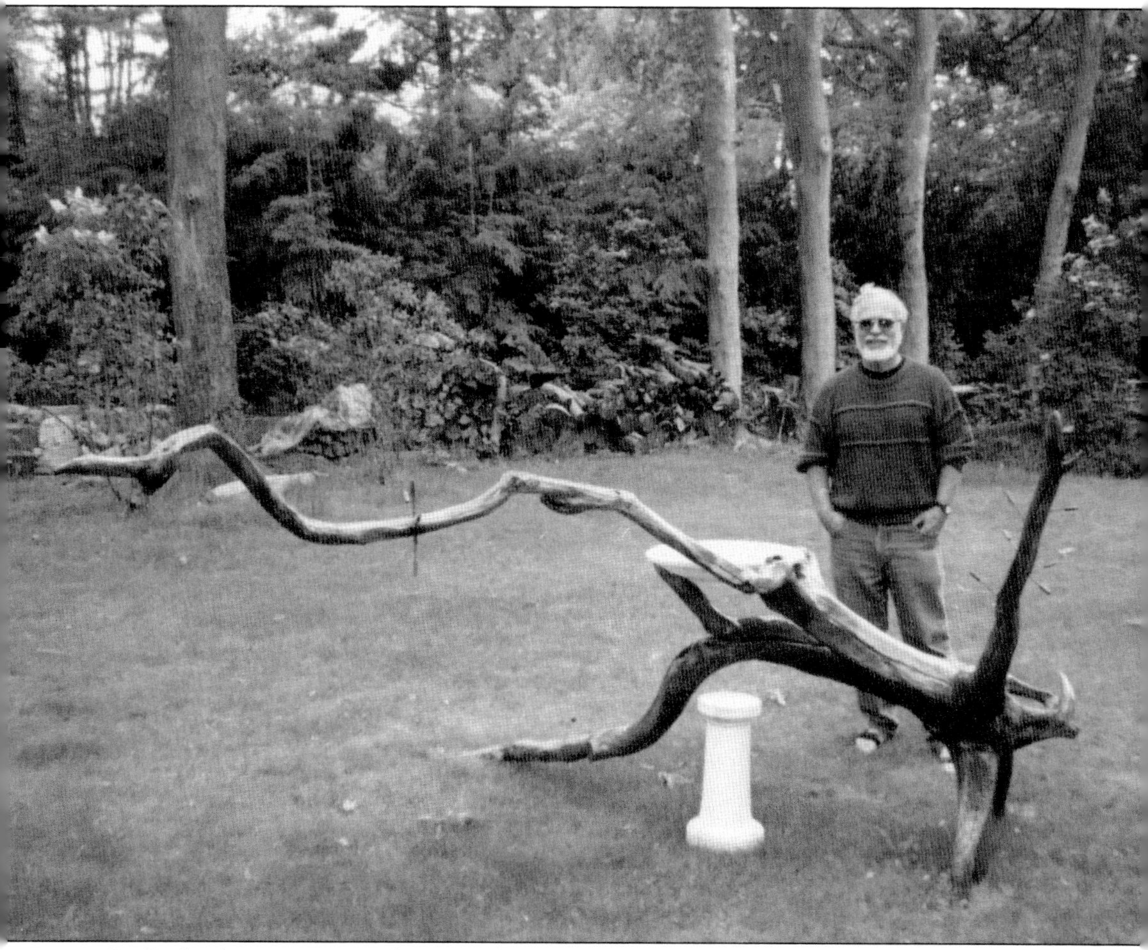

Bo Burbank, a Marion resident, stands in front of his sculpture titled *Mind, Body, Spirit.* He is a retired teacher of 40 years and chaired both the math and art departments at Mercersburg Academy in Pennsylvania. Since 1996, Burbank has lived in Marion full time. He works in a variety of media including sculpture, collage, oils, watercolor, and acrylics. His mixed media show of 40 works, titled Eclectic Visuals, at the Marion Art Center included paintings, drawings, two driftwood sculptures, and a collage using dried paint chips.

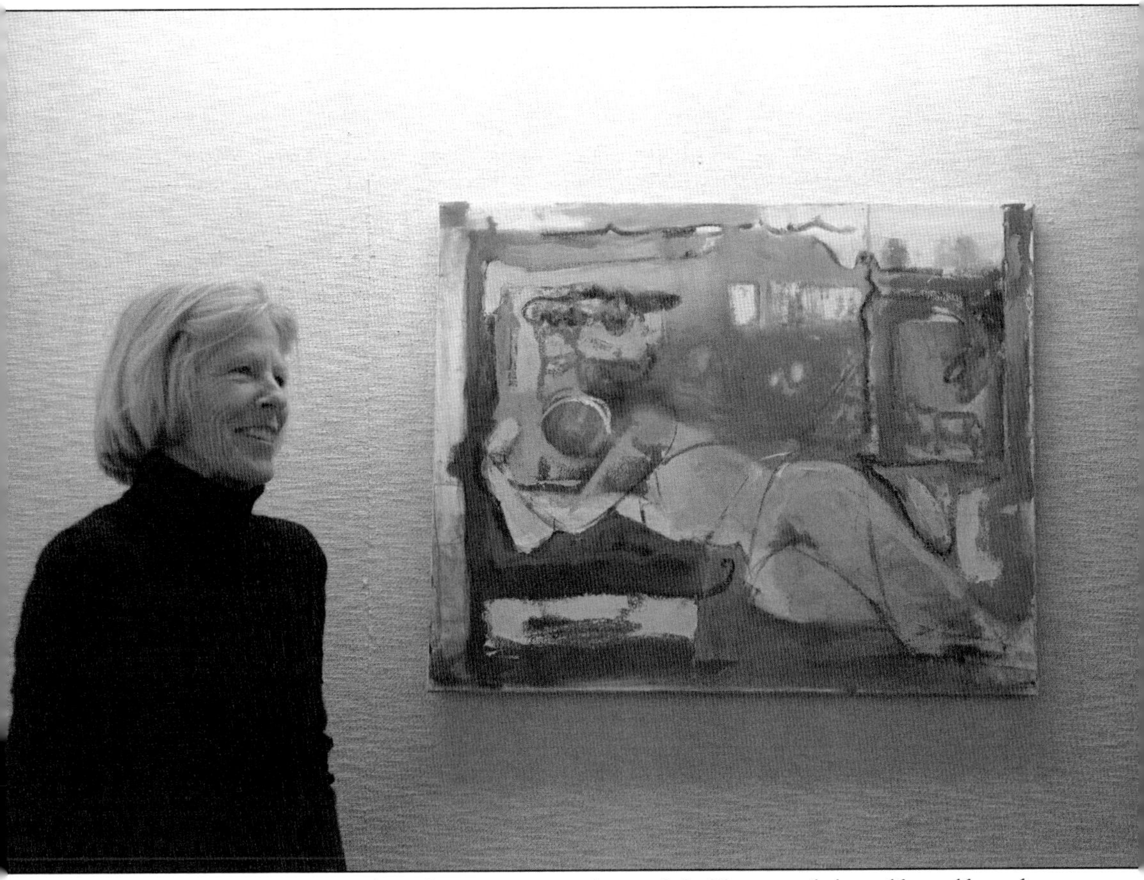

Hattie Notman, a Marion resident, began painting late in life. She regards herself as self-taught, but she has taken classes at the Boston Museum of Fine Arts. She paints with acrylics, watercolors, and oil and does both abstract and figurative work. She maintains studios in Marion and in Plymouth, Massachusetts.

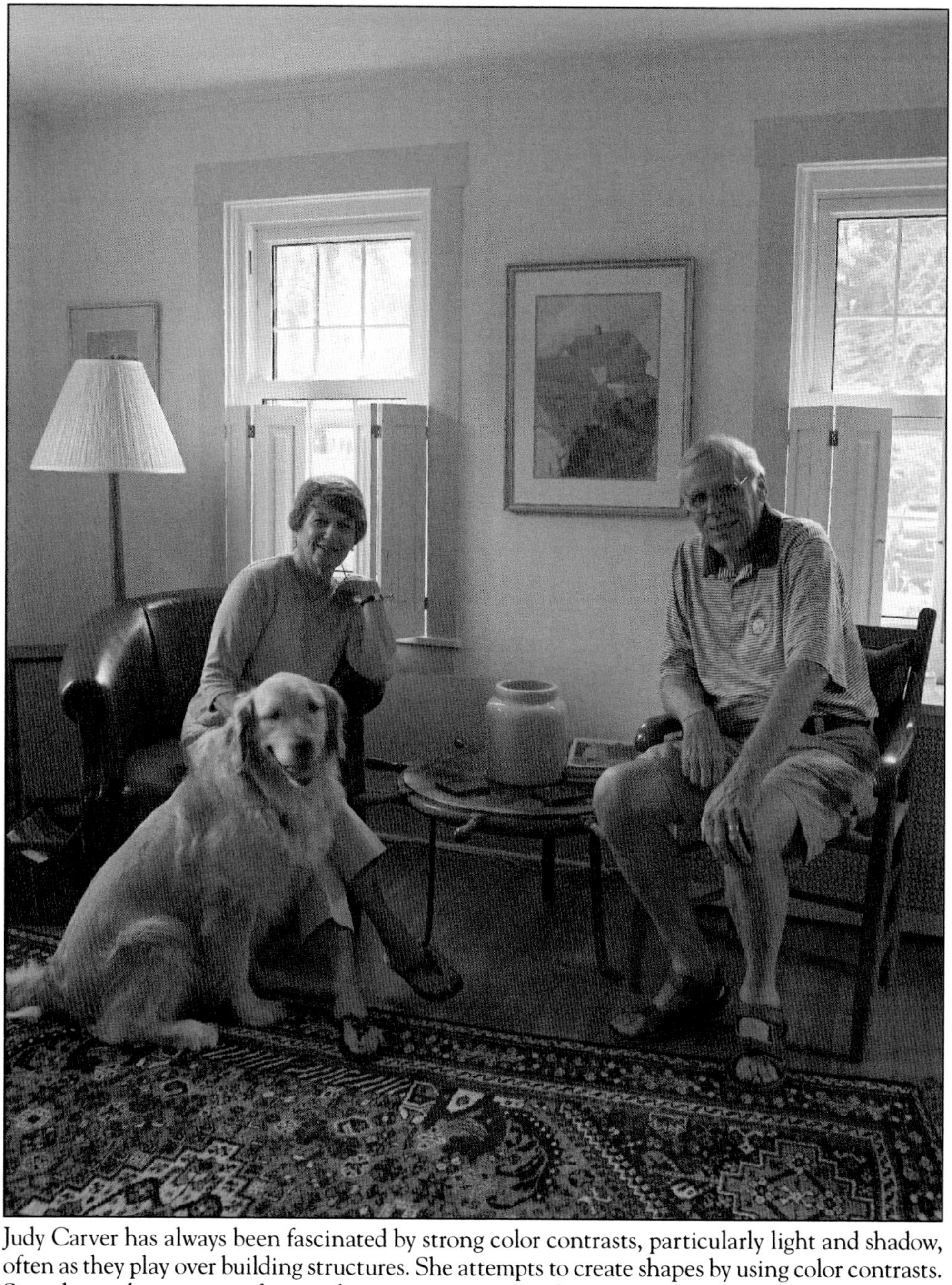

Judy Carver has always been fascinated by strong color contrasts, particularly light and shadow, often as they play over building structures. She attempts to create shapes by using color contrasts. Since her early retirement from real estate investment and management, she has taken watercolor classes at the Boston Museum of Fine Arts and the Rhode Island School of Design. Her work has been shown at the Dover Public Library and the Springbull Gallery in Newport, Rhode Island, as well as the Marion Art Center.

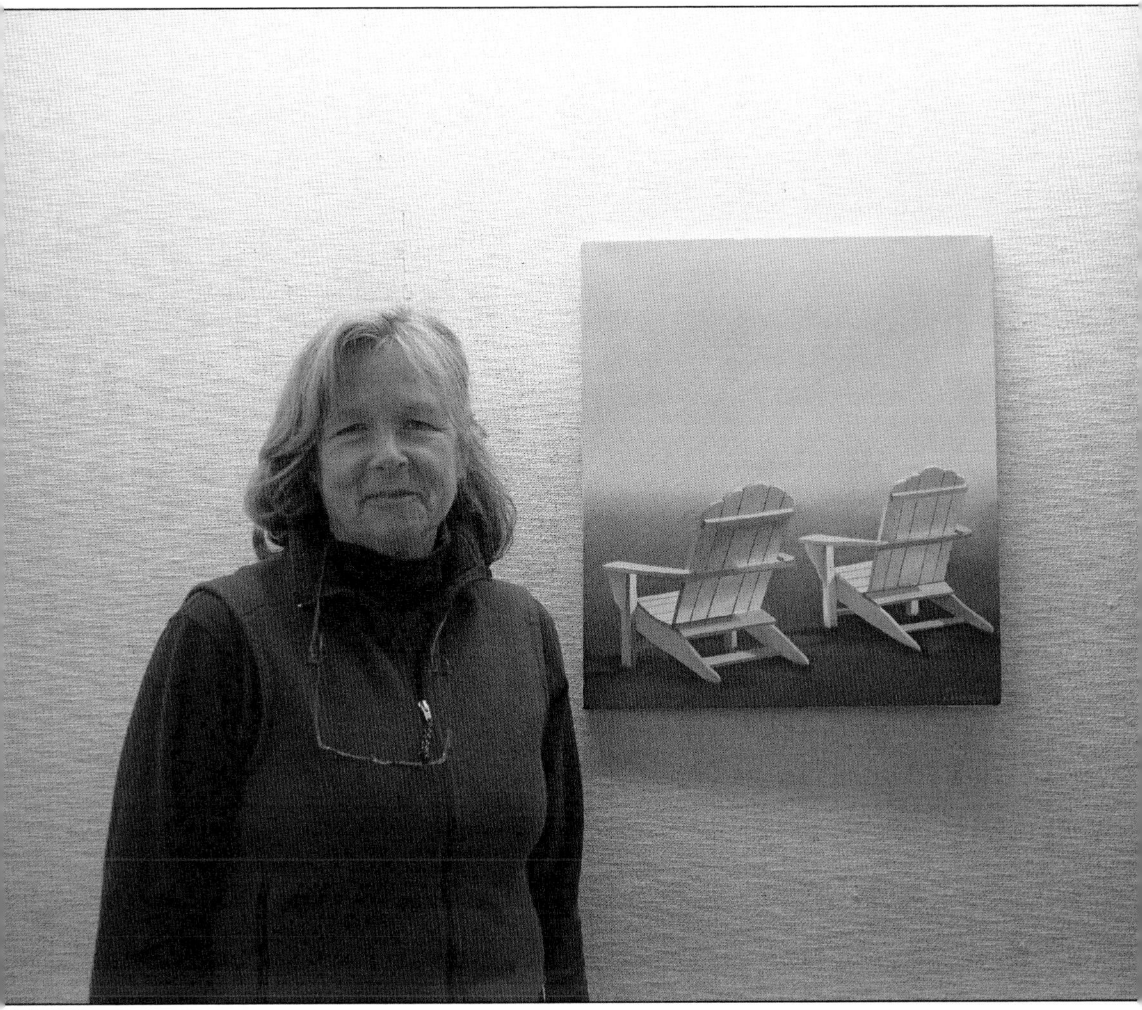

Laura Anderson, a professional artist who lives in nearby Mattapoisett, studied art at the Hartford Art School and the Rhode Island School of Design. Her work is in over 300 private collections throughout the United States and Europe as well as in the permanent collections of the De Cordova Museum, Fuller Museum, Massachusetts Mutual Life Company, Du Pont, Jackson and Company, Cabot Corporation, Fleet National Bank, and others. She has a studio in Mattapoisett and exhibits in several galleries including the Sherry French Gallery in New York City, the Case Gallery in Boston, and the Convergence Gallery in Santa Fe. She is a member of the prestigious National Arts Club in New York City where she has won several prizes.

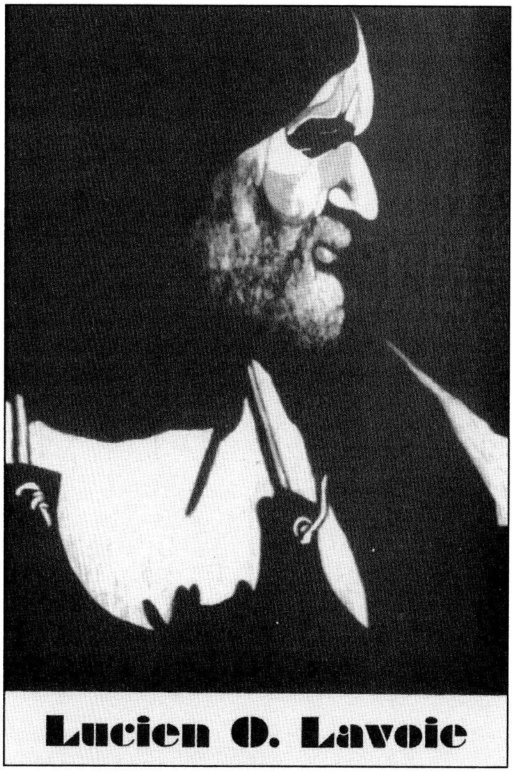

Lucien Lavoie graduated from Massachusetts College of Art and was chairman of the art department at Tabor Academy, where he taught for 40 years. He retired in 1994 and devoted the rest of his life to his art. He was versatile in many media including metal and wood sculpture, welding, and oil and watercolor painting. He also produced "aluminosities," relief sculptures drawn and hammered on heavy aluminum foil-like sheets. This self-portrait was included in his last show at the Marion Art Center before his death.

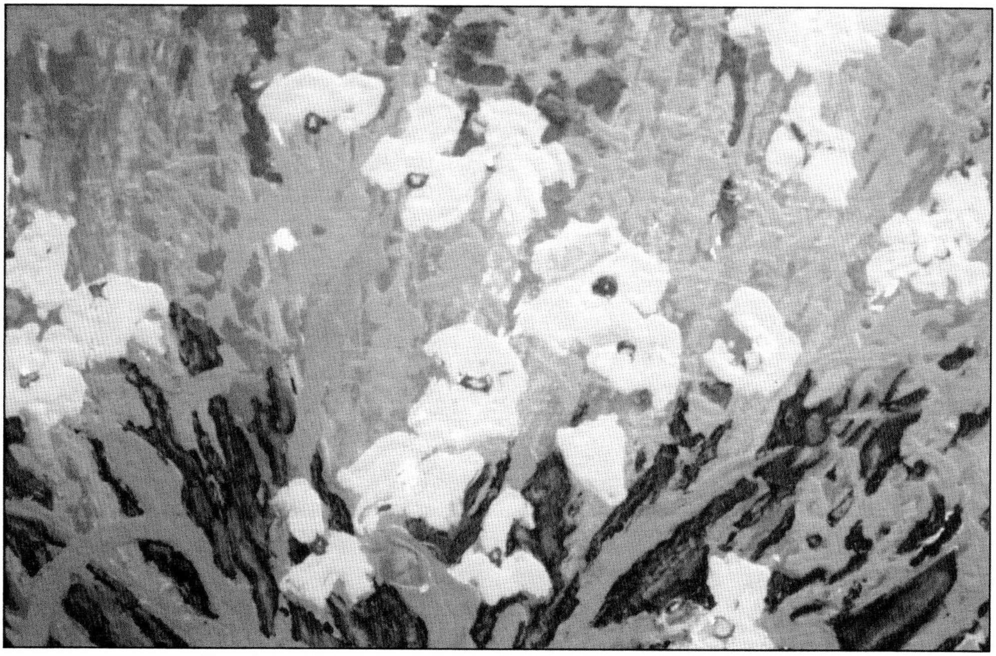

Virginia Lovejoy Allyn has been an artist for most of her life. She studied printmaking and oil painting at the University of Massachusetts in Dartmouth, and her favorite subjects are flowers, portraits, landscapes, and seascapes. She has a press in her Marion studio. This painting of her garden was shown at the Marion Art Center.

Three

Cecil Clark Davis

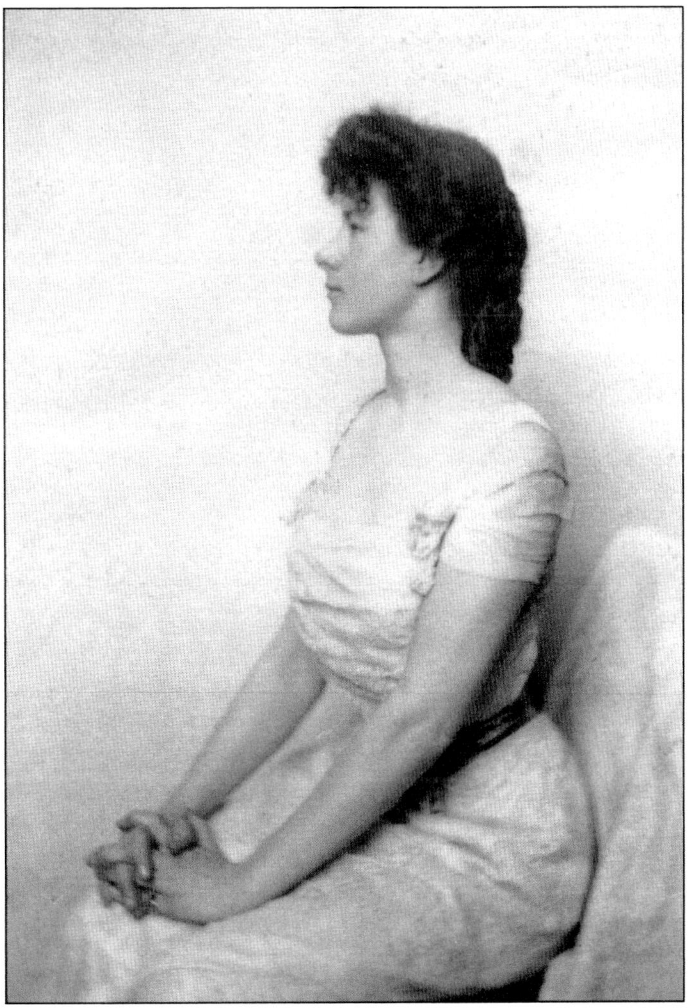

This is a photograph of Cecil Clark Davis, Marion's most famous painter. Over the course of her life (1877–1955) she developed into an award-wining portrait artist who painted many of the important people of her era, including flyer Charles Lindbergh, actor Lionel Barrymore, Arctic explorer Roald Amundsen, and inventor Alexander Graham Bell. The daughter of a successful Chicago industrialist who summered in Marion, Davis was interested in painting, sports, games, music, theater, and dogs. In 1899, her wedding to renowned journalist, novelist, playwright, and war correspondent Richard Harding Davis was reported from Marion as a social event of national interest.

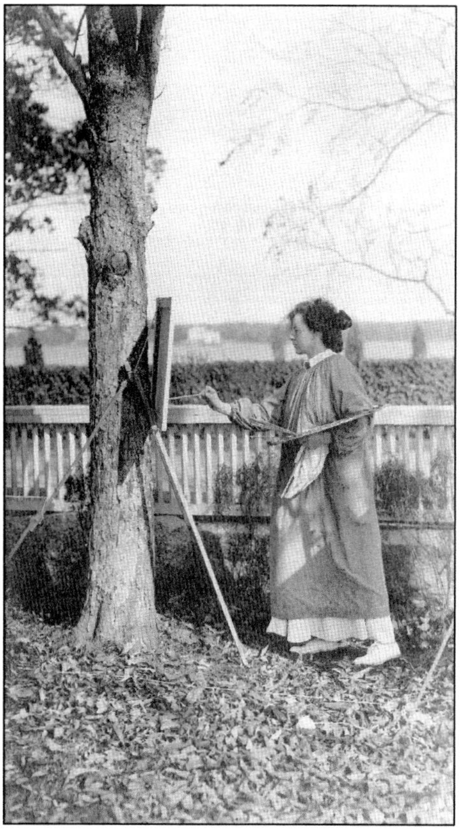

These two photographs show Cecil Clark Davis painting outdoors on Harbor Lane (now called Water Street) in Marion overlooking the harbor. She was mainly a self-taught artist, but many sources state that she was taught by the renowned John Singer Sargent. Davis kept a diary most of her life and according to an entry in her 1908 diary, she first met Sargent in London in December, noting that she found him a "simple forceful person." On January 3, 1909, her diary entry stated: "John Sargent came in after luncheon very nervous and perhaps shy, but a vast volcanic man—took him to the studio which he loved—thought the monochrome painting unnecessary. Admitted that no one could teach anyone anything but the technical part—mechanics of the trade. He played the piano for me charmingly and asked me to tea on Wednesday."

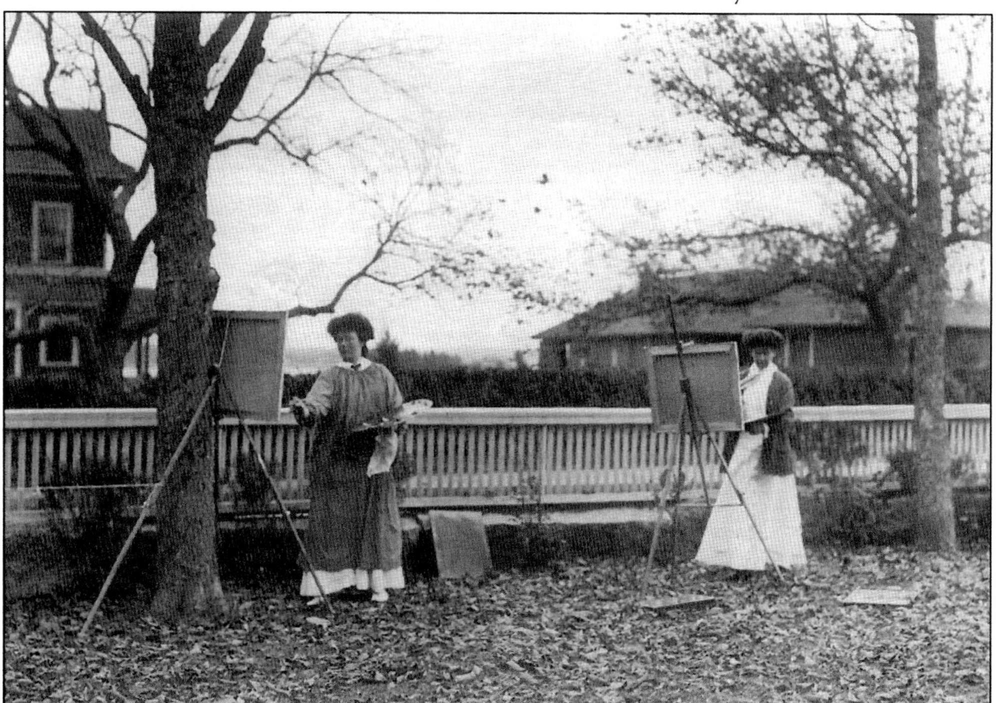

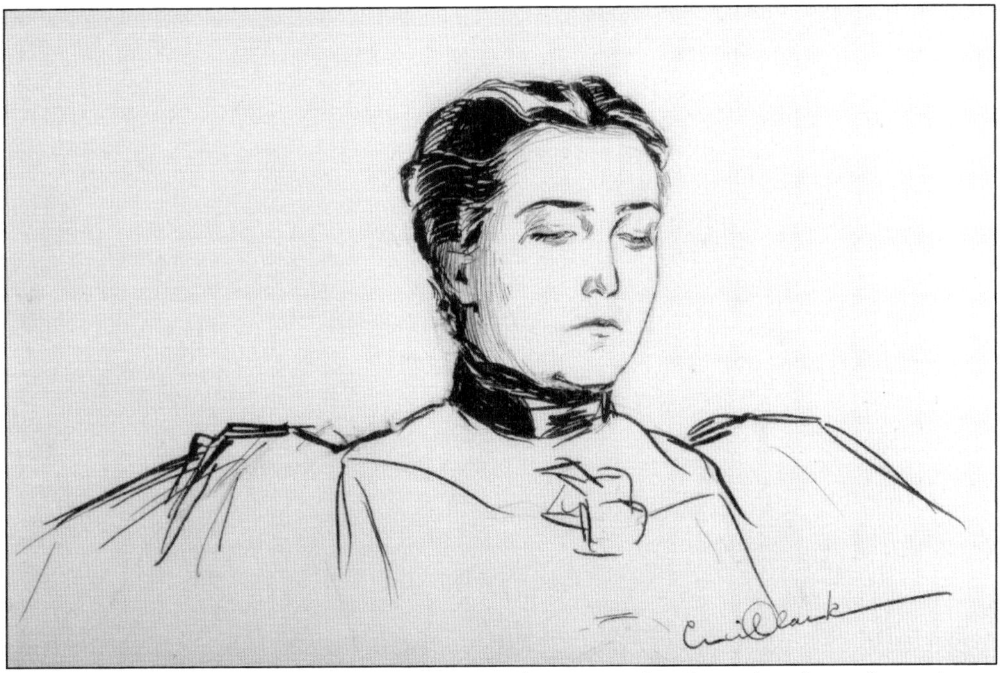

This is the earliest surviving artwork by Davis in the Marion Art Center's archives. It was drawn by Davis at age 13 when she was in Florence with her parents. It is titled *K. M. D.*

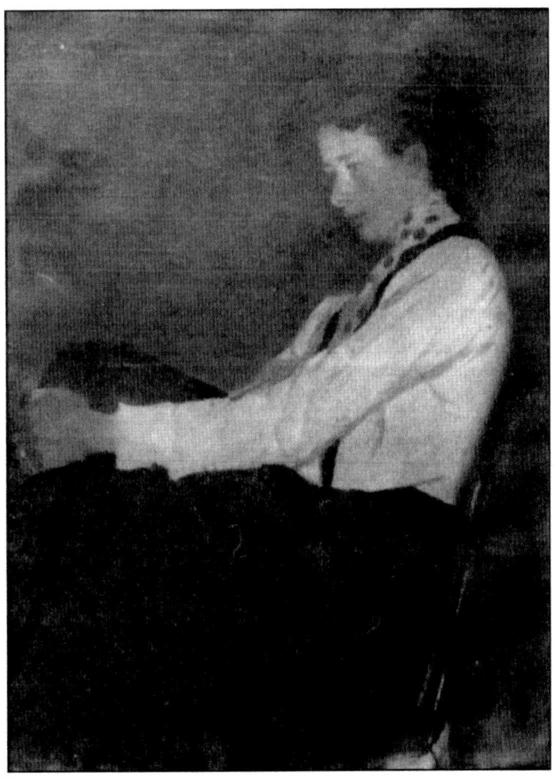

This portrait of Davis was painted by Ellen Emmett Rand in 1900 and is owned by the Marion Art Center. Rand, the cousin of Henry James, may have given art lessons to Davis. The portrait was a wedding present to Richard Harding Davis from the artist on his marriage to Cecil Clark Davis. It is so inscribed in the upper left corner of the portrait.

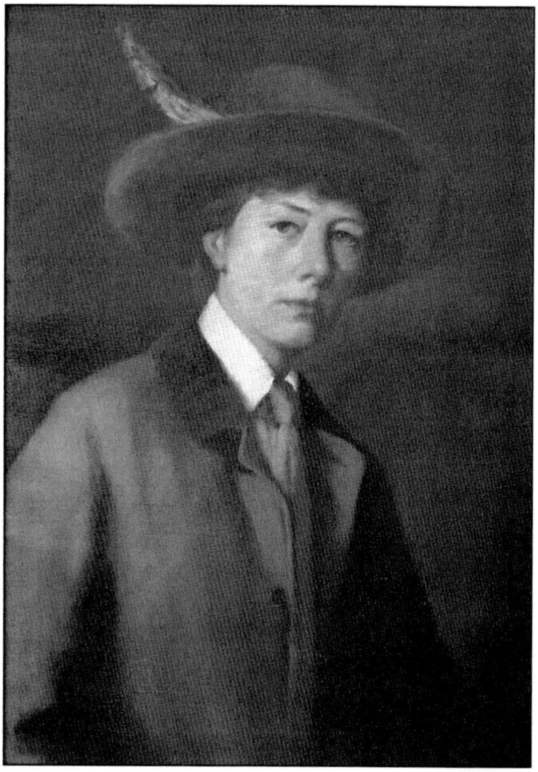

This is a c. 1909 self-portrait painted by Cecil Clark Davis. It was probably painted in London when she and Richard Harding Davis spent a year there. While in London, she became friendly with John Singer Sargent. Her January 6, 1909, diary entry stated: "Went to Mr. Sargent's at 3:30. A wonderful picture of Nancy Astor—alive—didn't care for the pose—background unfinished. He said that it would take him six months to do that and that he hated the mechanical labor and the thought of it. Met his sisters, Miss Sargent and Mrs. Osmond. He quite splendid—same fearless way of praising and condemning—not caring who hears. A really honest man at last. Showed me a bad drawing of Mrs. Reggie Brooks—doesn't admire her and couldn't do it—much annoyed about it."

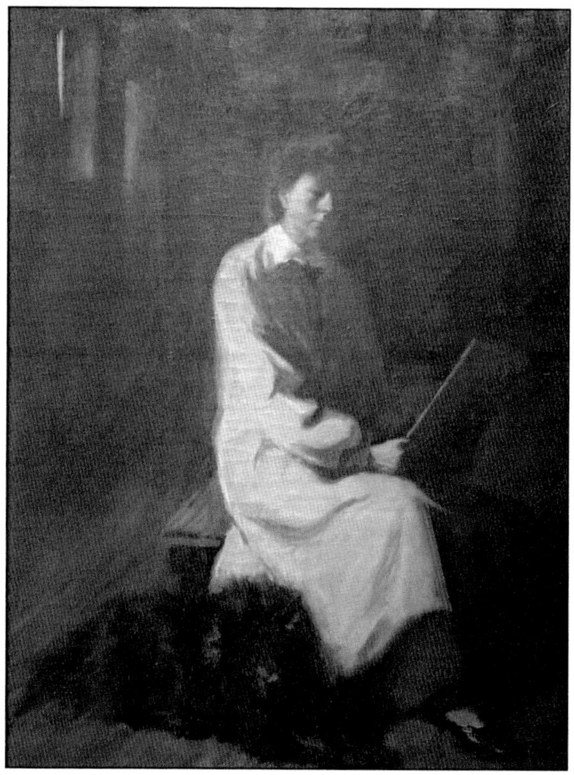

This is another self portrait titled *Self Portrait With Woo Sung*. It was painted in 1913 and is owned by the Sippican Historical Society in Marion. Davis had an innate ability for art and continually strove to improve her technique. She described herself as self-taught, although she studied briefly at the Art Institute of Chicago and had contact with other artists like Sargent and Ellen Emmet Rand. She had studios in New York, Chicago, London, Rio de Janeiro, and Santa Barbara, California, and won many prizes for her art, including the Portrait Prize from the Chicago Municipal Art League in 1918, gold medal of the Salon de Rio de Janeiro in 1920, and the Portrait Prize from the National Association of Women Painters and Sculptors and 1926. Often doubtful of her artistic abilities, she nevertheless persevered to improve them, painting constantly.

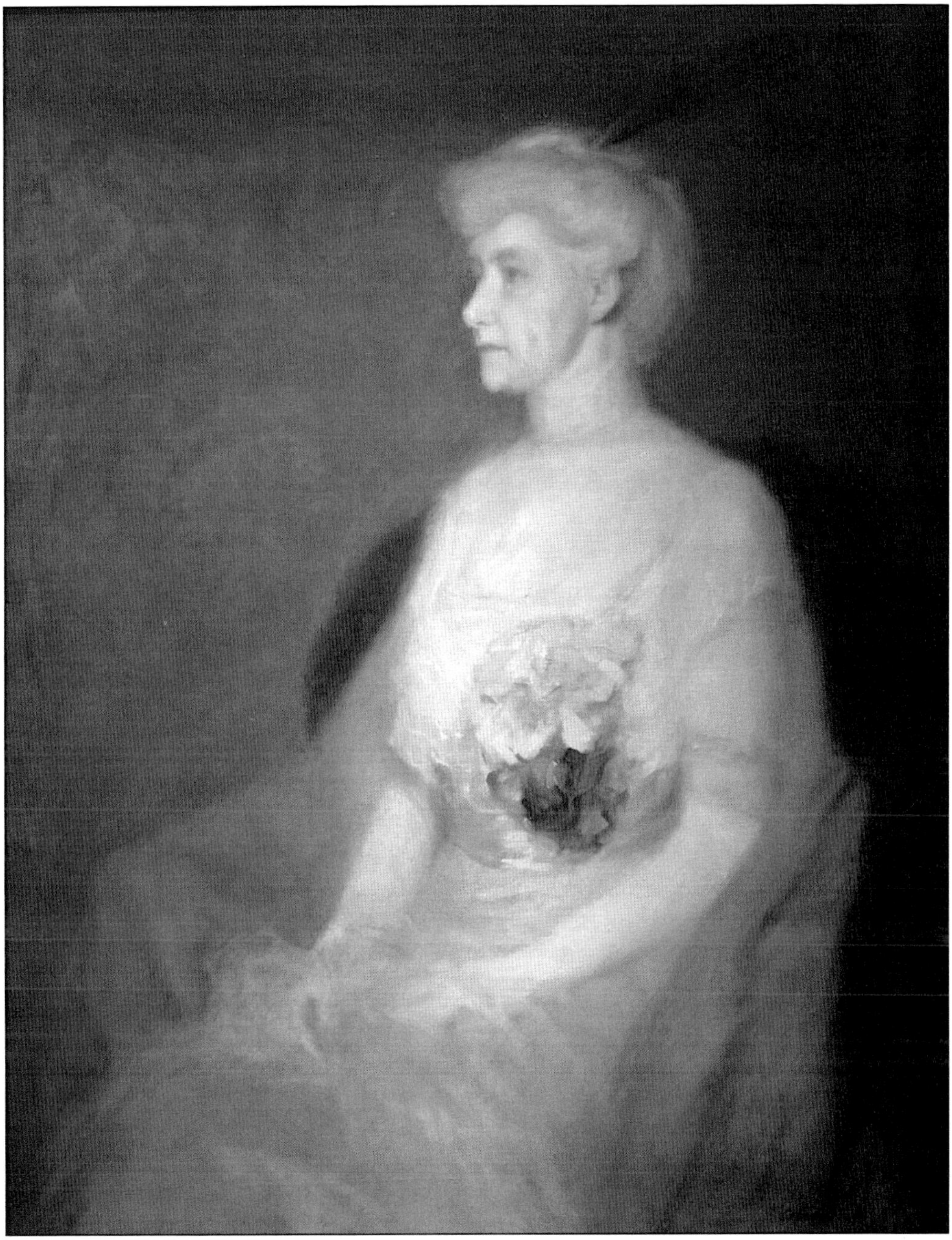

This portrait is *Mrs. John Marshall Clark*, mother of the artist, and was painted in 1916. It is owned by the Sippican Woman's Club in Marion. The Clarks were a wealthy Chicago family who summered in Marion in the family's rambling 23-room cottage on Harbor Lane (now called Water Street). Benefiting from well-to-do doting parents, Davis was exposed to artists and writers and some of the period's best thinkers early in her life. The artist's mother was a concert pianist who performed at Carnegie Hall. She also chaperoned and played for dances at the casino, which was part of the Sippican Hotel in Marion. She and Richard Harding Davis were good friends and she saved all his letters to her.

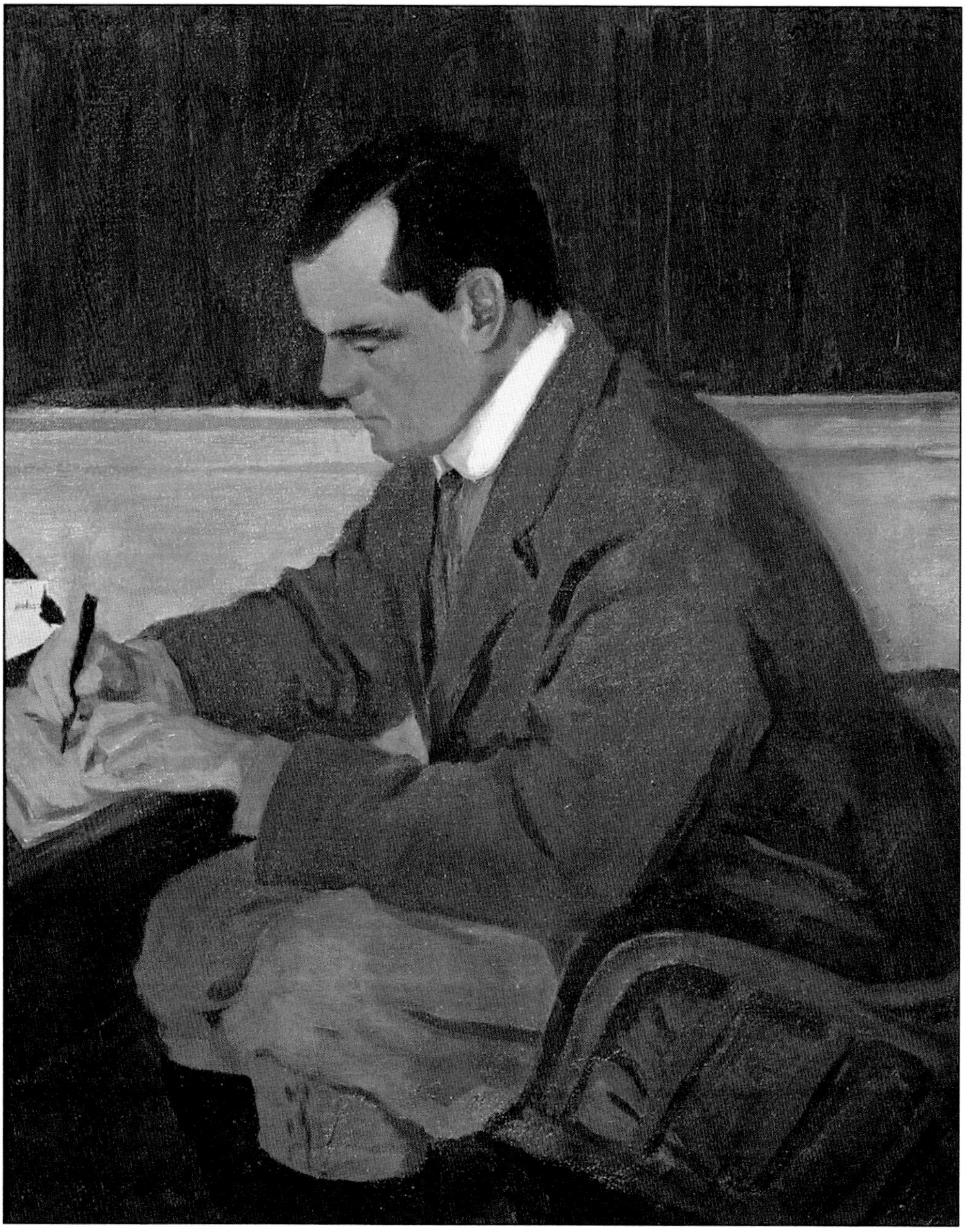

This portrait is of Richard Harding Davis, the husband of Cecil Clark Davis. In 1899, Cecil married the renowned journalist, novelist, playwright, and war correspondent. Their wedding was reported from Marion as a social event of national interest. His journalist assignments led the pair into a marriage of world travel, which gave Cecil access to a vast array of international art and artists. Later divorcing Richard, Cecil devoted the rest of her life to painting. This portrait was painted in 1906 and is in the collection of the Sippican Historical Society in Marion.

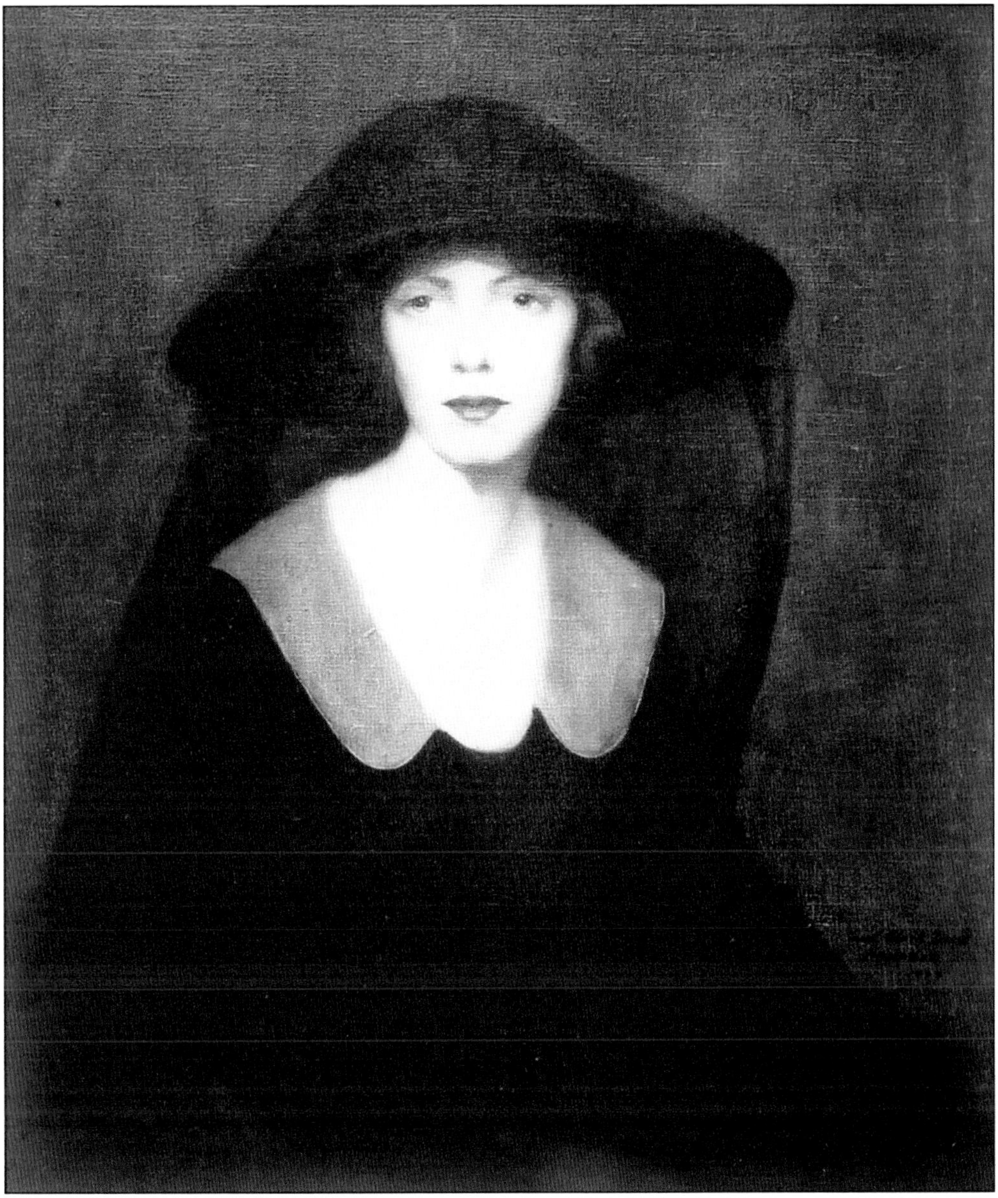

This portrait is of Dai Davis (shown in mourning), wife of Charles Belmont Davis, Richard's brother. It was painted in 1916, the year that Richard died.

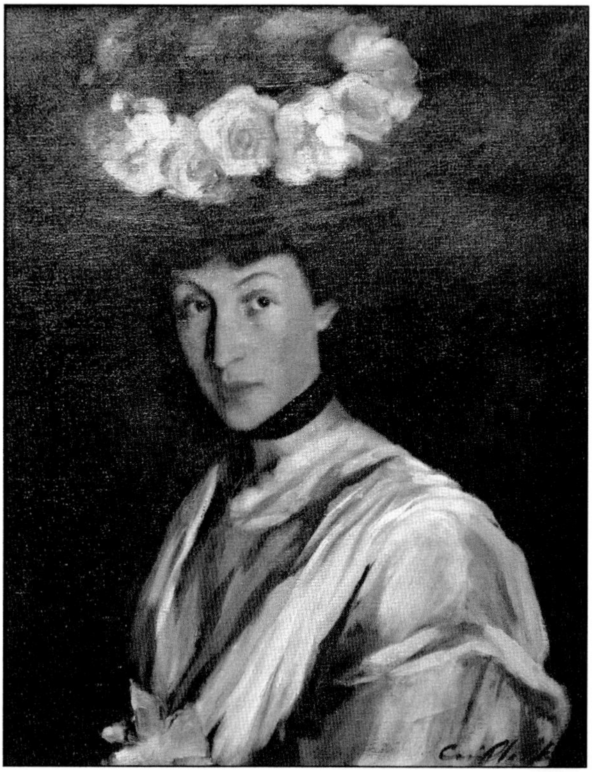

Marjorie Thayer with Hat was an oil painting by Cecil Clark Davis painted in 1908. Thayer married the artist's brother, Bruce Clark, and became her sister-in-law.

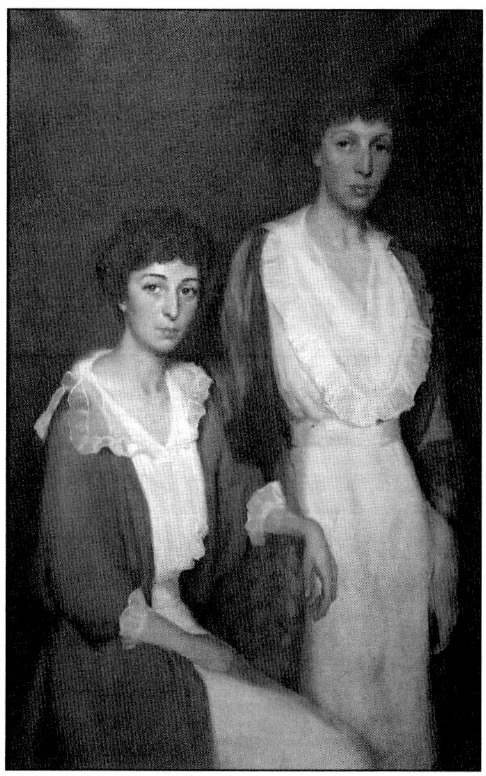

This very unusual double portrait is of sisters Mildred and Marjorie Thayer and was painted in 1916. Mildred Thayer married Paul Burdett, one of Davis's tennis partners at the Sippican Tennis Club in Marion. This portrait is in the collection of Albert Ford.

Soldier Paul Burdett was painted by Davis in 1918 and is in the collection of the Sippican Historical Society in Marion.

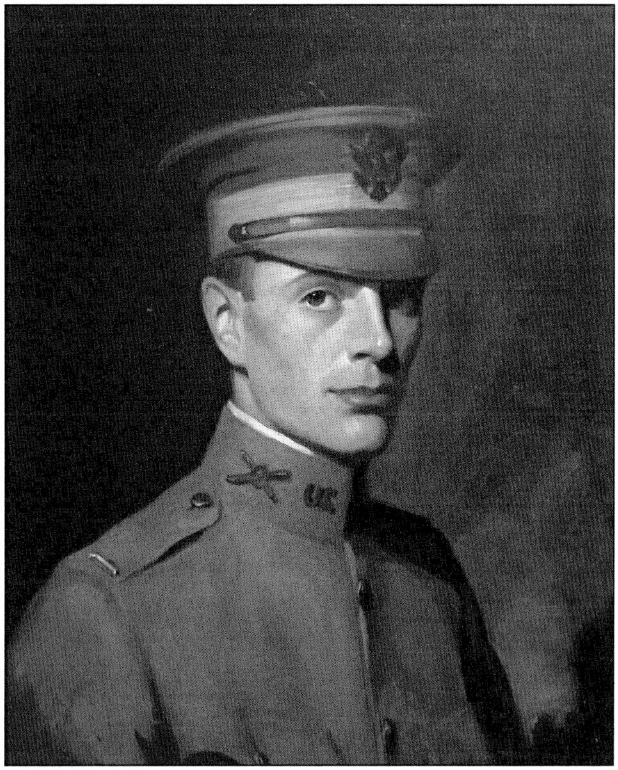

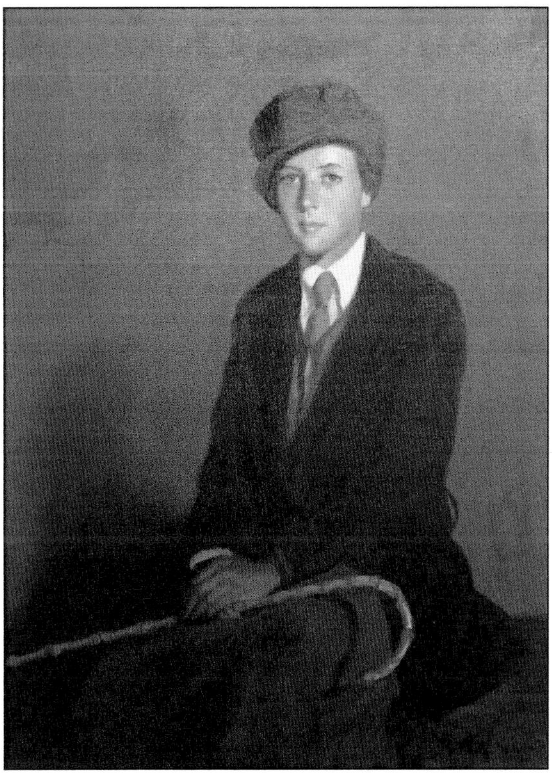

Margaret L. Cutler was painted in 1914 and is in the Cutler family collection. Peggy Cutler was a friend of the artist and they enjoyed riding horses together. The Cutler family still lives in Marion.

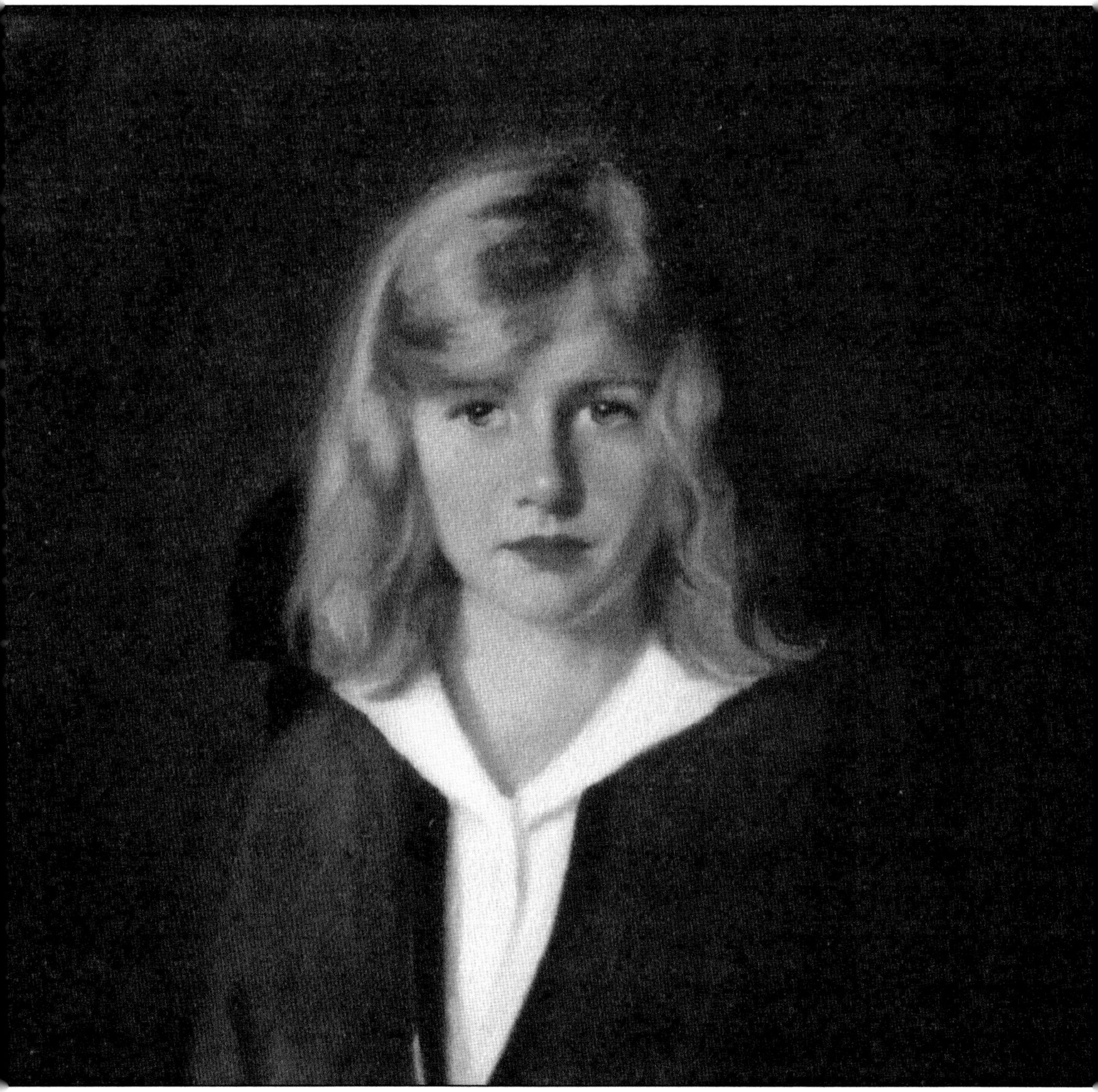

This portrait of Elizabeth "Mopsie" Richardson was painted in 1914. Richardson lived in Providence in the house where she was born. She once had a successful gift shop called M's. She was the cousin of Mrs. Amory Houghton and the "aunt" of Elizabeth Houghton Weinberg of Marion. She owned a small home on Main Street in Marion.

This portrait, *Mrs. Amory Houghton*, was painted in 1933. The Houghton family summered in Marion and were the founders of Corning Glass Works.

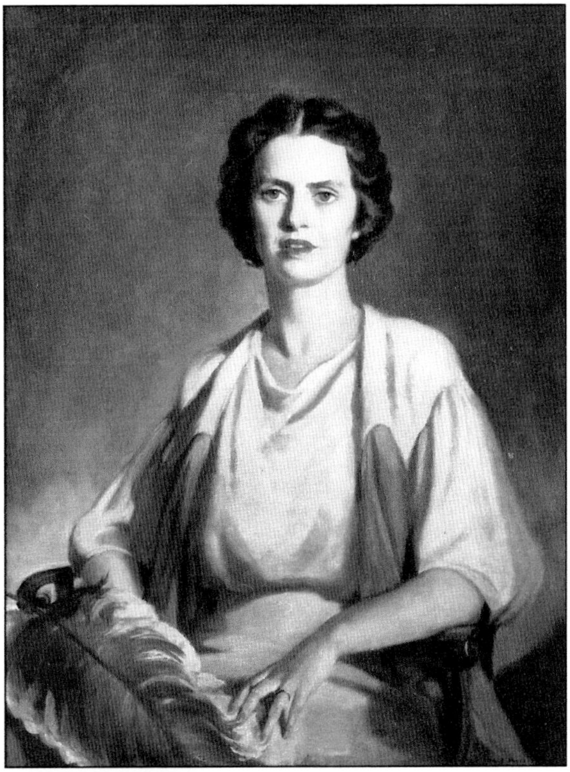

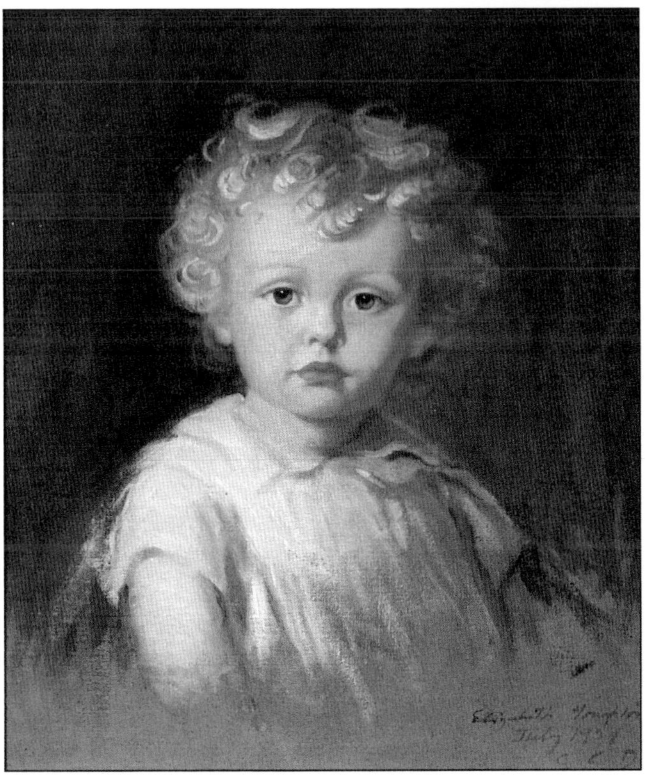

Elizabeth, the daughter of Mrs. Amory Houghton, posed for this portrait in 1924. The Houghtons were summer neighbors of the Clarks in Marion. Elizabeth Houghton Weinberg still lives in Marion.

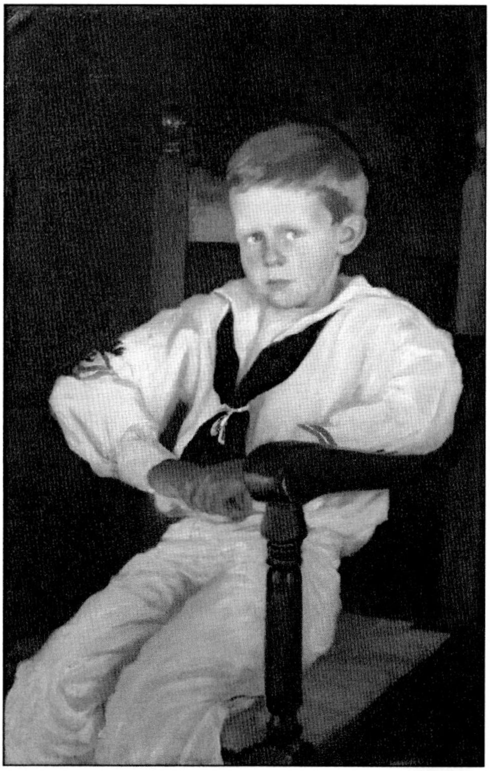

Cecil Clark Davis painted this portrait of Parker Converse in 1905. The squirming boy in the sailor suit was later to become a very successful businessman and owner of the Converse Rubber Company in Malden, Massachusetts. He owned a large point of land in Marion called Converse Point, named after him, where the family still lives today.

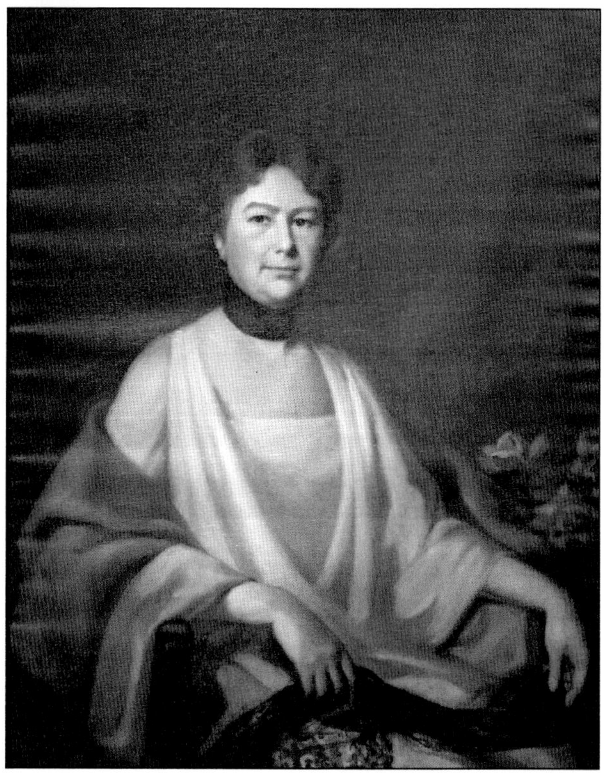

This portrait of Myra Tucker Hood was painted by Davis in 1928 and is in the collection of the Marion Art Center. The Hood family owned a large home on Butler's Point in Marion. Myra was the beloved grandmother of Elizabeth Weeks, Vee Angle, and Frederic Hood. She had a great sense of humor and sometimes dressed up as the Easter Bunny on the Fourth of July. When the family was invited to the house for dinner, Myra might serve the meal backwards, with dessert first, much to the delight of the children. She was a lady of society originally from Providence, Rhode Island.

Frederic Hood II, the grandson of Myra, posed for this portrait in 1926. He lives in South Dartmouth, Massachusetts, today.

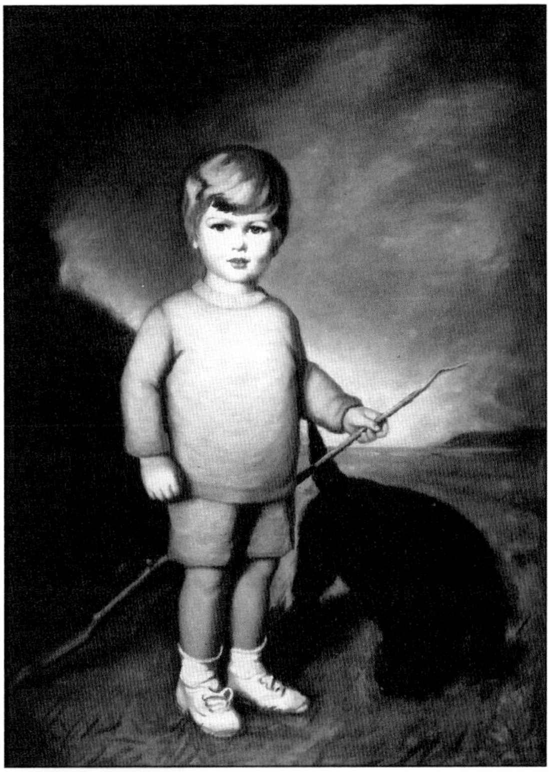

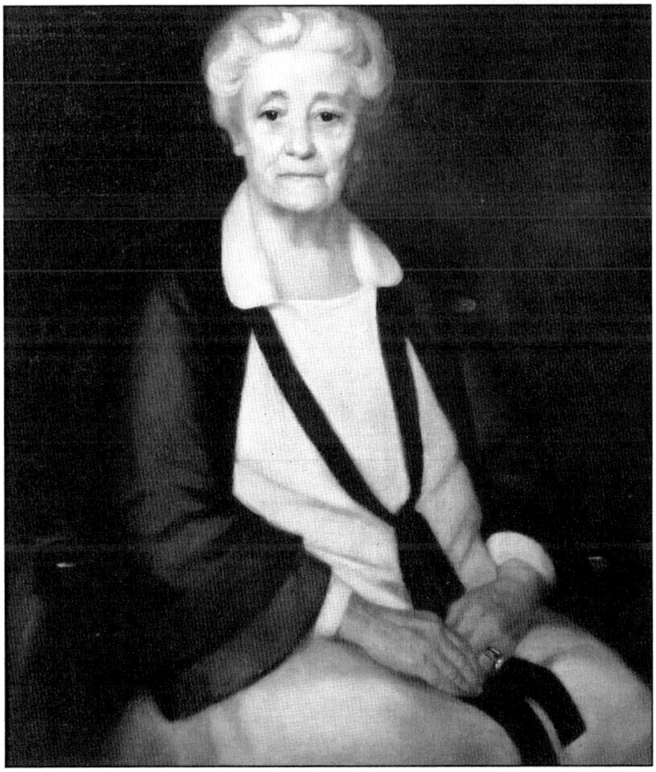

Davis painted this portrait of her Marion neighbor, Mrs. Knowlton, in 1930. The Knowlton family still lives in Marion today.

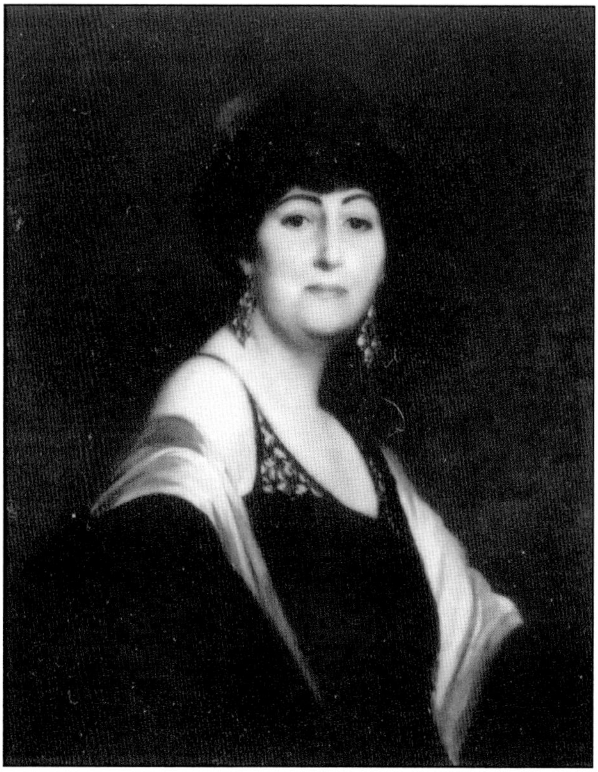

The Cudahy family was a prominent Chicago family who summered in Marion along with the Clark family. This portrait of Elizabeth Cudahy is owned by the Cudahy family who still reside in Marion today.

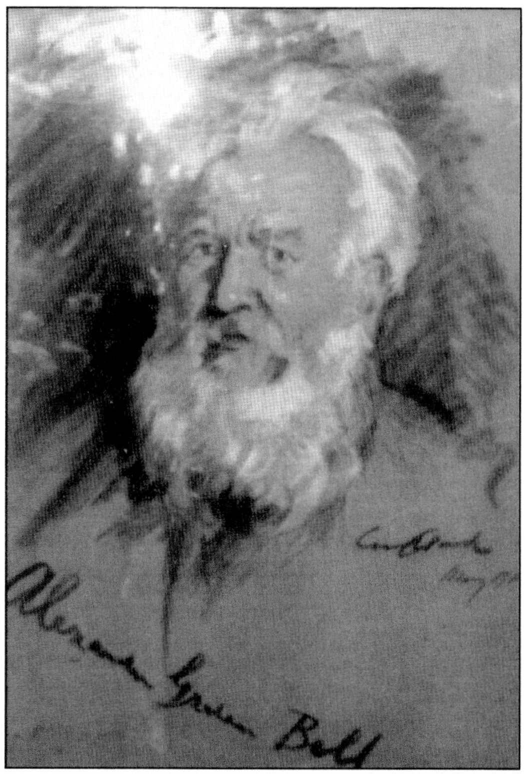

Cecil Clark Davis sketched this portrait in charcoal and chalk of Alexander Graham Bell in 1898. Bell and John Marshall Clark, the artist's father, were business partners in Chicago. He was a close friend of the family.

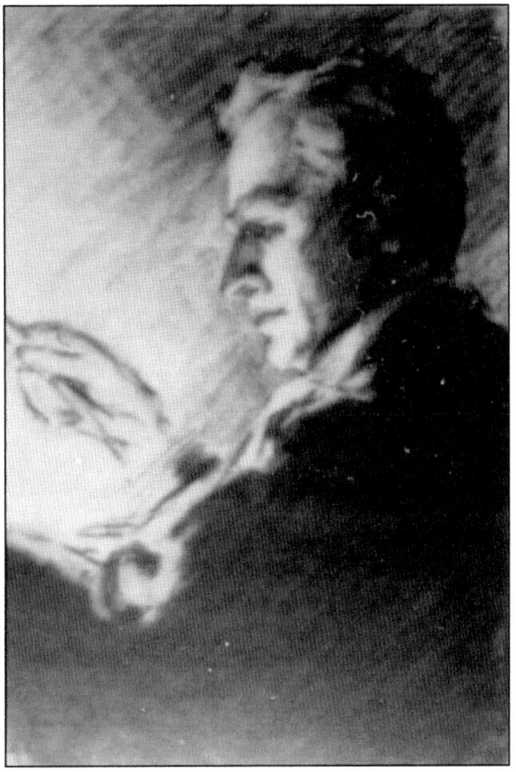

Davis painted Walter Damrosch in 1908 and his wife Margaret in 1920. Walter was conductor of the New York Philharmonic orchestra and was instrumental in creating Tanglewood and other musical retreats and centers in the Greater New York area. He gave Davis a pass to attend all rehearsals and performances at any time. She kept a box of his letters that reflect the close relationship they had throughout their lives.

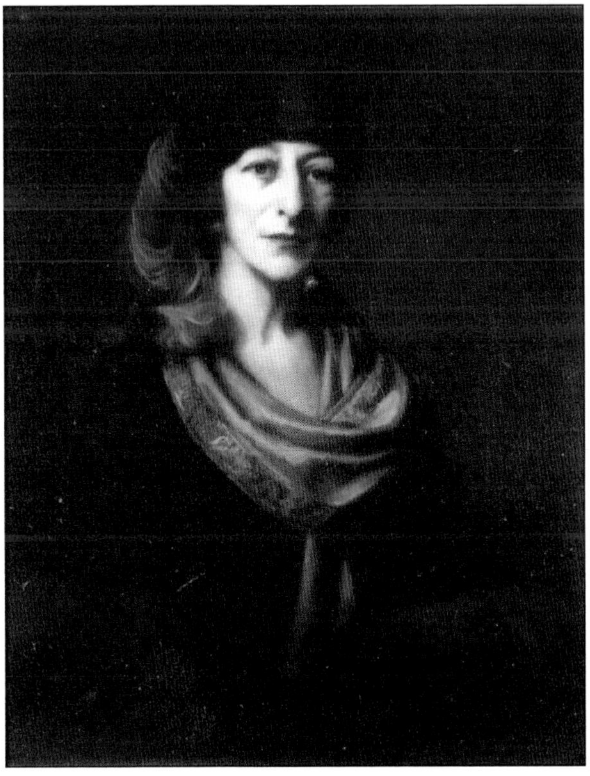

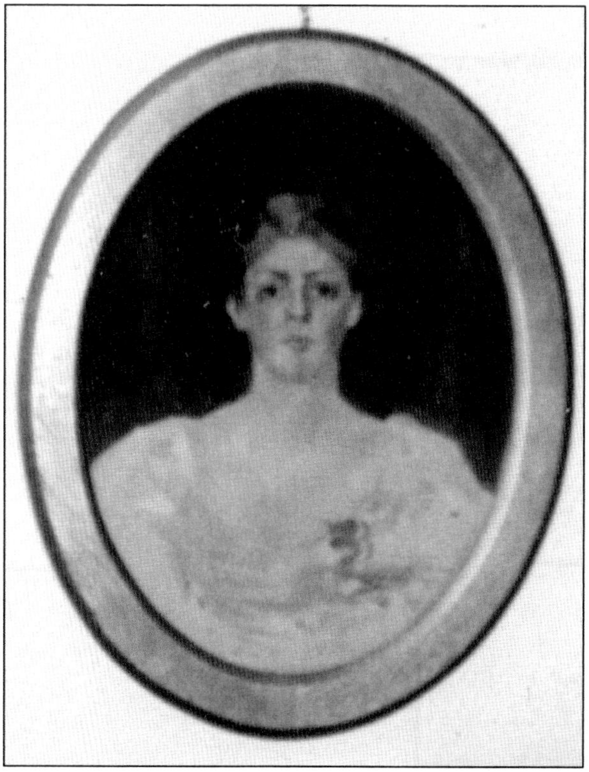

This early portrait of actress Ethel Barrymore was painted in 1896 by Cecil Clark Davis. Barrymore was a close friend of Richard Harding Davis (their families were both from Philadelphia) and was the bridesmaid in his wedding to Cecil and also in his wedding to Bessie McCoy. Barrymore, born in 1879, was the second child of the actors Maurice Barrymore and Georgiana Drew. Her brothers John and Lionel were also actors.

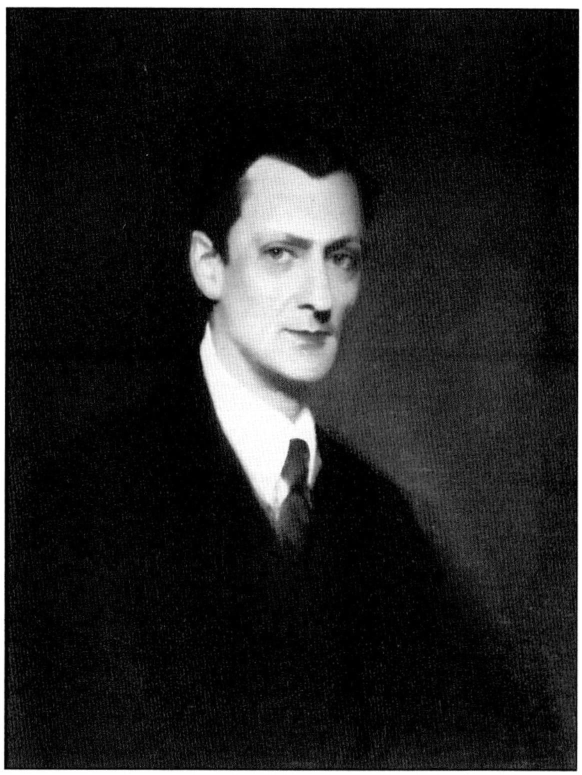

Davis painted this portrait of Lionel Barrymore in 1919, and it is in the collection of the Marion Art Center. The Drews and Barrymores summered in Marion and were good friends of the Clarks and Davises. The Barrymores were an institution in the theater and later in movies. Lionel is best known today for his role as the villain in *It's a Wonderful Life*.

Davis drew this portrait of Sarah Bernhardt, the popular French stage actress, in May 1896, when Davis was only 19 years old. Bernhardt, born in 1844, was over age 50 in the portrait. Bernhardt was also photographed by Nadar, one of the earliest photographers.

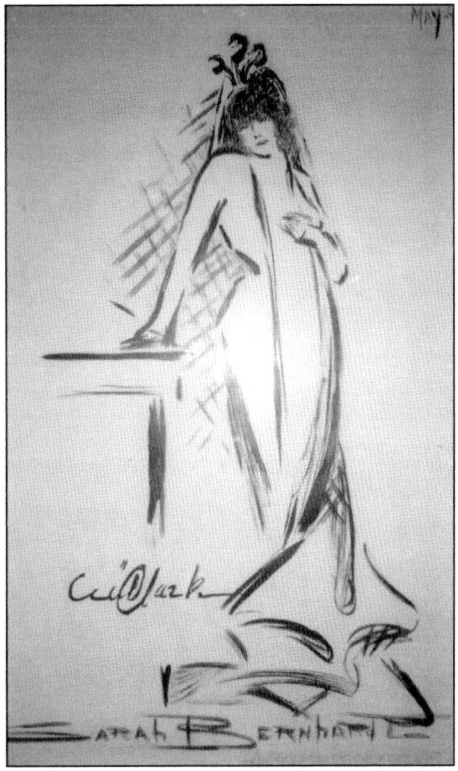

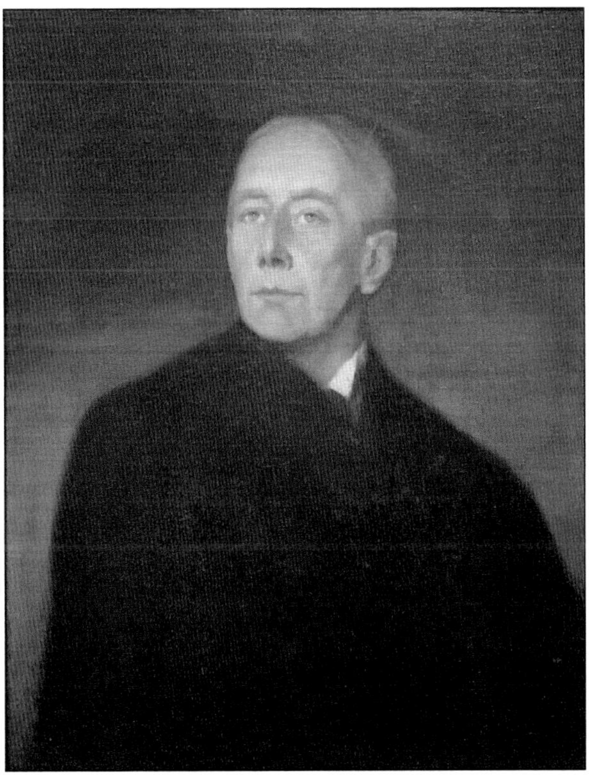

In 1916, Davis painted this portrait of Roald Amundsen. This is the only portrait that the Arctic explorer ever posed for. Actually, Amundsen was only able to sit for a couple of hours, once or twice. Christian Abrahamson posed for the cloak.

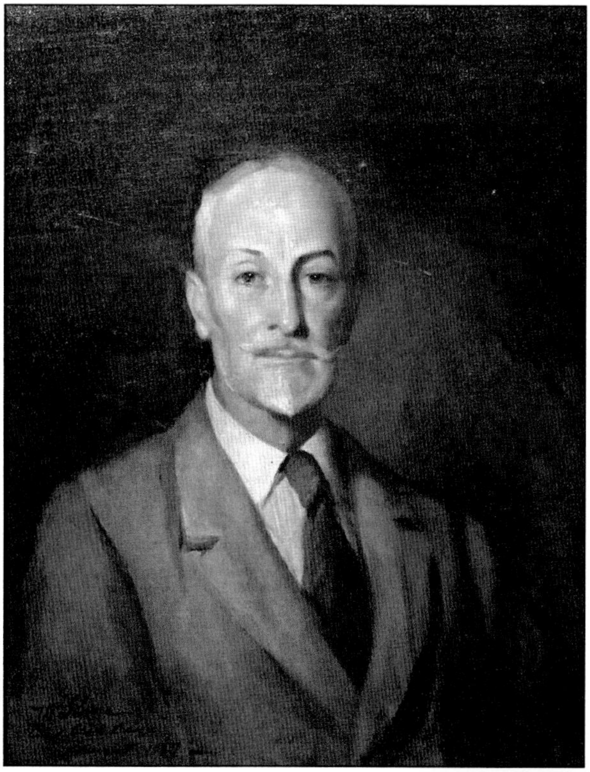

Tabor Academy in Marion owns this portrait of Adm. William Sowden Sims painted by Cecil Clark Davis in 1927. Sims sought to modernize the U.S. Navy in the late 19th and early 20th centuries. During World War I he commanded all U.S. naval forces operating in Europe. He also served twice as president of the Naval War College. His account of the United States naval effort during World War I, *The Victory at Sea,* won the 1921 Pulitzer prize for history.

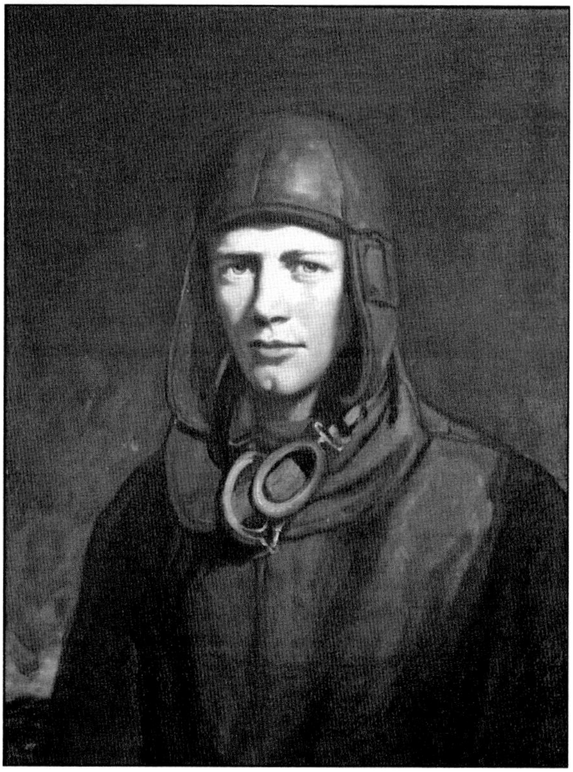

Tabor Academy also owns this portrait of Charles Lindbergh painted in 1927. This painting was done from a photograph. Lindbergh is famous for his solo transatlantic flight in *The Spirit of St. Louis.* The portrait hung in Lillard Hall at Tabor Academy in Marion for many years. In the late 1930s, Hitler and the Nazi party in Germany gave Lindbergh an award for his contributions to aviation. Captain Lillard, the headmaster at Tabor, was angered by Lindberg's Nazi leanings and threatened to turn the painting to the wall. When Davis heard of this, she sent Frederica Poett to retrieve the portrait, and she hid it in her studio where it was finally found after her death in 1955.

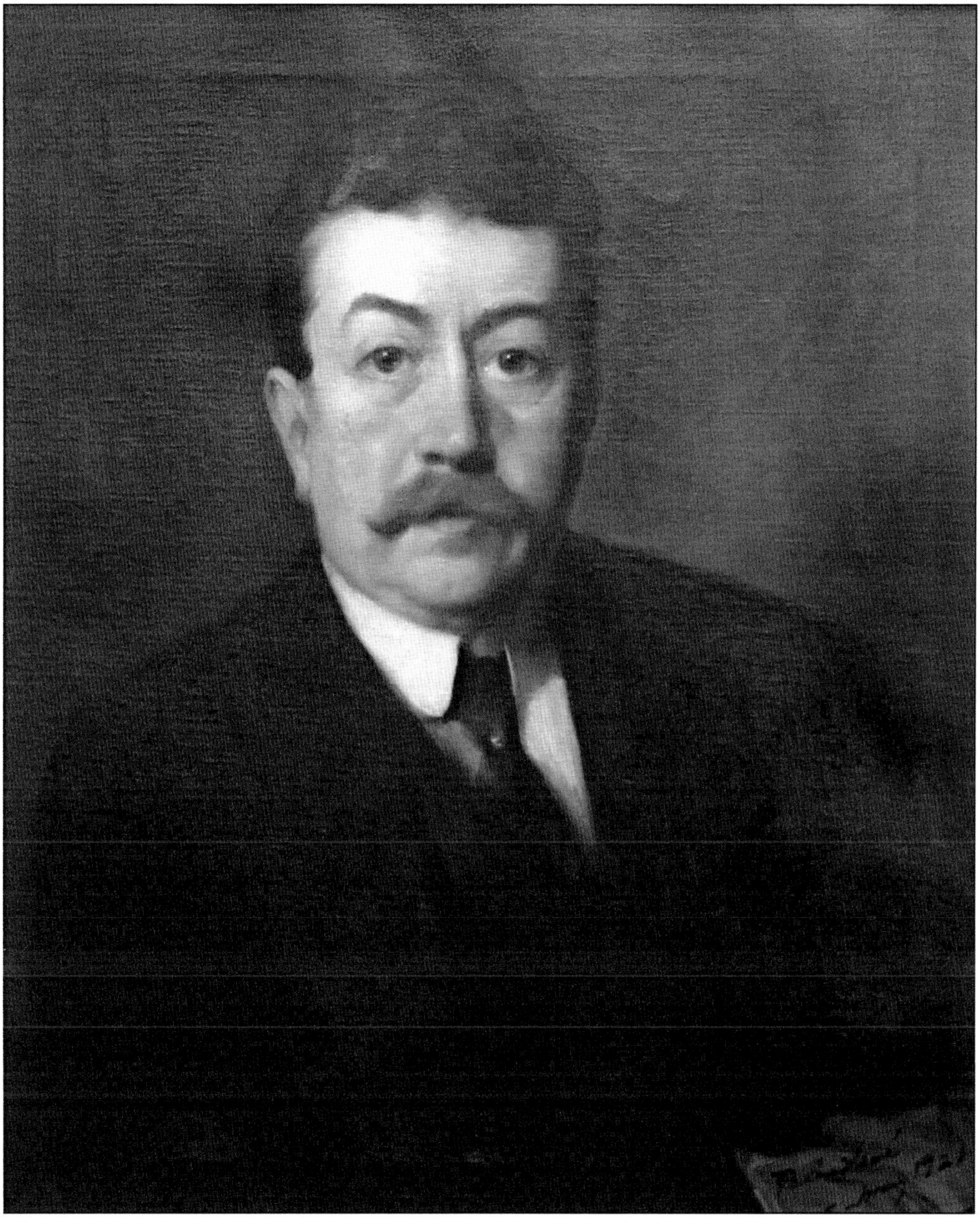

Davis painted this portrait, *Paul Painleve, Premiere of France*, in 1921. The portrait is in the collection of the Sippican Historical Society.

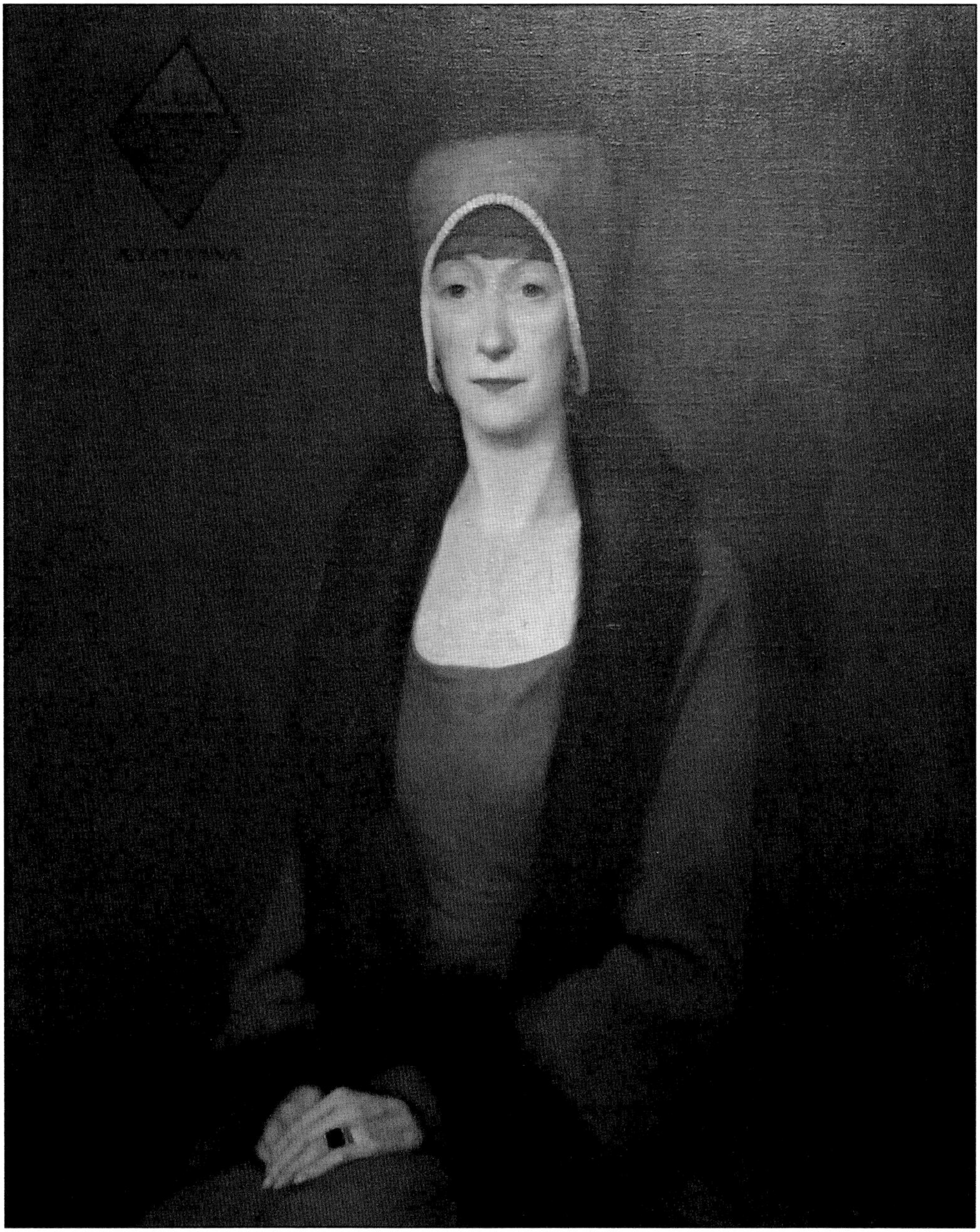

This portrait, *Therese d'Hennesdahl*, was painted in 1921 in Paris, where d'Hennesdahl lived at 60 rue de Varenne and gave French lessons. It is in the Arms family collection.

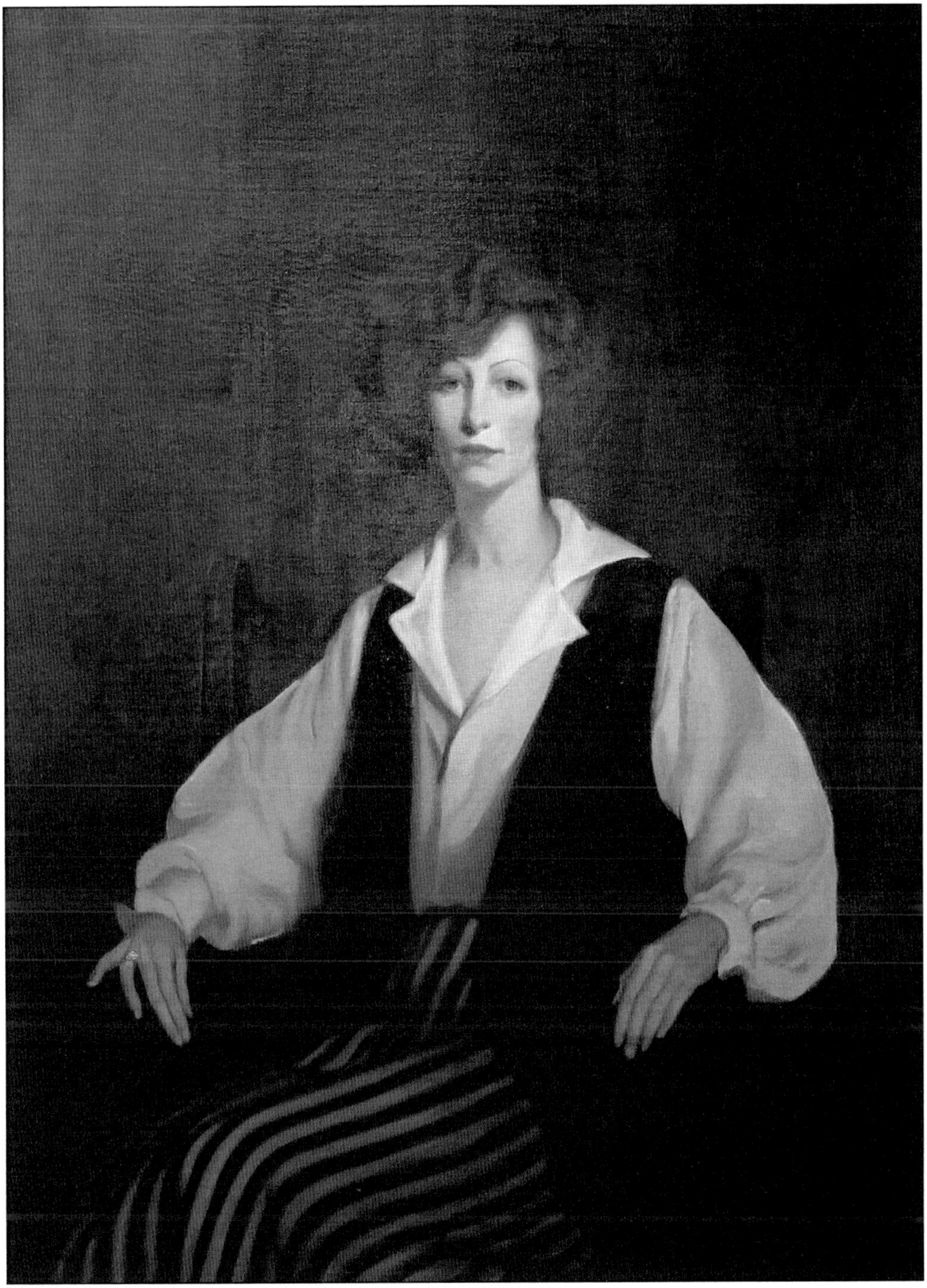

The Redhead, painted in 1922, is in the Arms family collection.

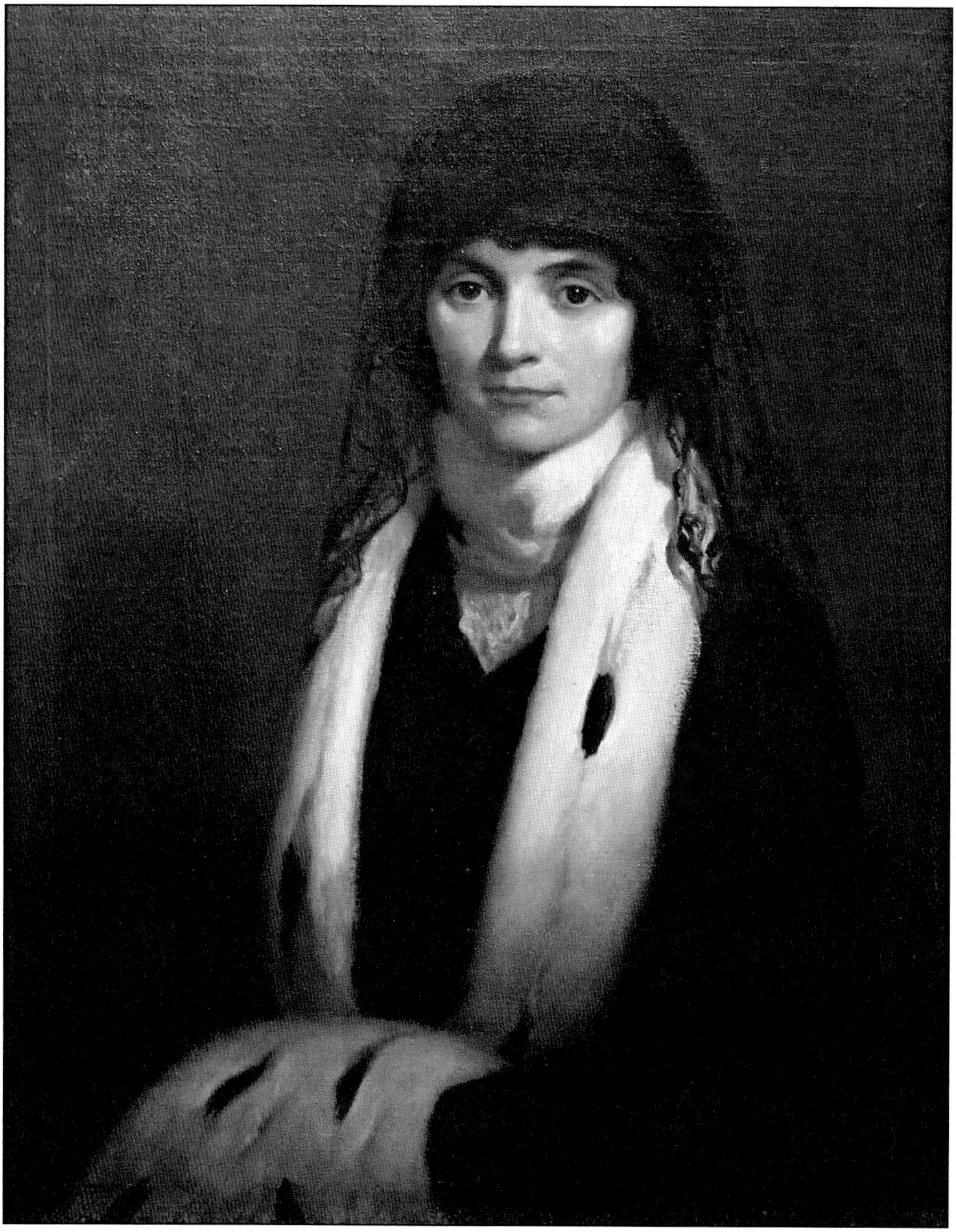

Marte Hennigan, painted in 1926 by Cecil Clark Davis, is in the Arms family collection.

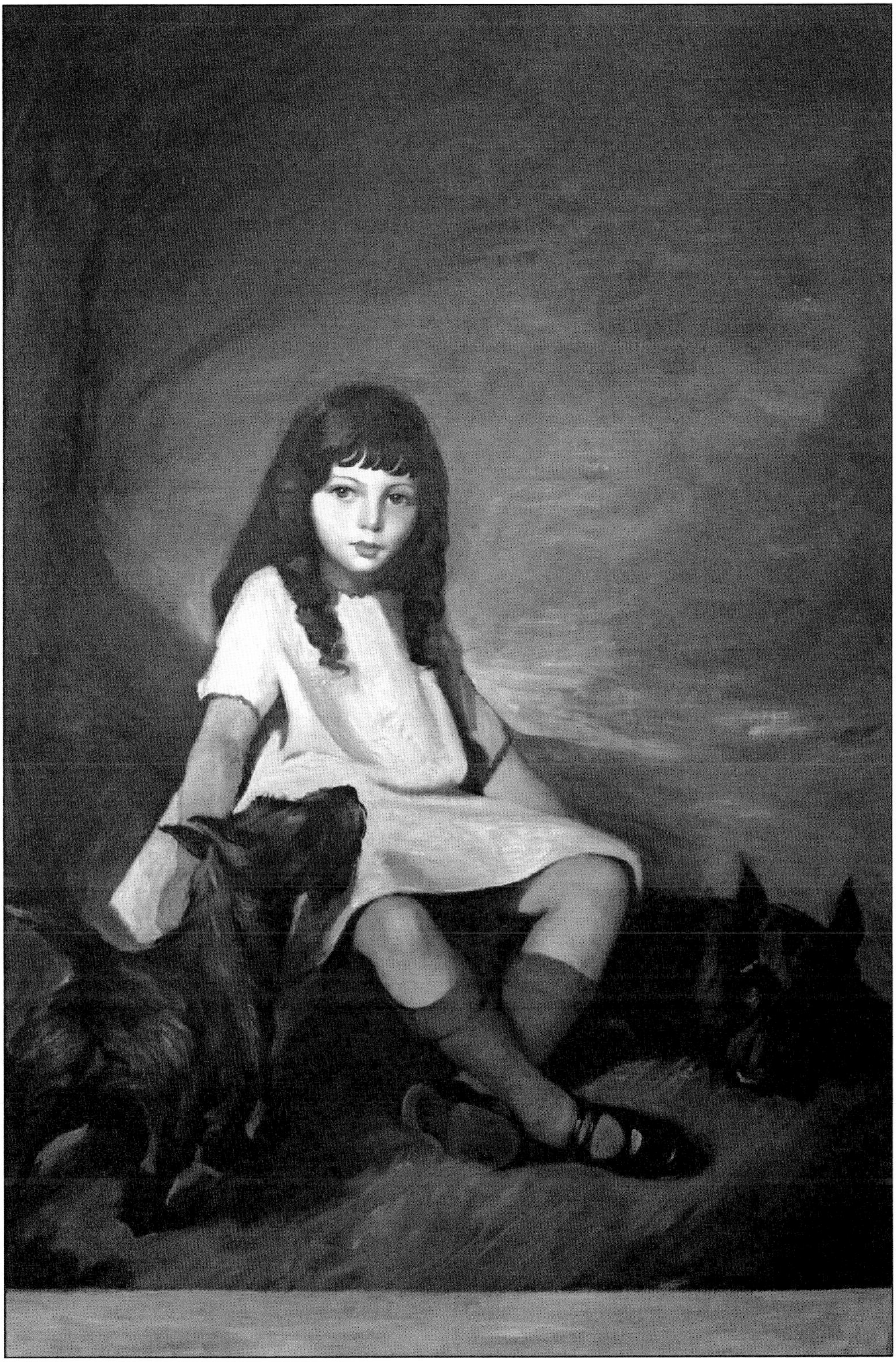

Girl with Scotties, painted in the 1930s, is in the collection of Tabor Academy.

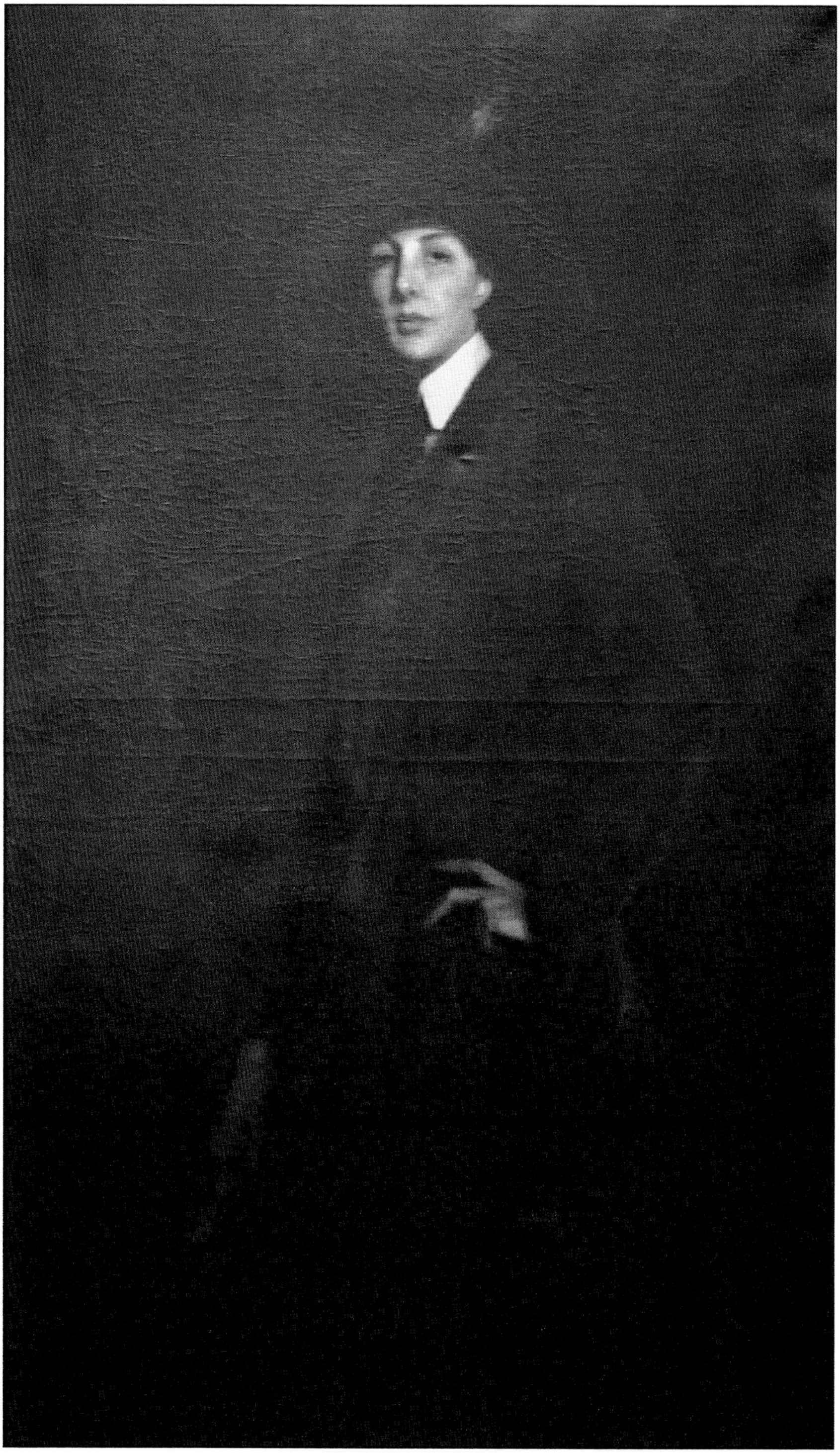

The collection of the Marion Art Center contains this 1911 portrait of Lily Clark Silver-Smith painted by Cecil Clark Davis. Davis's address book, now in the collection of the Marion Art Center, contains a recipe for gin given to her by Newton Smith, Lily's husband.

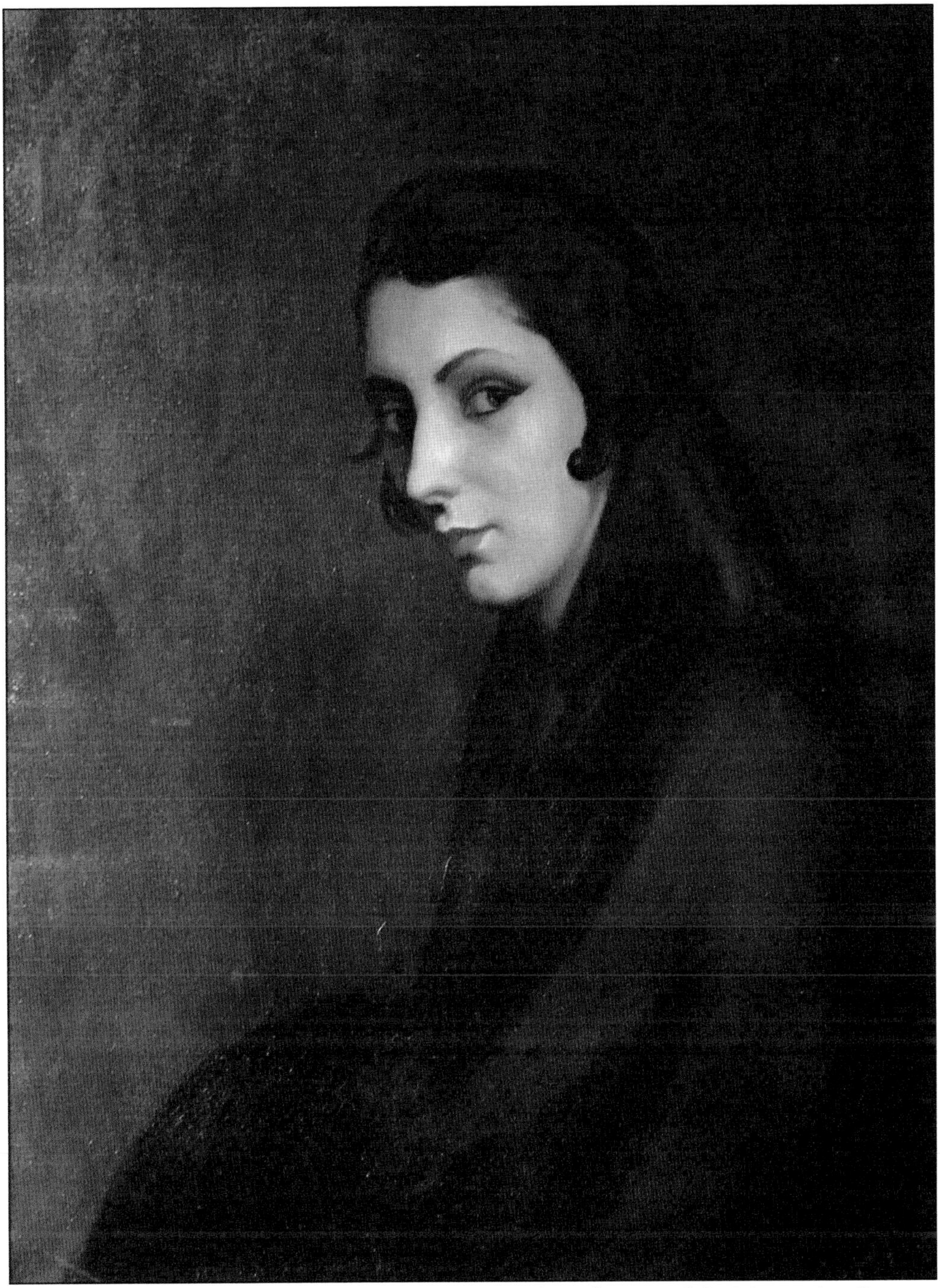

Woman with Dark Hair was painted in 1922 and is in the collection of the Marion Art Center.

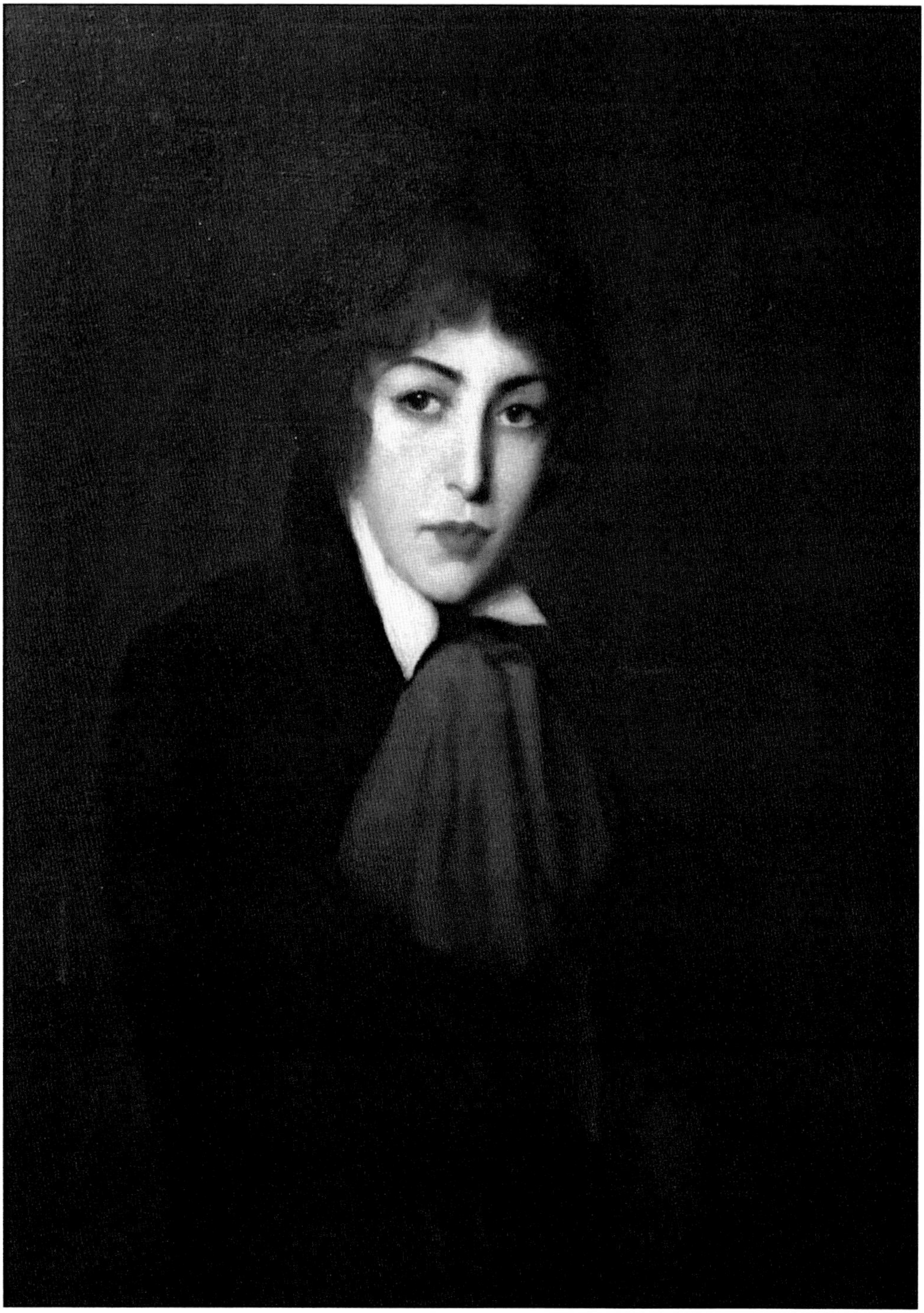

Marie Delanoir was painted in 1916 and is in the collection of the Marion Art Center. Delanoir was a professional model. This portrait won a prize at the Art Institute of Chicago.

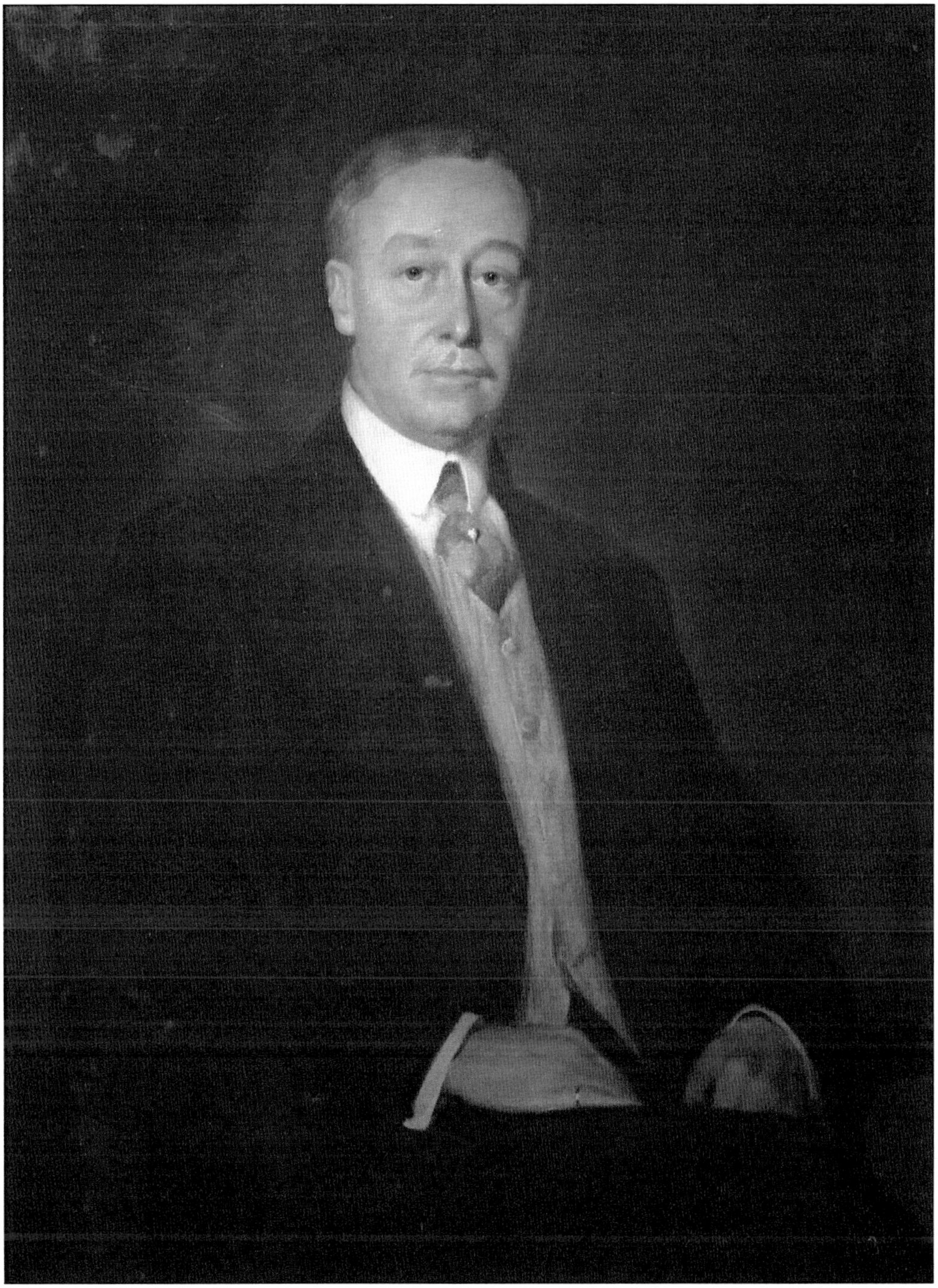

Mr. Larsen, painted in 1917, is in the collection of Tabor Academy. Cecil Clark Davis played tennis with Larsen and admired his skill at tennis. Later she found out that he was the Danish national tennis champion!

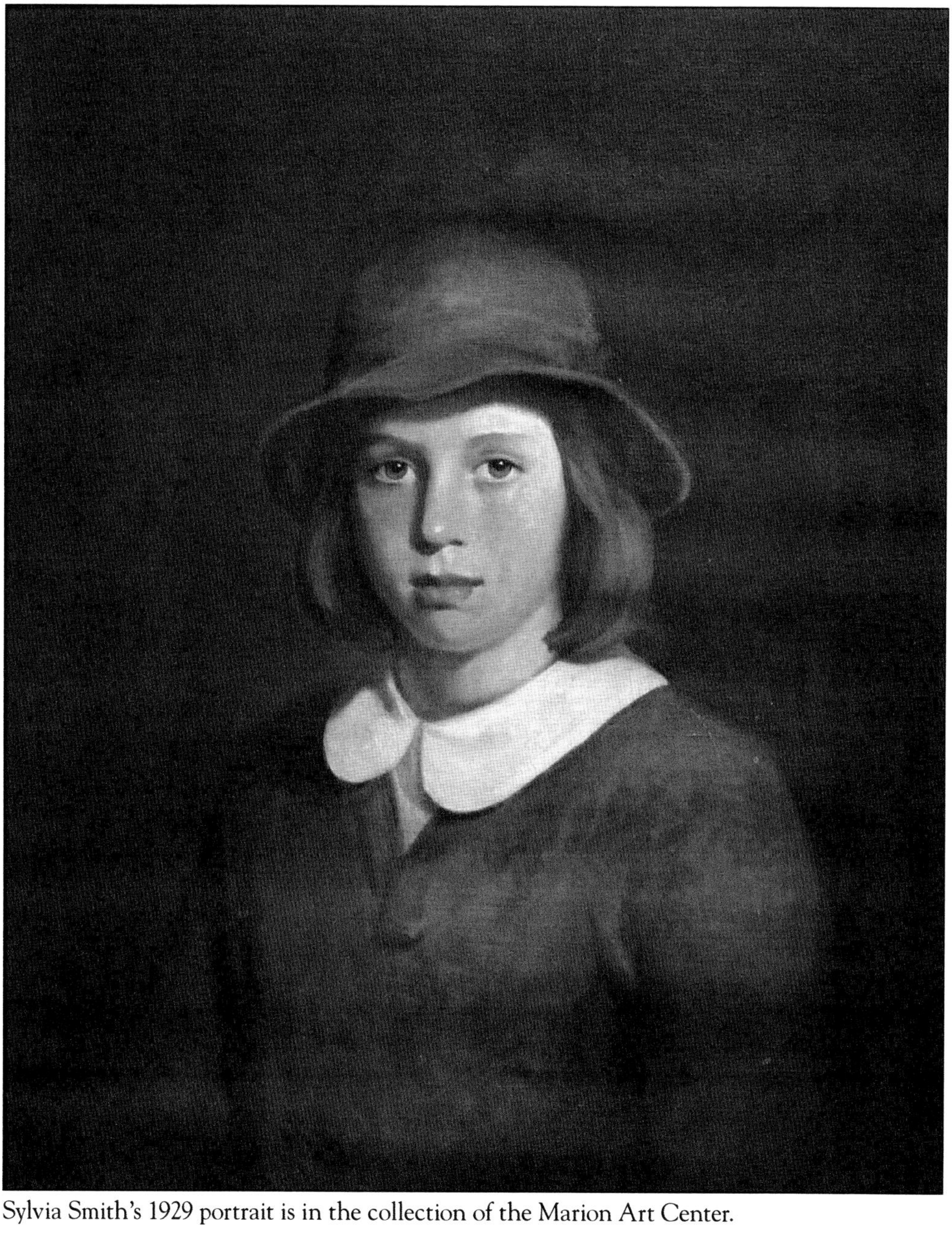

Sylvia Smith's 1929 portrait is in the collection of the Marion Art Center.

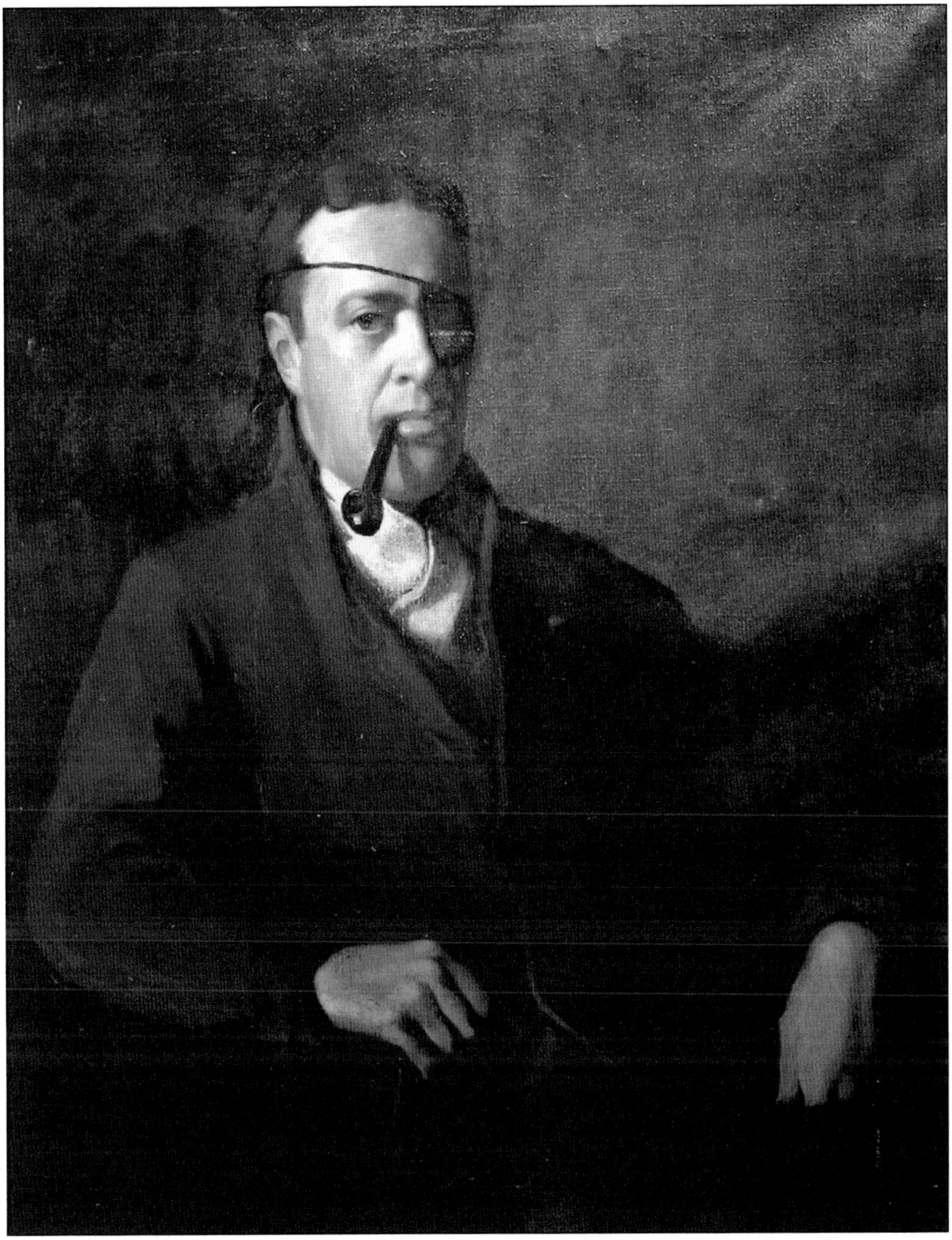

This portrait of Schuyler Smith was painted in 1921 and is in the collection of Tabor Academy. His nickname was the "Beekeeper." He was also one of Davis's tennis partners, especially for the Fourth of July tournaments.

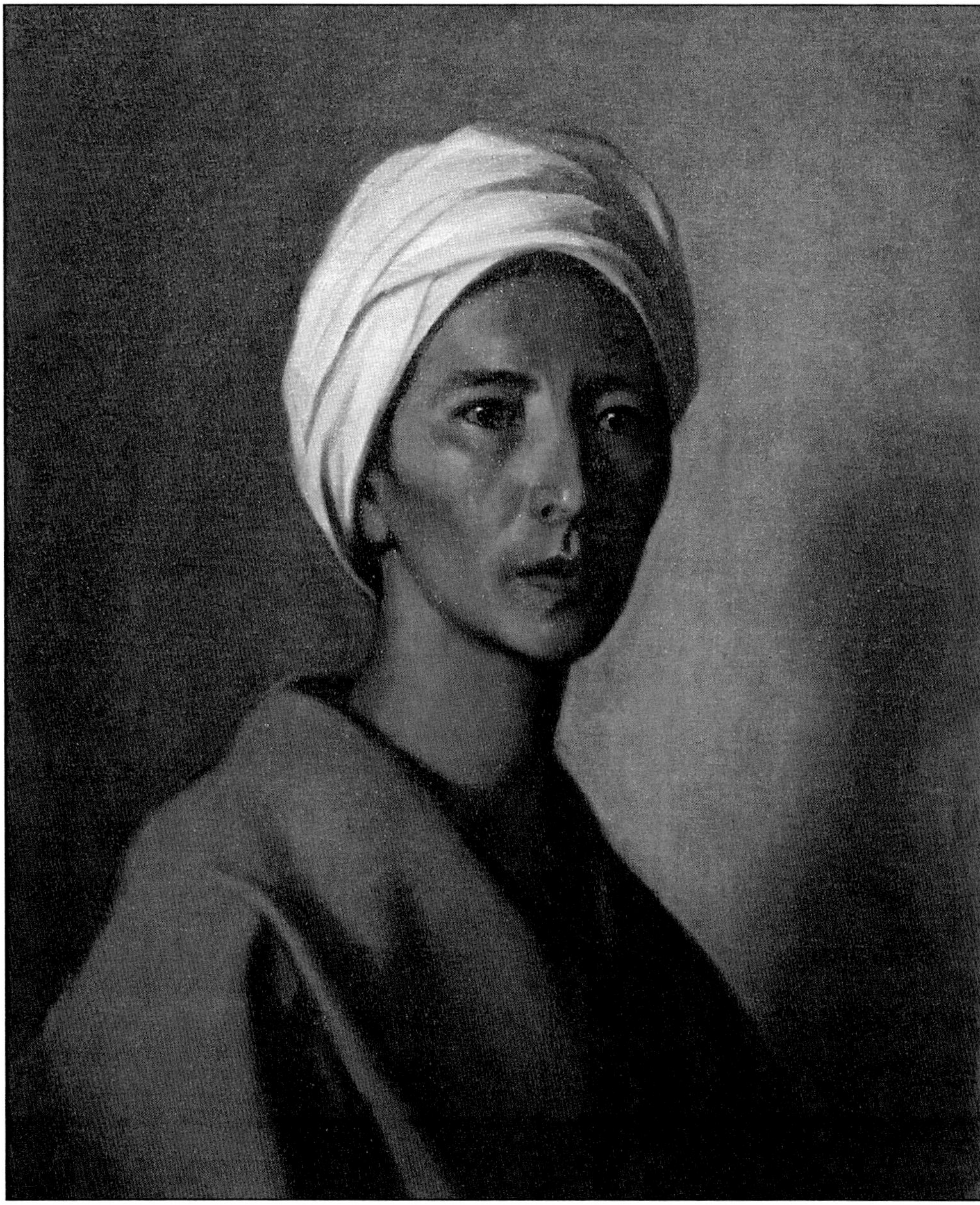

Bertha Miller in Yellow Turban, painted in 1935, is in the collection of the Marion Art Center.

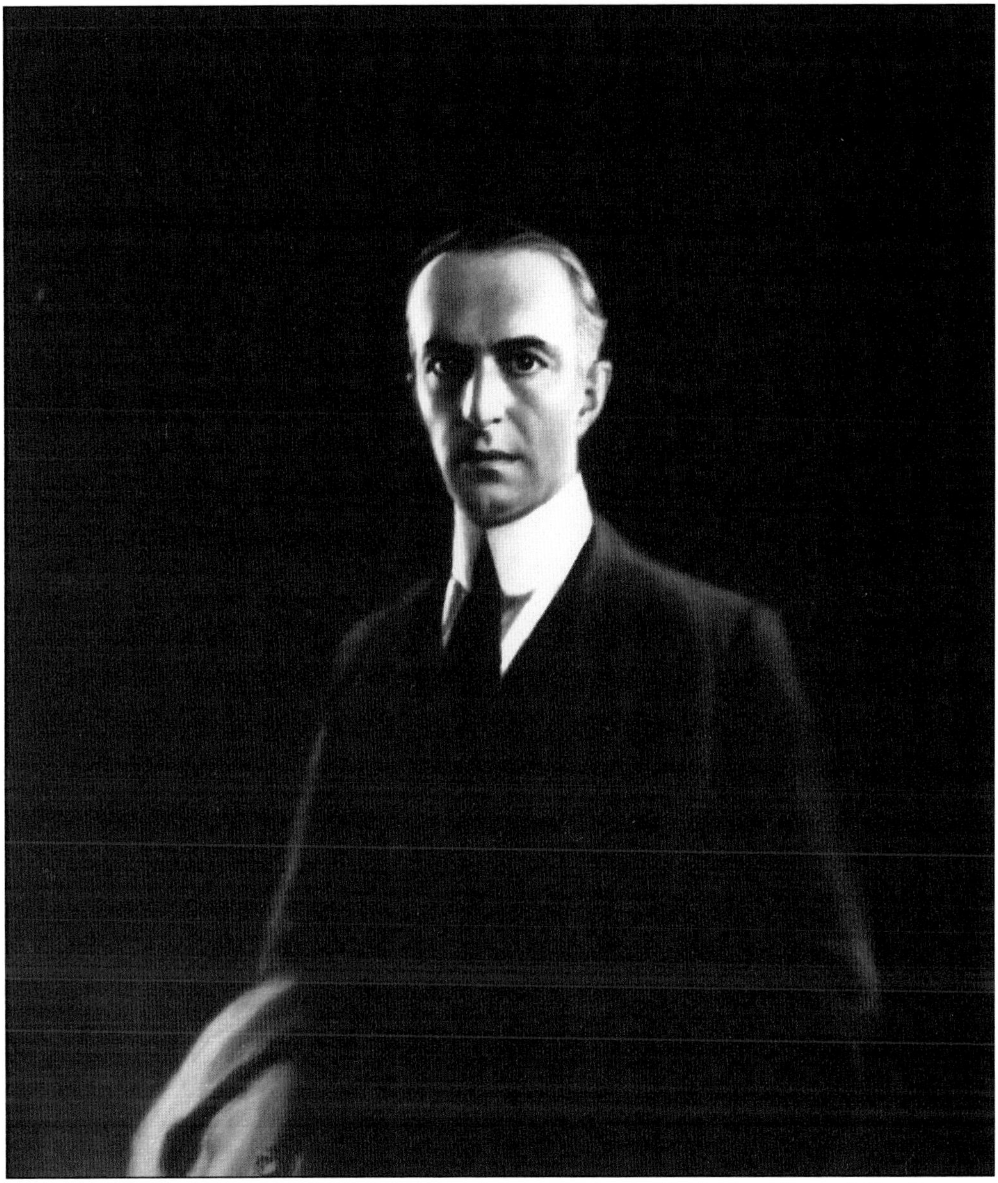

This portrait is of Elmer Schlesinger, a Manhattan lawyer with the law firm of Chadbourne, Stanchfield and Levy. He was a longtime Chicagoan and onetime vice president and general counsel of the U.S. Shipping Board. He married Countess Eleanor Patterson Gizycka, Chicago publisher Joseph Medill Patterson's sister. He was divorced from Halle Schaffner of Chicago, daughter of founder Joseph Schaffner of Hart, Schaffner and Marx, tailors.

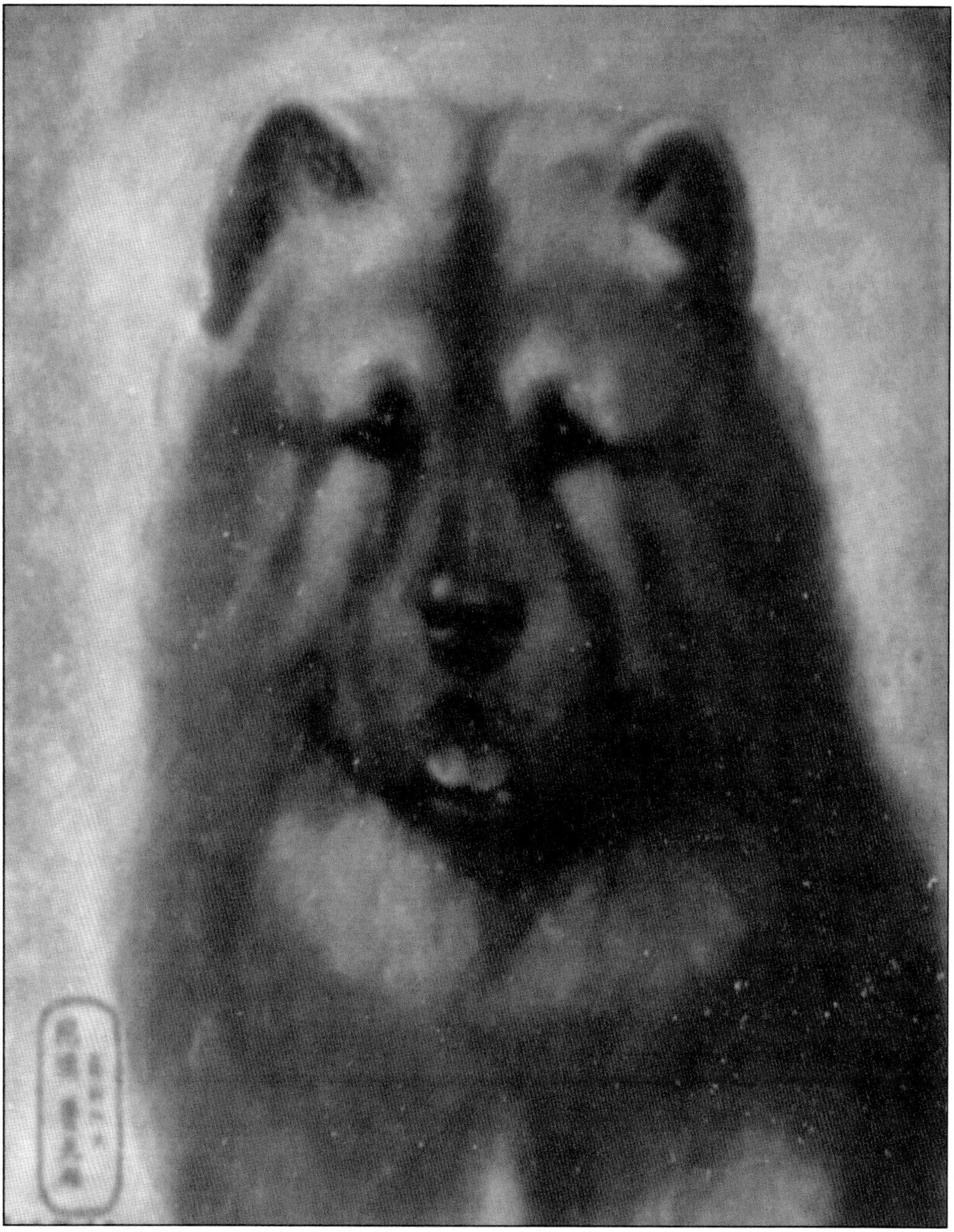

Cecil Clark Davis loved all of her 35 dogs, but traveled with only two or three of the smaller ones. This is a portrait, painted in 1908, of her chow chow, which traveled with her to London where she and Richard Harding Davis lived for a year. Cecil became friendly with John Singer Sargent in London and noted several visits with him in her diary. On January 21, 1909, Cecil wrote: "Mr. Sargent came to luncheon—said my picture of Mrs. Walker was monotonous in tone in the shadows—liked the Gibbons better. . . . Sargent said he hated portrait painting because of the impossible people that he had to try to please and that his trump card of saying to them that 'he was trying to make the best of them' he could never use. Said that with advancing age he was losing his nerve. Asked me to play chess with him."

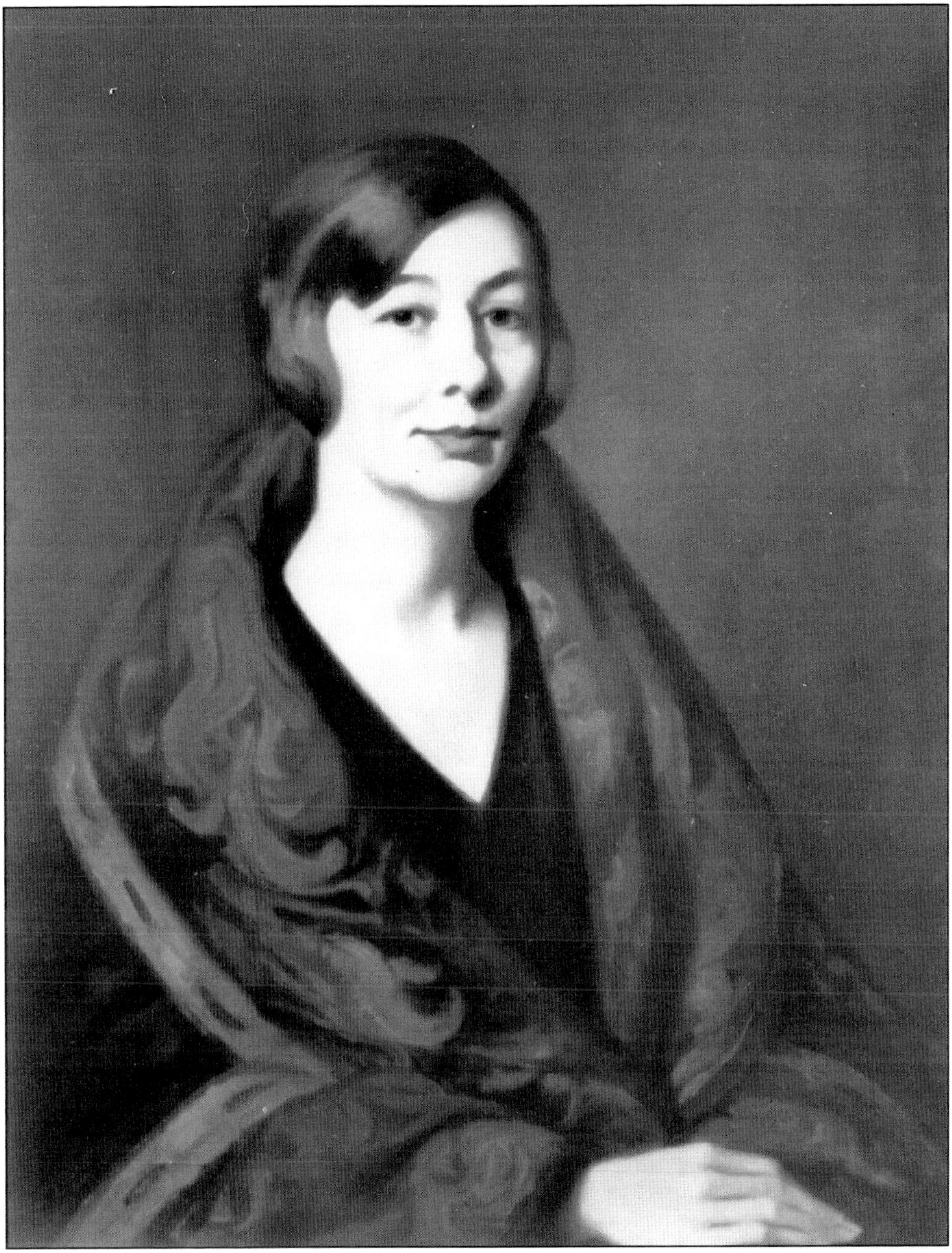

This undated portrait painted by Davis is in the Poett collection in Santa Barbara, California. This portrait may be of the Janet referred to in her diary entry for February 24, 1909: "John Sargent came here at twelve. Liked my picture of Janet. . . . He returned after luncheon to see Janet in the pose—rearranged the pose—said my painting of the head was nice, and to be brave, have courage to start on a larger canvas 54 x 48. Drew Janet for me in the new pose—lovely drawing—all movement. She was thrilled."

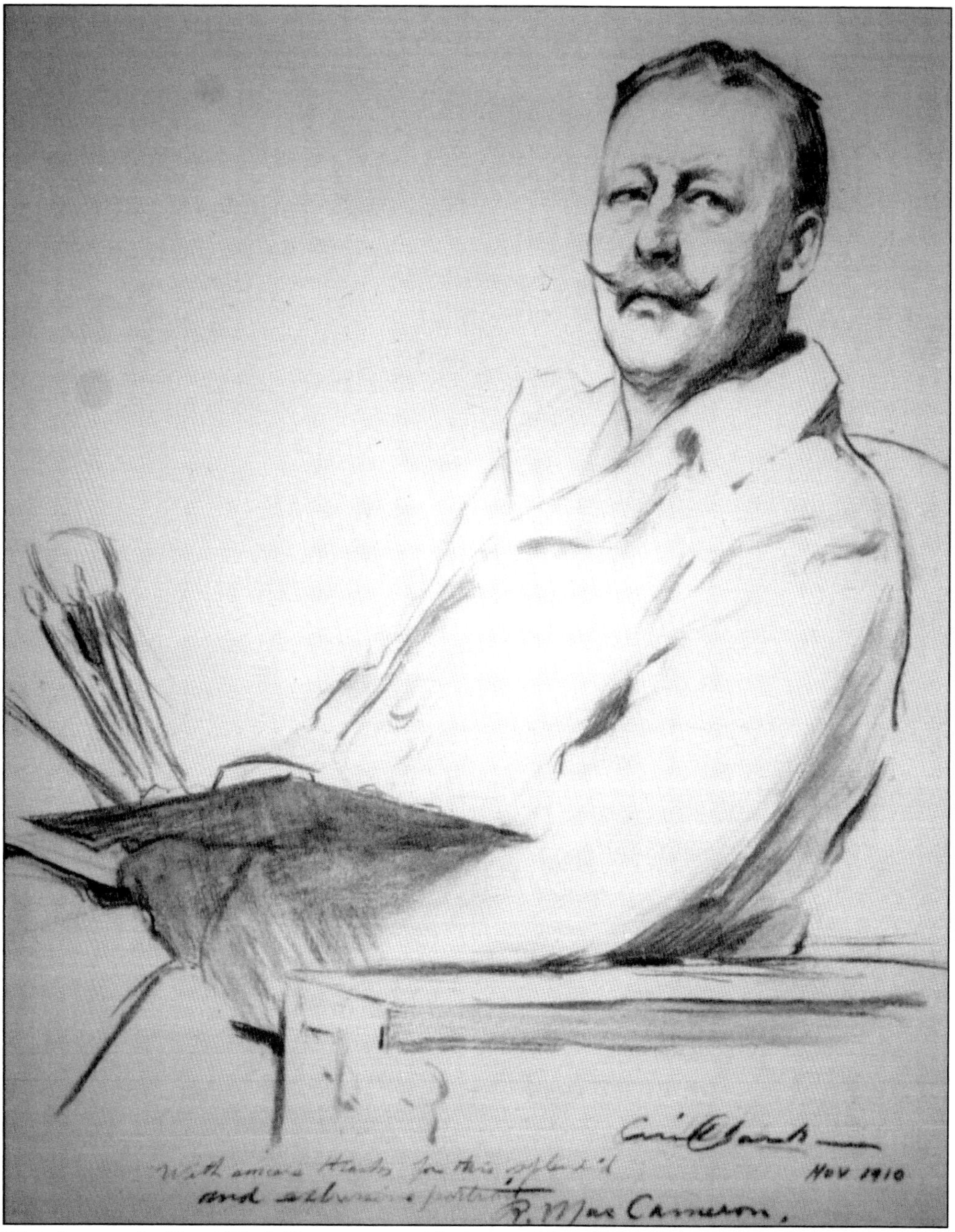

This drawing by Cecil Clark Davis is signed by her and dated November 1910. Written along the bottom of the drawing is the following: "With sincere thanks for this splendid and expressive portrait. R. Mac Cameron."

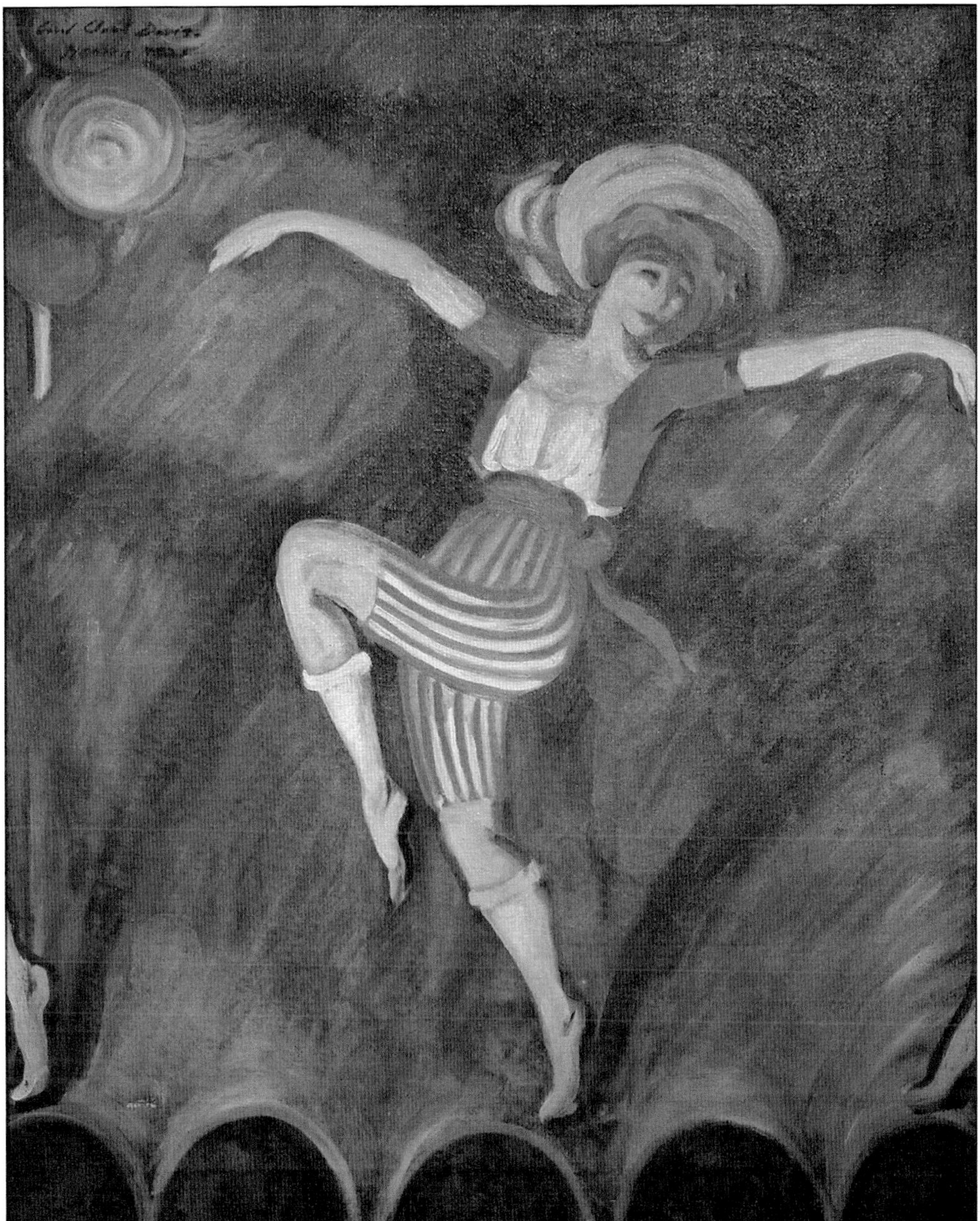

This portrait by Davis, painted in 1925, is called *The Dancer* and is in the collection of the Marion Art Center. It may be of Bessie McCoy, the Broadway dancer who sang and danced and was known as the "Yama Yama Girl." Richard Harding Davis was enthralled by her and married her when she was only 19 years old.

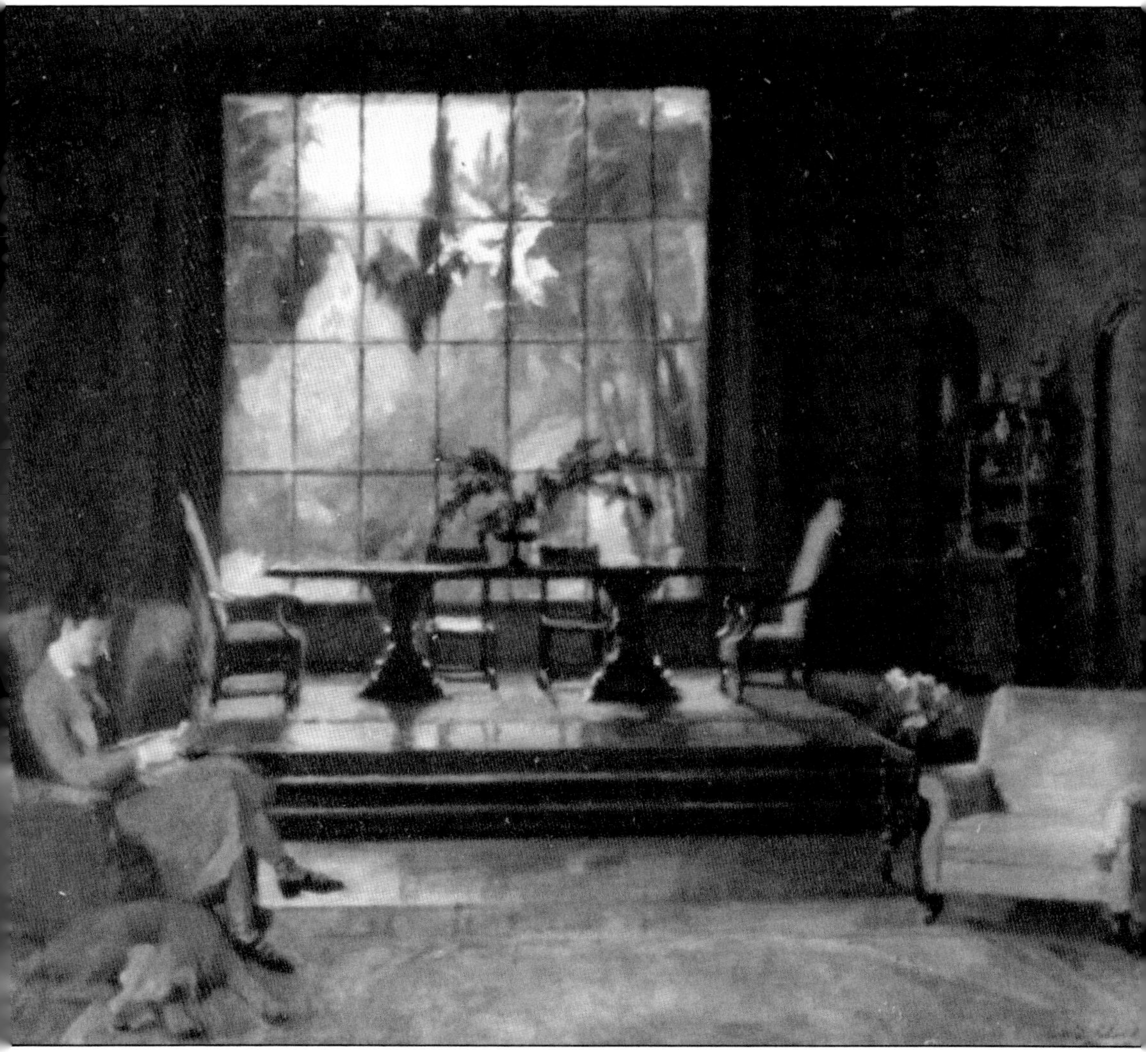

This interior painting by Cecil Clark Davis shows her employee and companion, the late Frederica Poett, sitting at left in Davis's studio in Marion.

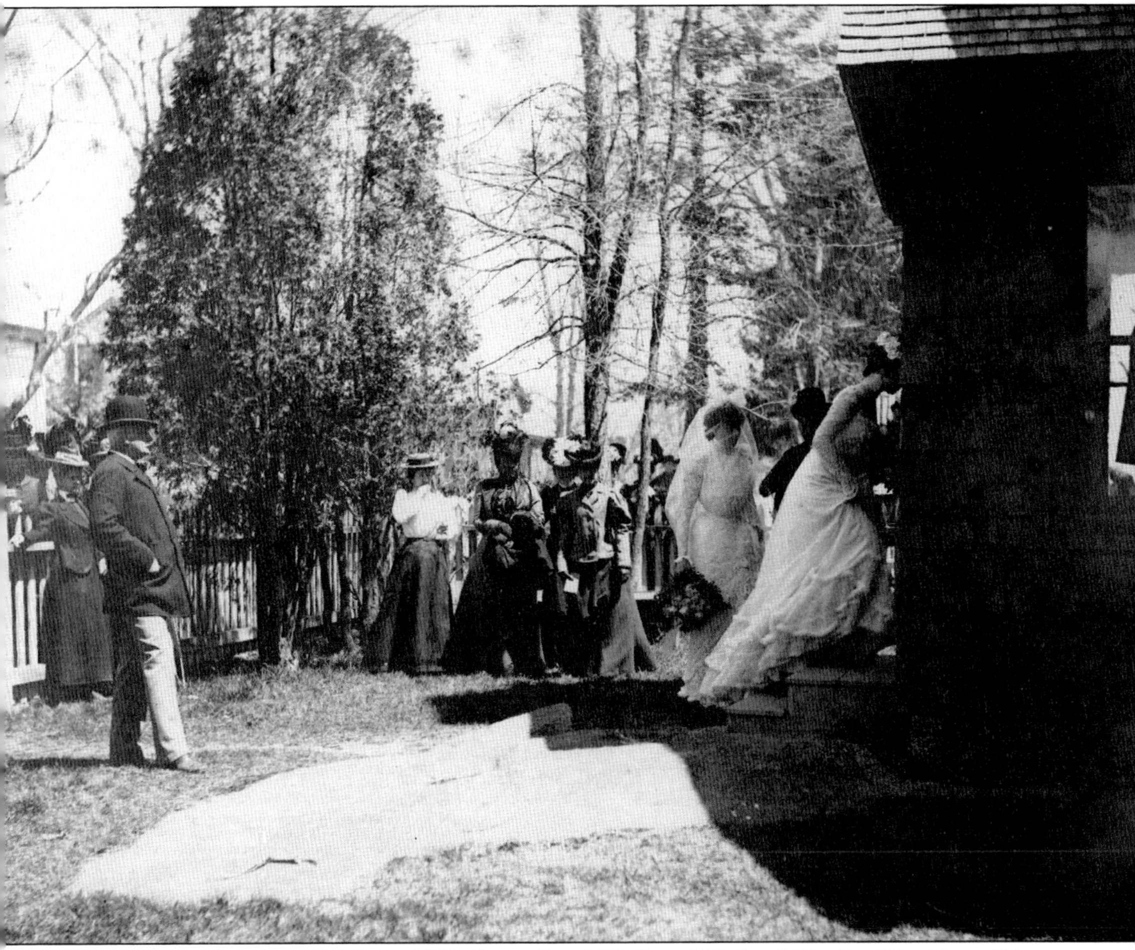

This photograph, taken on May 4, 1899, shows Cecil Clark and Richard Harding Davis's wedding party entering St. Gabriel's chapel before the wedding ceremony.

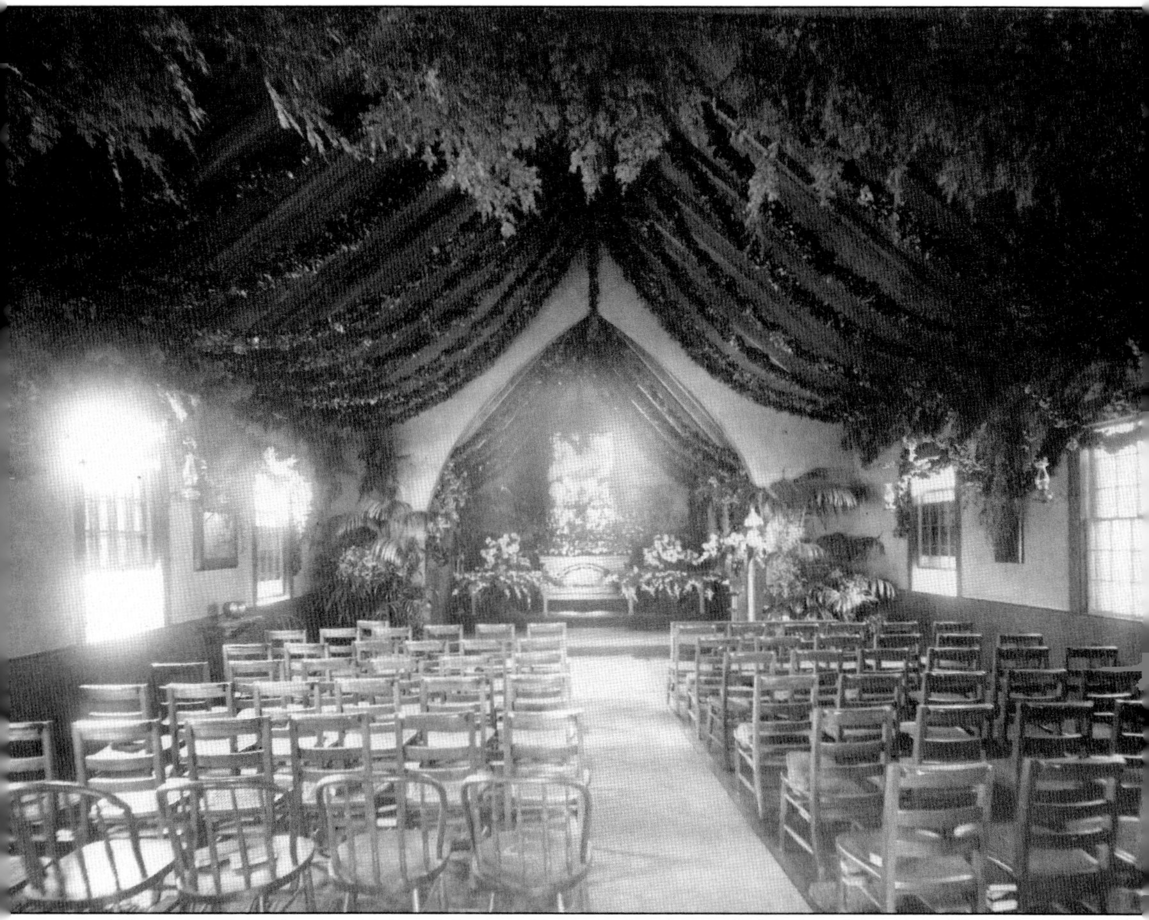

This photograph shows the decorated interior of St. Gabriel's chapel right before the wedding ceremony.

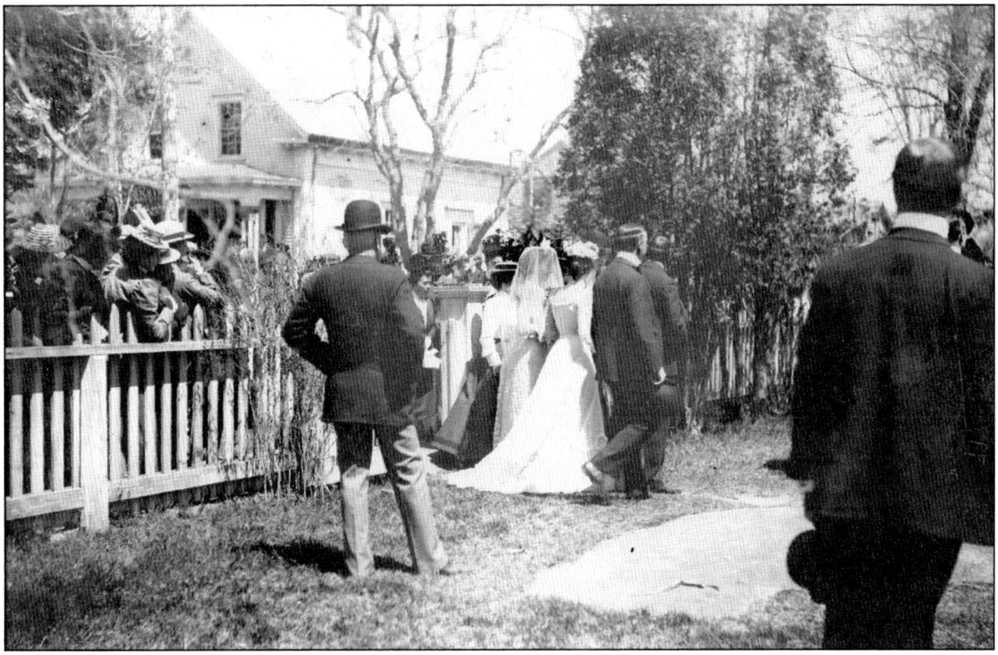

This photograph shows Cecil and Richard Harding Davis leaving the church after the wedding to walk to the Clarks' home on Harbor Lane (now called Water Street), a block away, for the wedding reception.

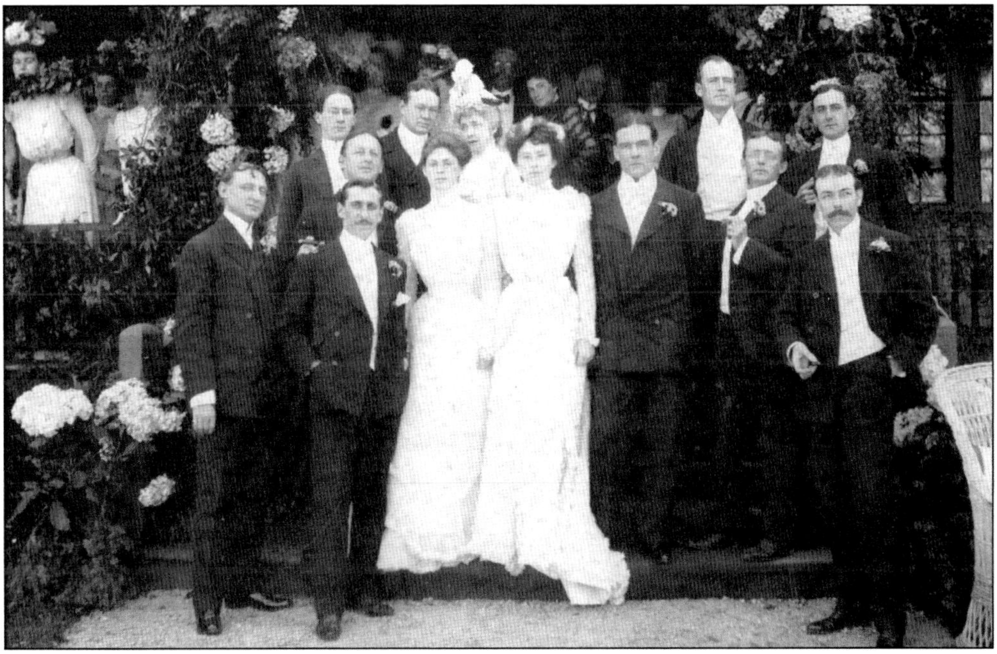

The wedding party poses in this photograph. The wedding party included well-know figures such as Ethel Barrymore (the young woman on the left, next to Cecil) and Charles Dana Gibson (second row, second from right), the artist who created the Gibson girl illustrations. Gibson used the likeness of Richard Harding Davis for the man who accompanied the Gibson girl, who was similar to Cecil—beautiful, athletic, and independent.

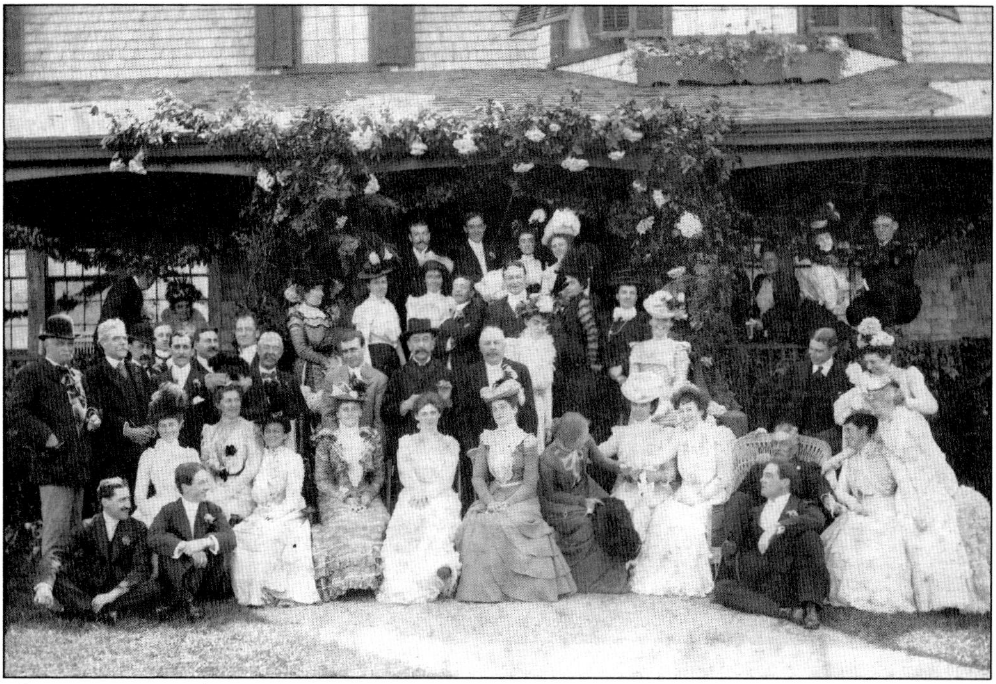

This portrait was taken at the reception at the Clark home on Harbor Lane. It is unusual in that the two actresses, Ethyl Barrymore and Sissy Loftus, are in the center. The bride is fifth from right (next to her father-in-law in the wicker chair), the groom is seated in front of his father, and the two mothers are on the far right.

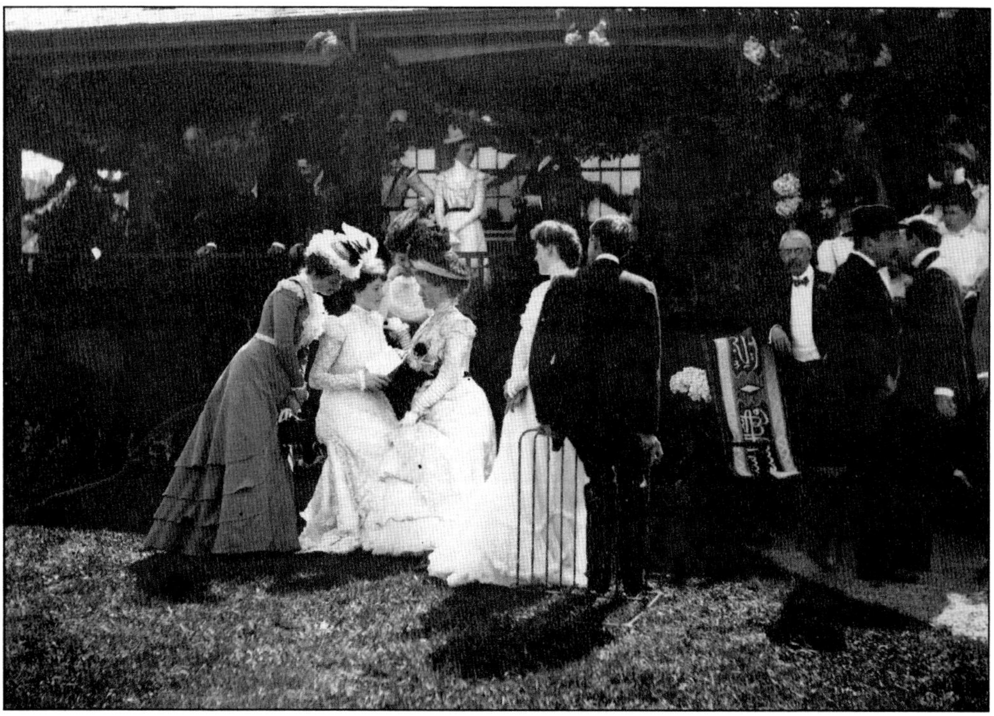

This is another photograph taken at the wedding reception at the Clark home.

This photograph was taken on the dock of the Clark home. Cecil Clark Davis throws something into the water for her small dog to fetch.

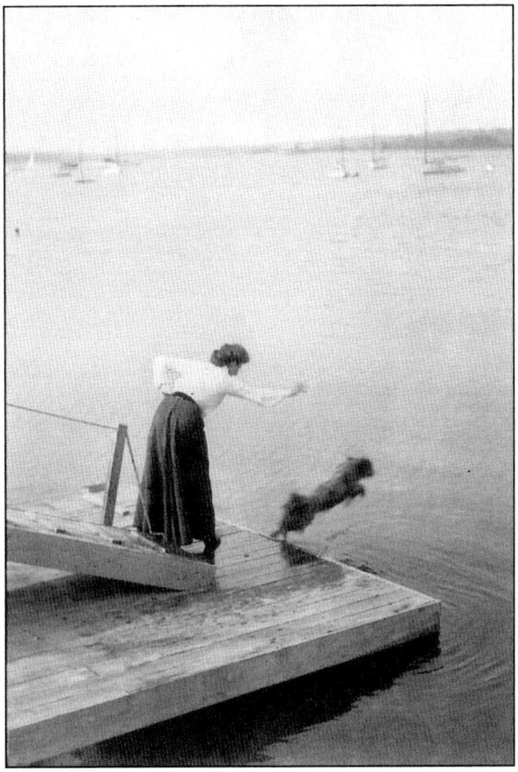

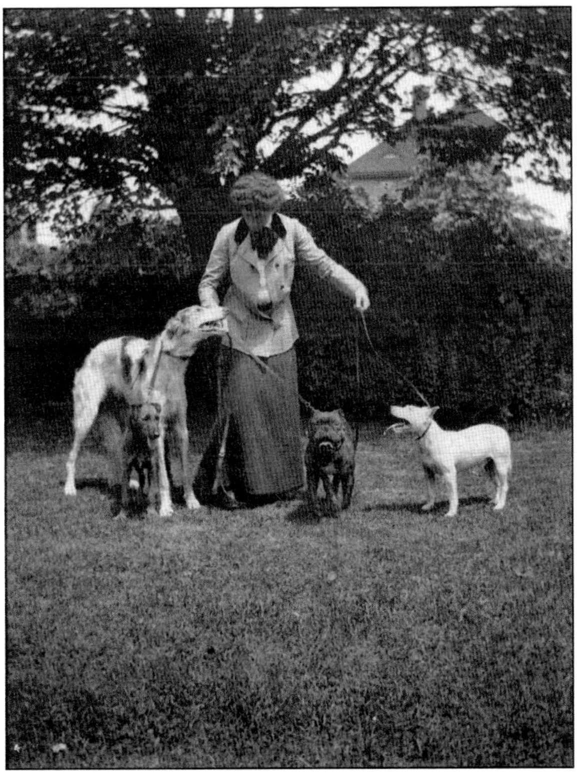

Here is another photograph of Davis and some of her beloved dogs.

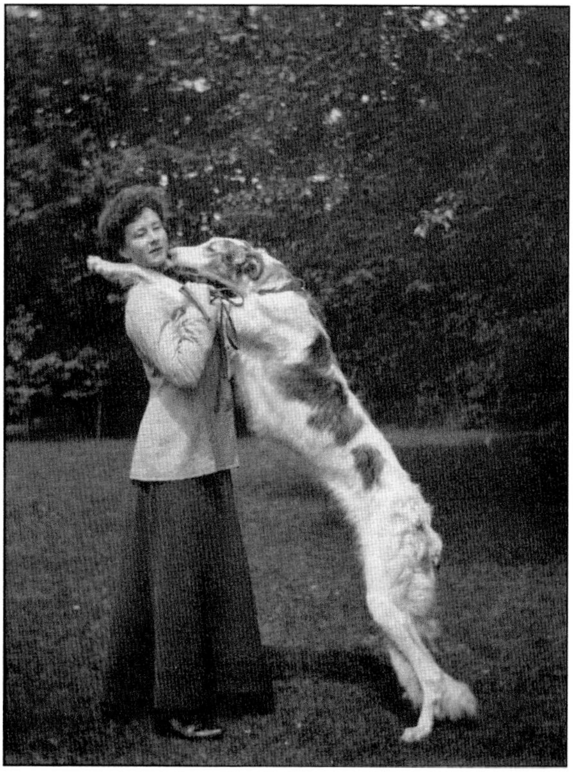

Cecil Clark Davis receives a kiss from one of her large dogs.

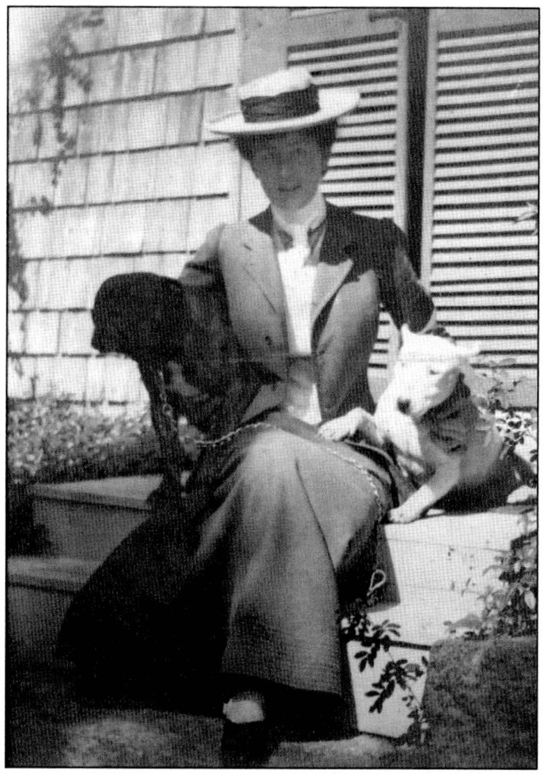

Davis poses with two of her dogs on the steps of her home in Marion.

This photograph shows Davis with two of her other dogs at her home in Marion.

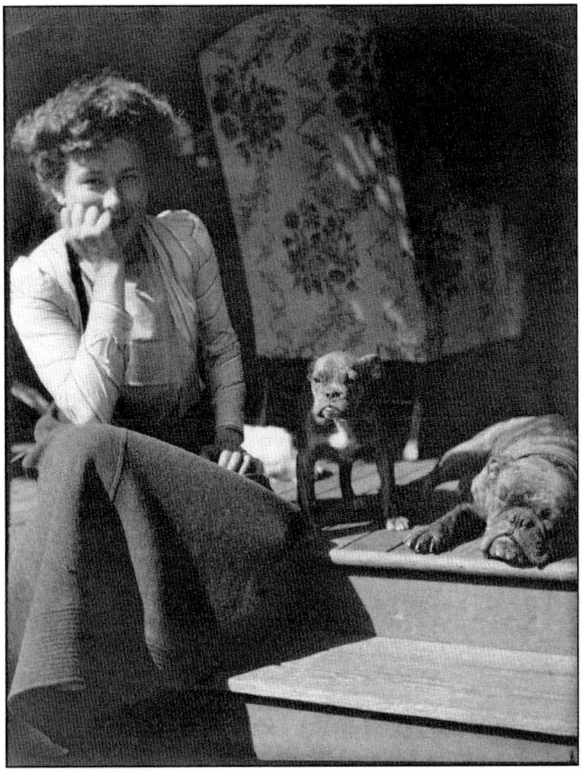

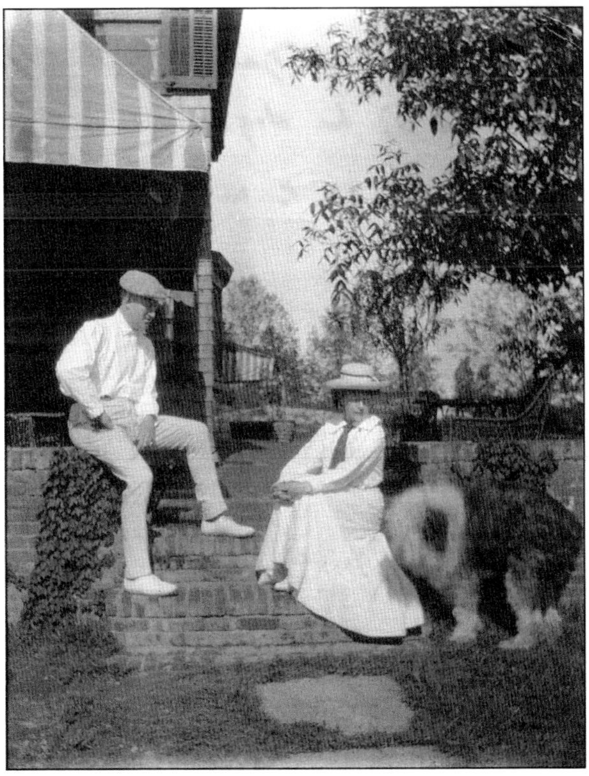

Davis loved to play tennis at the Sippican Tennis Club just down the street from her Marion home. She and her tennis partner, Paul Burdett, are shown in their tennis clothes (along with one of her dogs) on the steps of her Marion home.

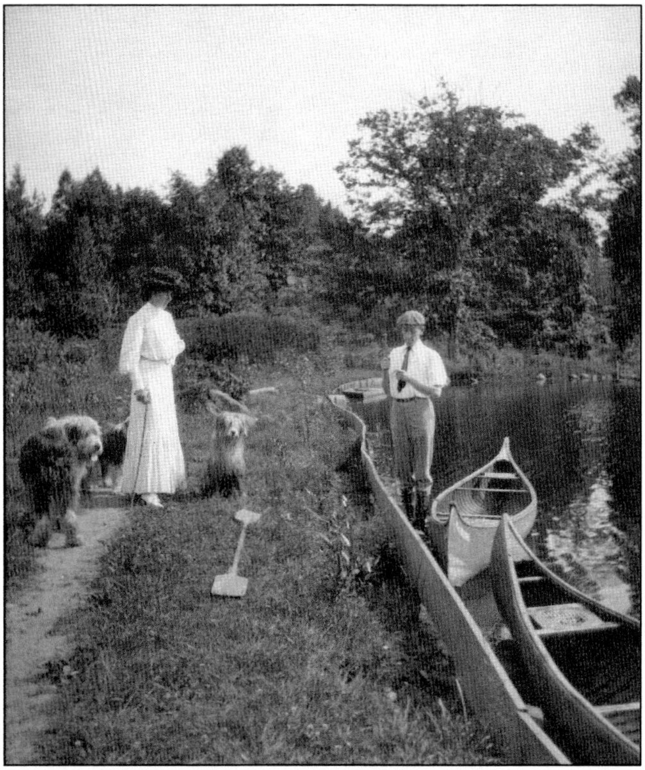

Cecil Clark Davis and her dogs have just finished canoeing or are about to set off from the shore.

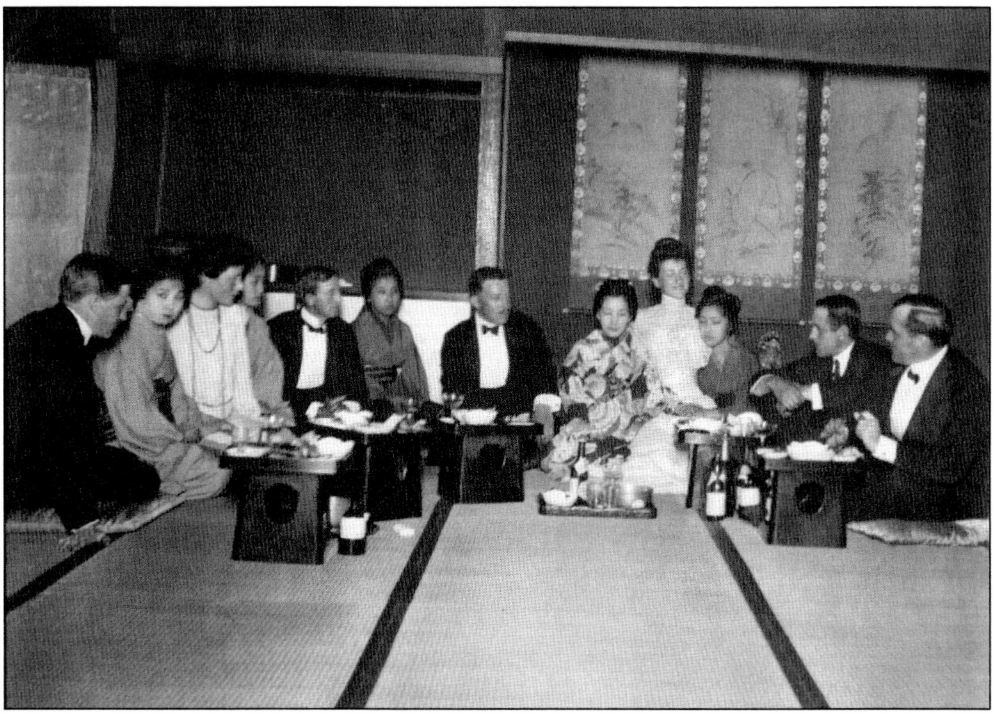

Cecil Clark Davis traveled all over the world with her war correspondent husband, Richard Harding Davis. Here they are in Japan.

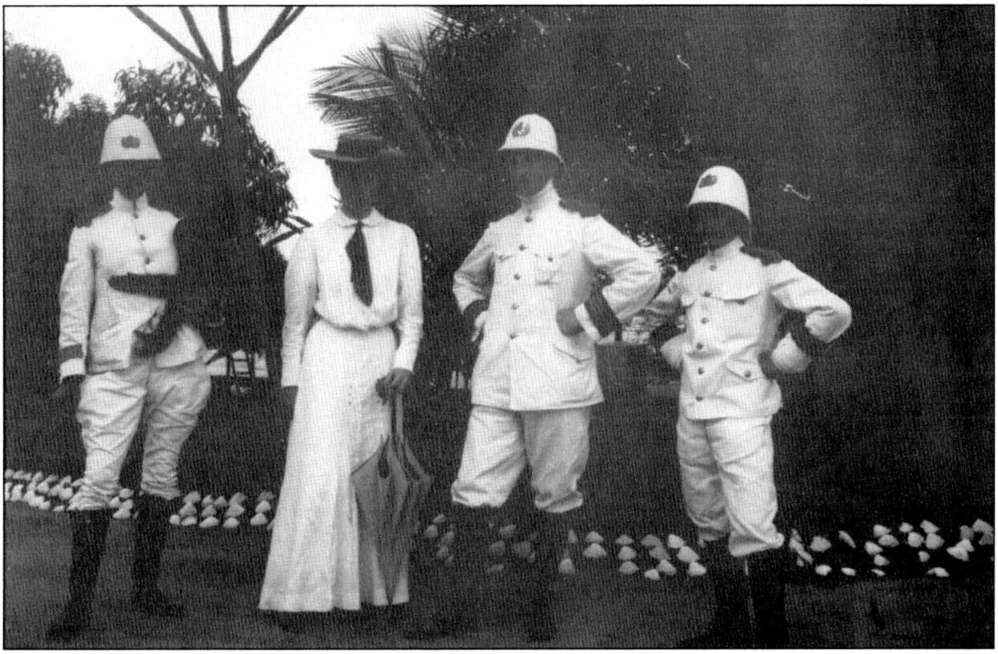

These photographs were taken of Davis on her travels to South Africa. The gentleman on the left in the top photograph is holding a monkey. Note the small bulldog under the table in the image below. The Davises travelled with cases of champagne and evening clothes.

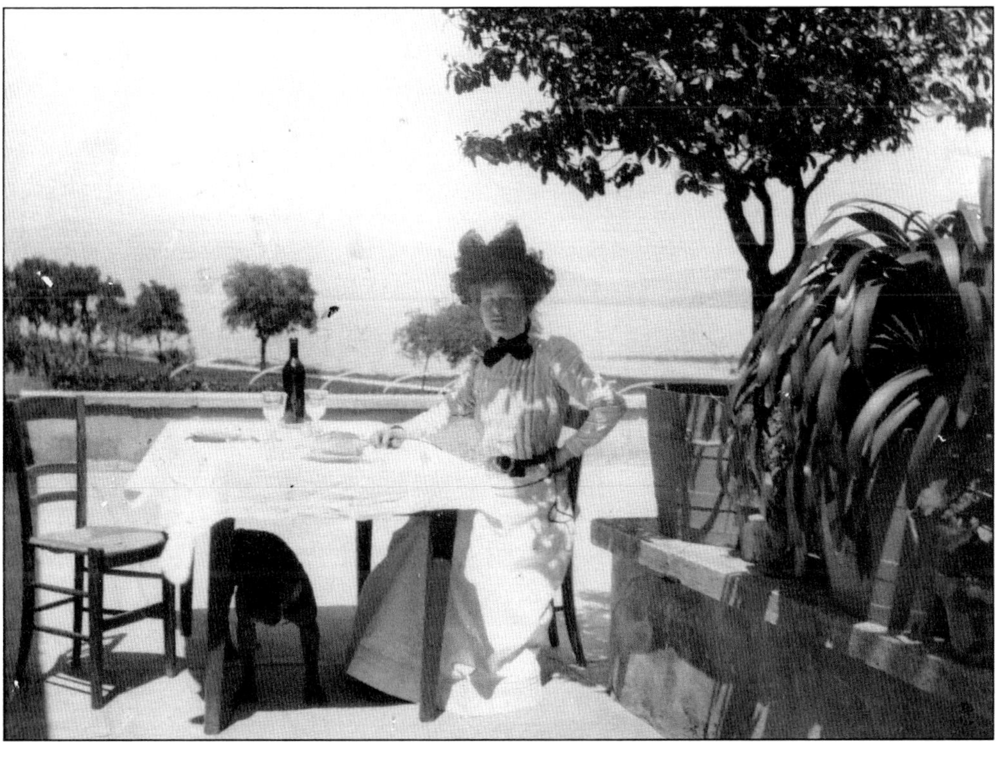

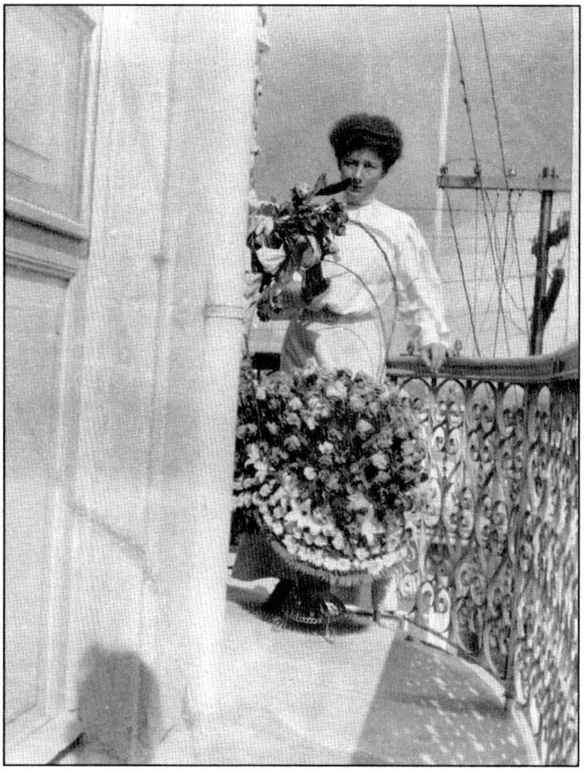

This photograph shows Cecil Clark Davis aboard a ship.

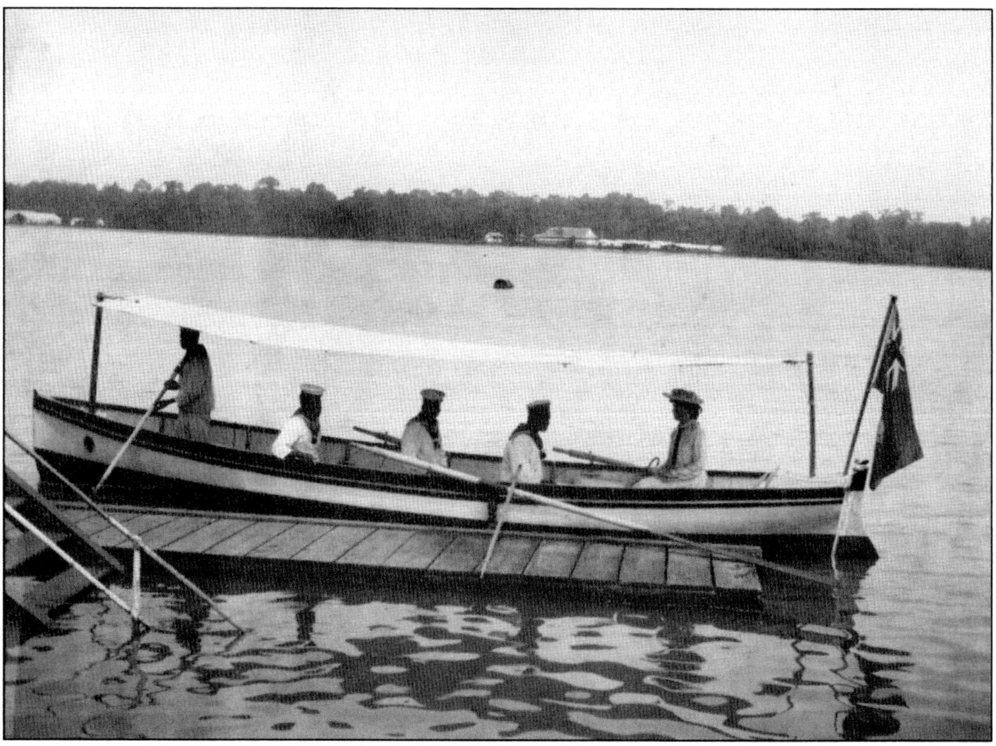

Here Davis is being rowed ashore during her travels.

Four

Other Activities

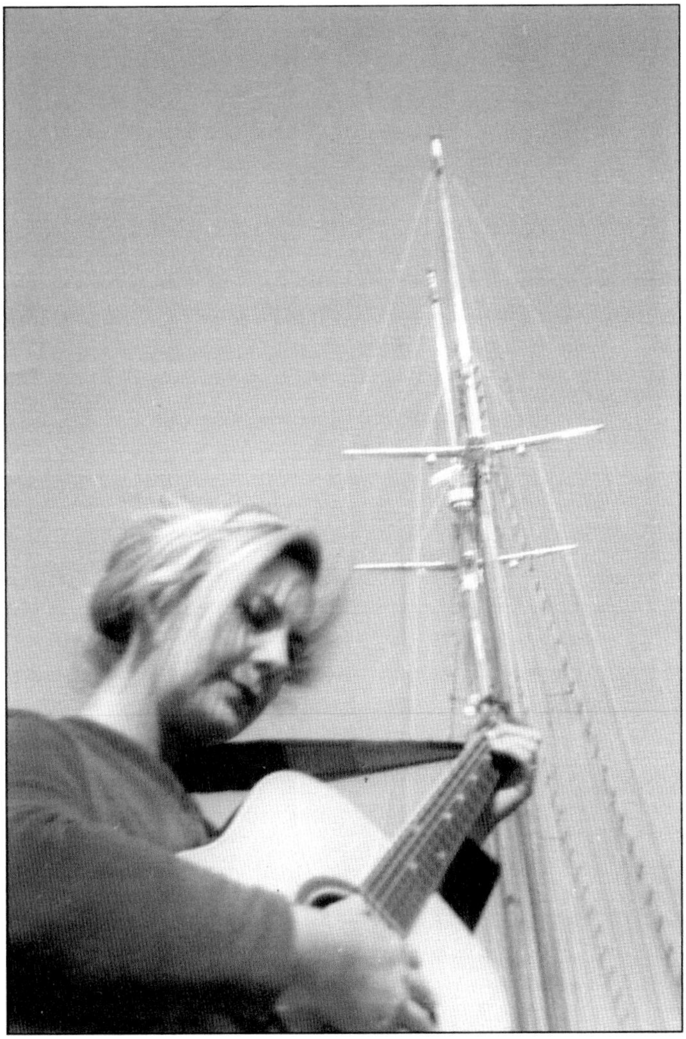

This photograph of Barbara Carns was taken in April 1965. Not only was Barbara a professional folk singer, she was also an officer of the Marion Art Center for years. She also organized coffeehouses in the art center.

Every year the Marion Art Center has a "Holiday Shop" where local artists sell their work to the public. In 1965, the Marion Art Center exhibited art associated with Christmas carols, which was on loan from the Boston Museum of Fine Arts.

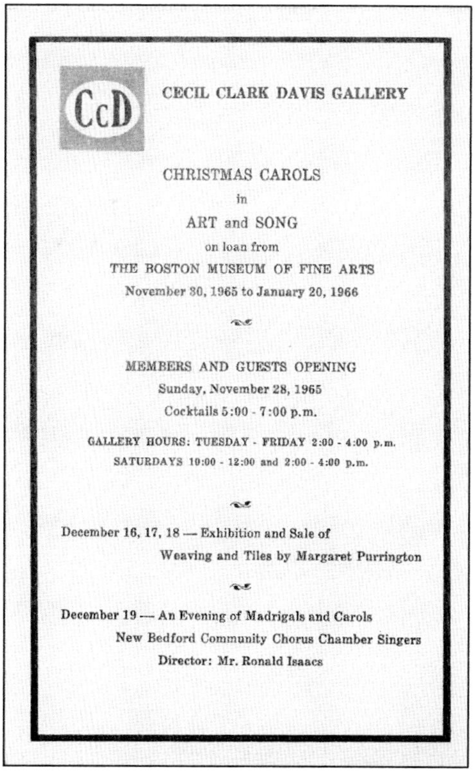

CcD CECIL CLARK DAVIS GALLERY

CHRISTMAS CAROLS
in
ART and SONG
on loan from
THE BOSTON MUSEUM OF FINE ARTS
November 30, 1965 to January 20, 1966

MEMBERS AND GUESTS OPENING
Sunday, November 28, 1965
Cocktails 5:00 - 7:00 p.m.

GALLERY HOURS: TUESDAY - FRIDAY 2:00 - 4:00 p.m.
SATURDAYS 10:00 - 12:00 and 2:00 - 4:00 p.m.

December 16, 17, 18 — Exhibition and Sale of
Weaving and Tiles by Margaret Purrington

December 19 — An Evening of Madrigals and Carols
New Bedford Community Chorus Chamber Singers
Director: Mr. Ronald Isaacs

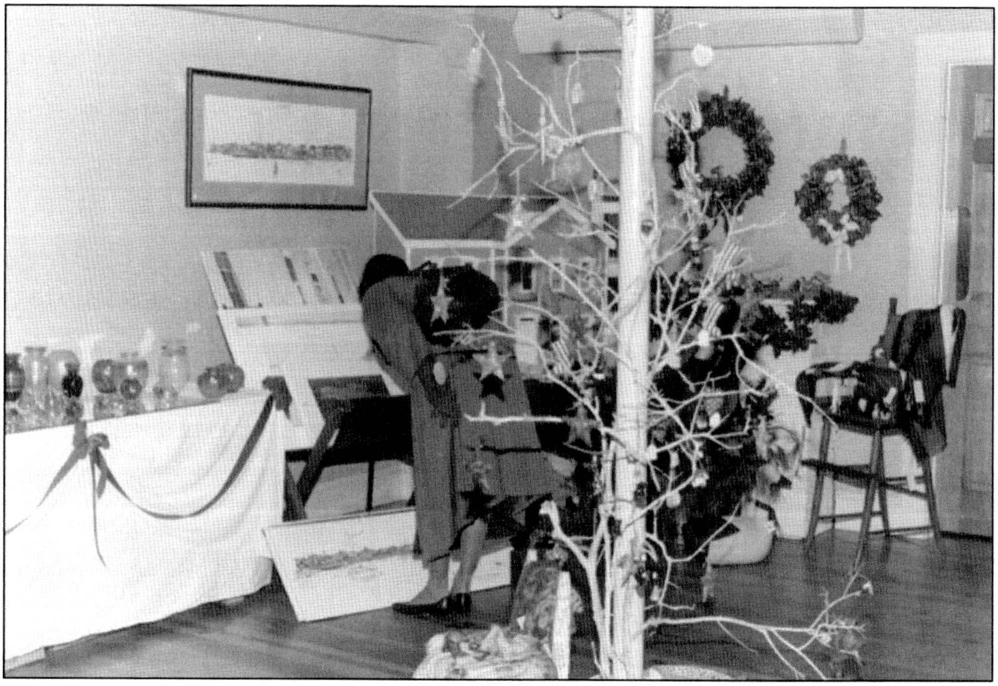

This photograph shows some of the many articles made by local artists that are for sale in the art center's Holiday Shop each year. Not only does the Holiday Shop support local artists, it offers unique handmade gifts for sale with a percentage going to the Marion Art Center.

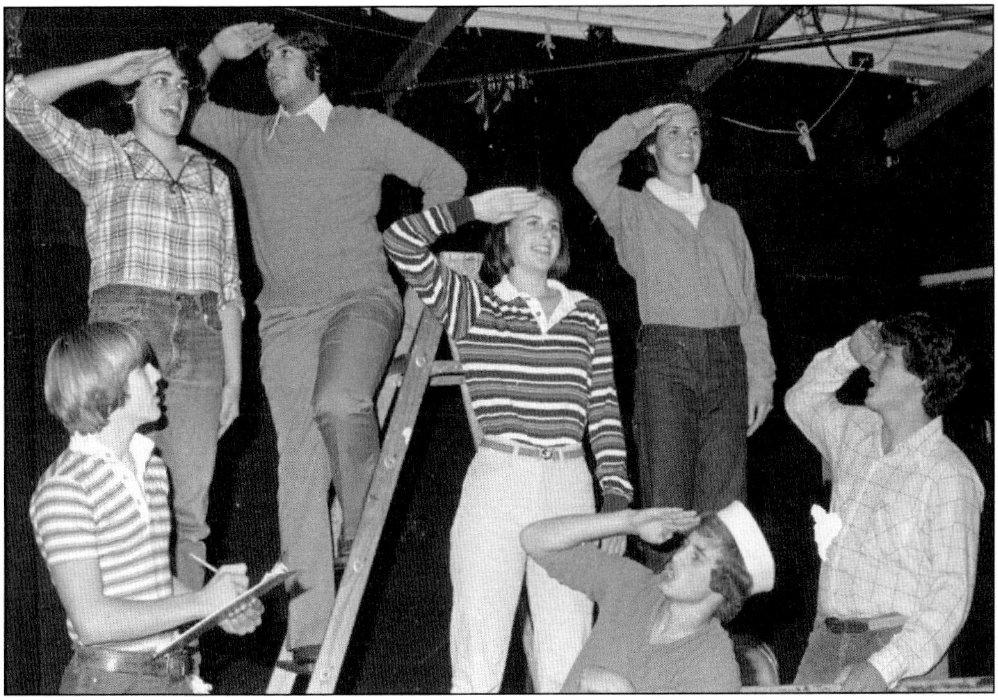

From its very beginning, the Marion Art Center has supported a Young People's Theater in order to train aspiring actors and actresses. This photograph shows a rehearsal of *Dames at Sea* starring Chris Gaucher, Sandy Brown, and others, which was performed in 1977.

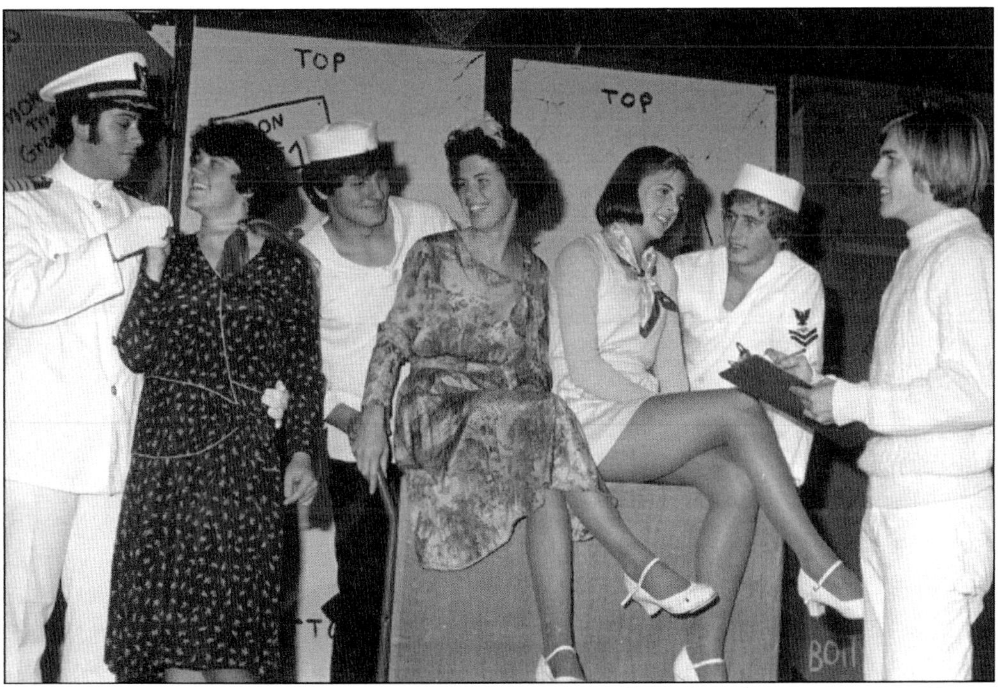

This photograph shows the Young People's Theater actors dressed in their costumes for *Dames at Sea*. It was directed by Nancylee Gaucher.

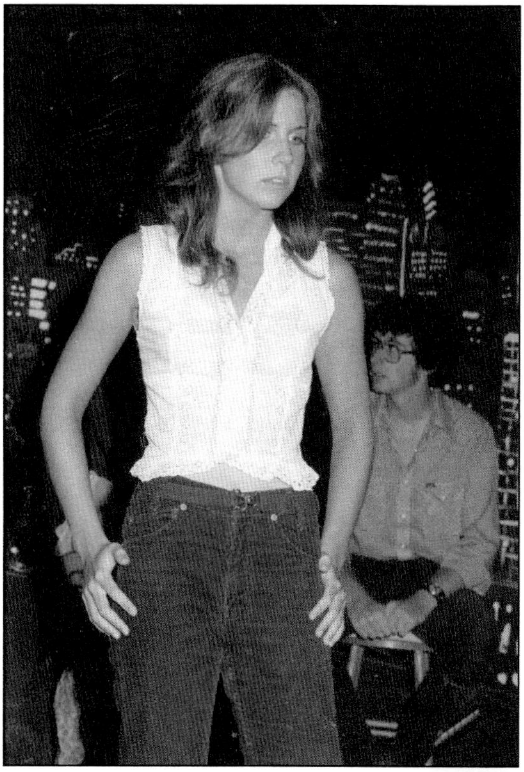

In 1979, the Young People's Theater performed *Feiffer's People*. This photograph shows Perdita Finn at a practice rehearsal. The play was directed by Kate Benton.

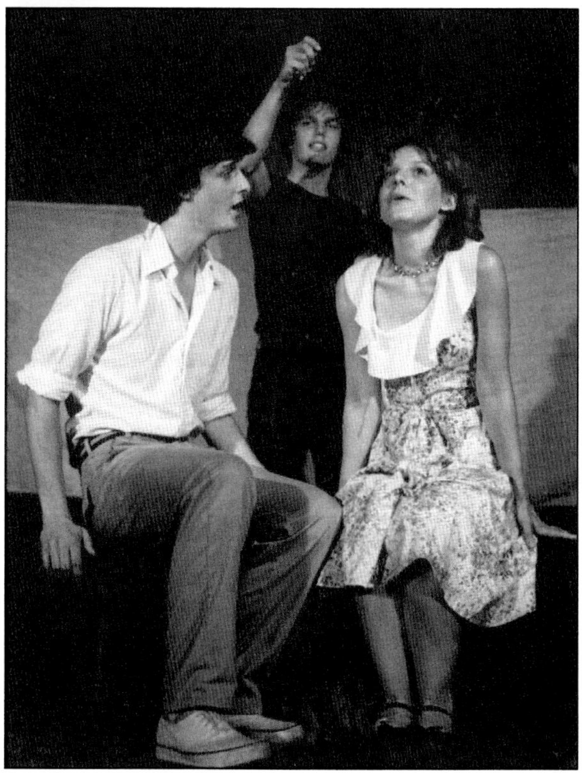

In 1979, the Young People's Theater also performed *The Fantastiks*. Here Andy Winters, the Boy, sings to Sally Jones, the Girl.

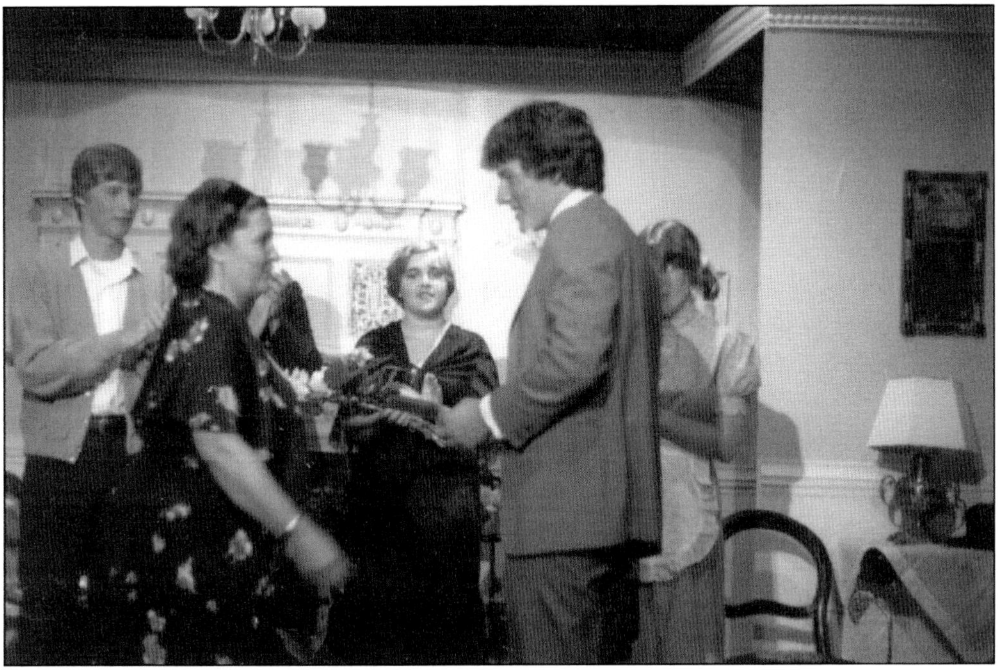

This photograph shows Christopher LeBlanc of the Young People's Theater receiving an award from the director, Nancylee Gaucher. Christopher LeBlanc went on to a professional career in Hollywood and New York City.

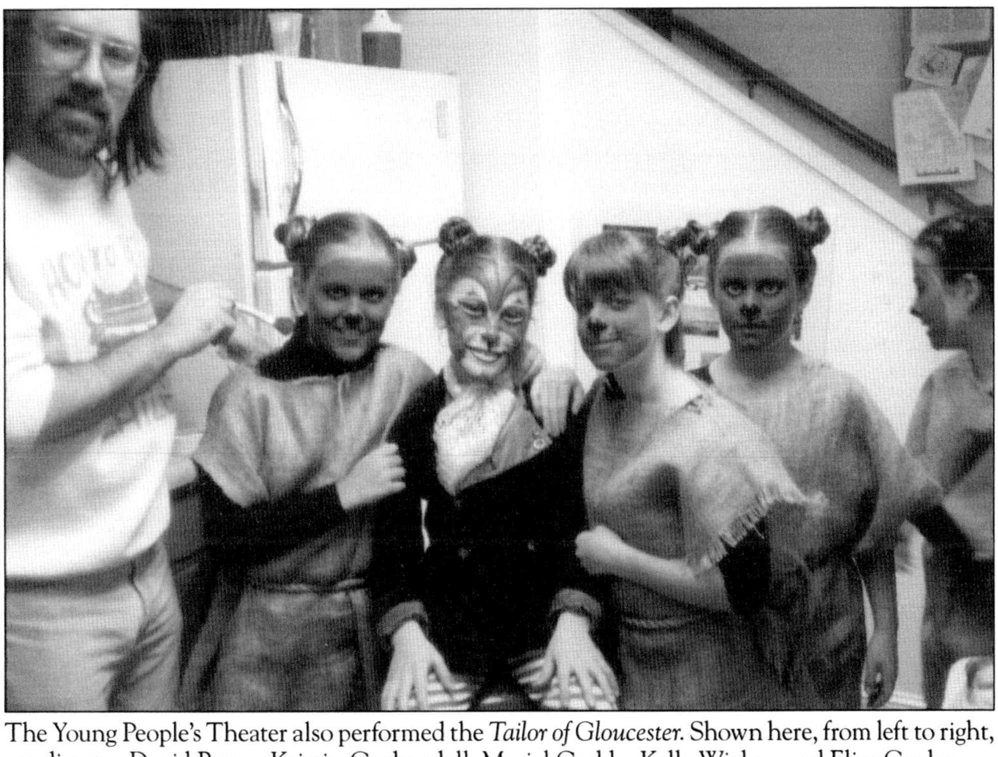

The Young People's Theater also performed the *Tailor of Gloucester*. Shown here, from left to right, are director David Boyce, Kristin Coykendall, Mariel Goddu, Kelly Wicker, and Elise Cooke.

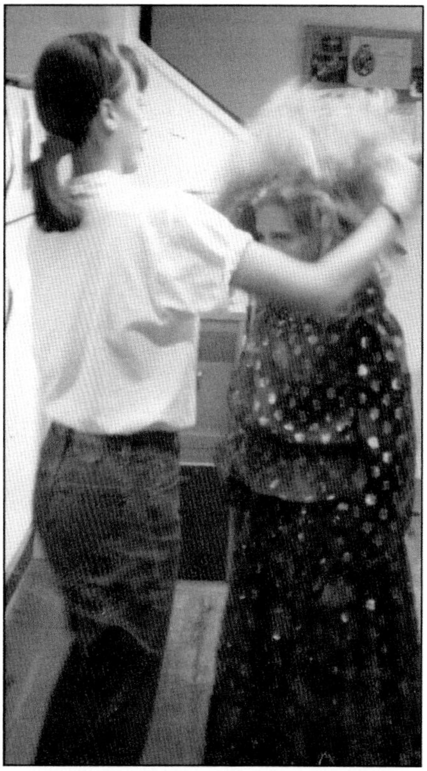

The Young People's Theater also performed *Comedy of Errors*. This photograph shows the director, Jessica Shephardson, assisting Mariel Goddu with her costume.

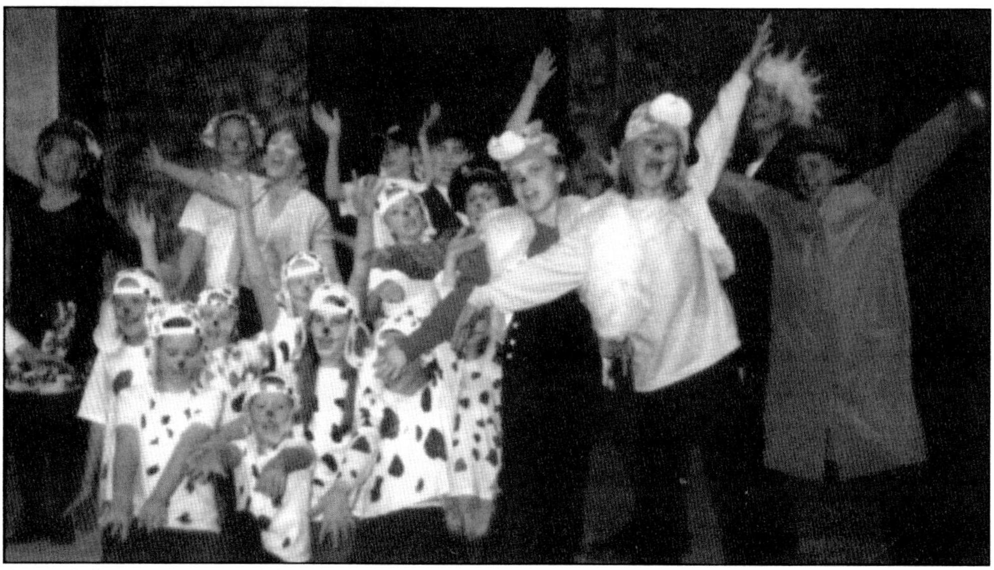

One of the most successful productions of the Young People's Theater was the performance of Disney's *101 Dalmatians* in May 2006. The cast included Emily Kistler, Maddy West, Connor West, Hannah Olson, Gary Taylor, Kim Hrasky, Cassie West, Courtney McLeod, Maura Lonergan, Elizabeth Lonergan, Kyra Lorden, Charlotte Van Voorhis, Olivia Levine, Meghan Hoeg, Will Taylor, Madison Schultz, Chloe Seroussi, Dede Nyhart, Michelle Kelley, Jacob Miller, Cal Heavey, Lucas Parker, Anne Magauran, Ruth Olson, Fiona Lonergan, and Bea Arnfield. Nancy Sparklin was the musical director and the directors were Wendy Bidstrup and Michele Kelley.

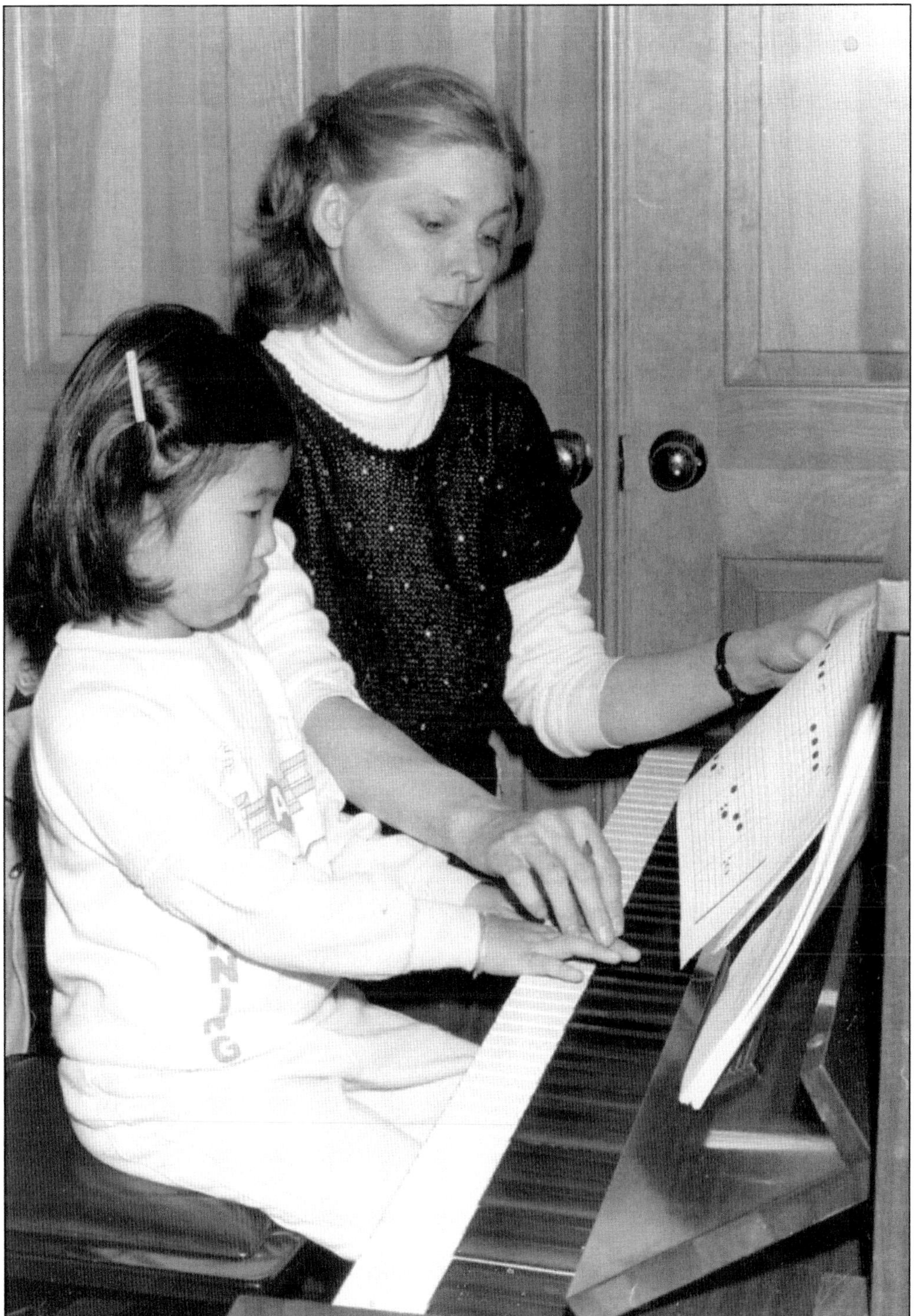

The Marion Art Center also provides piano, singing, guitar, dance, art, and other lessons for children. This photograph shows piano instructor Marilyn Brown giving piano lessons to Beth Grossart.

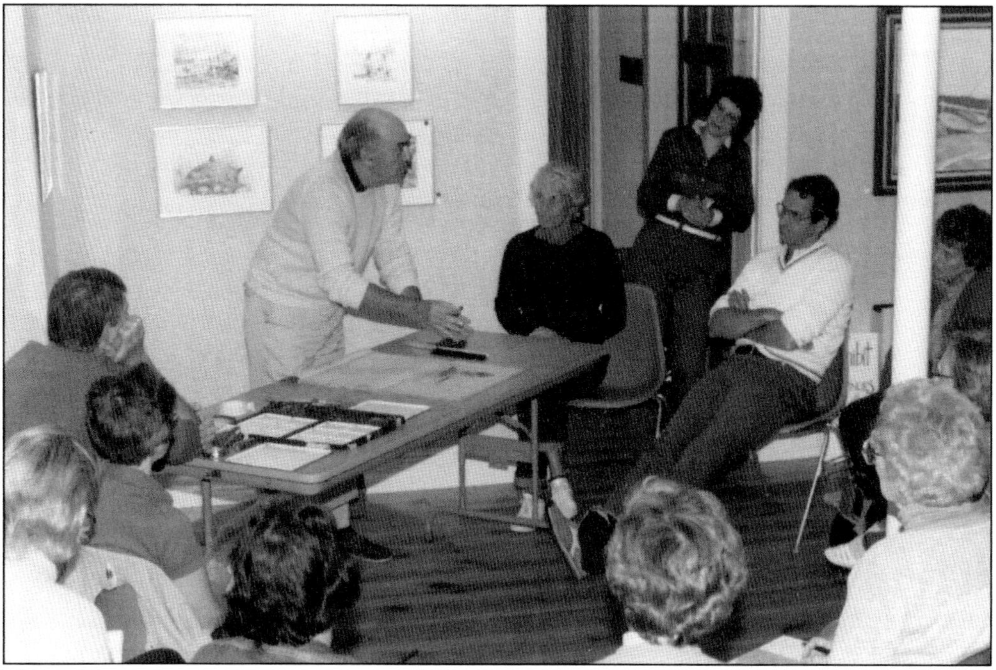

The Marion Art Center sponsors workshops by experienced artists for its members. This photograph shows artist Ray Ellis giving a watercolor workshop in 1985.

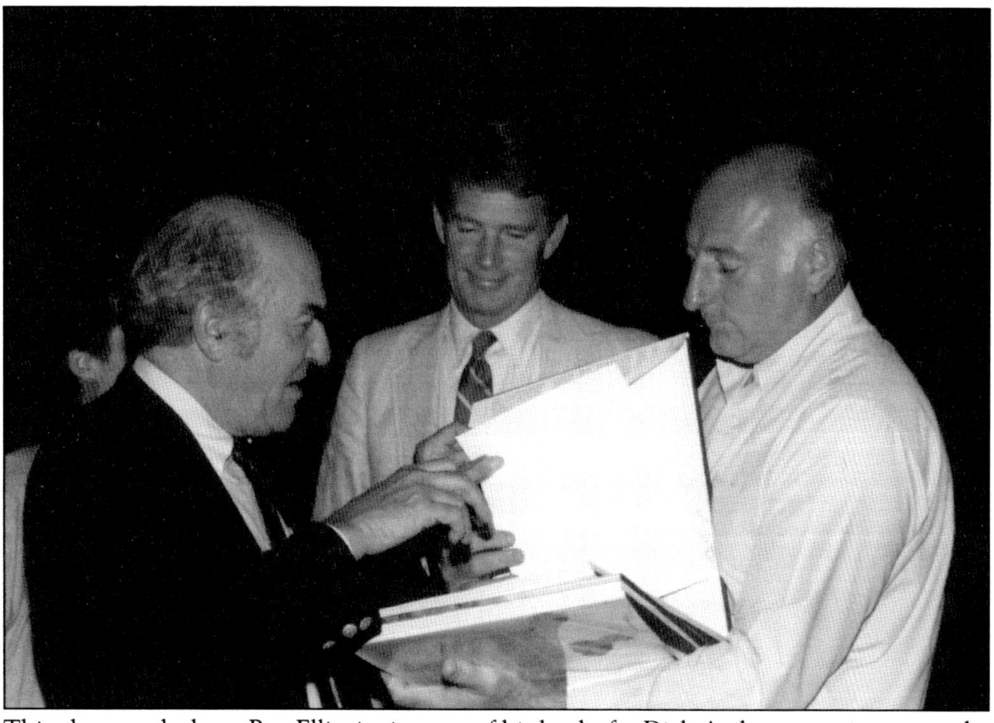

This photograph shows Ray Ellis signing one of his books for Dick Arthur, a participant in the workshop. Standing in the middle is Charlie Parsons, a friend of the artist, who lives in Marion and is a successful watercolor artist who has had many shows at the Marion Art Center.

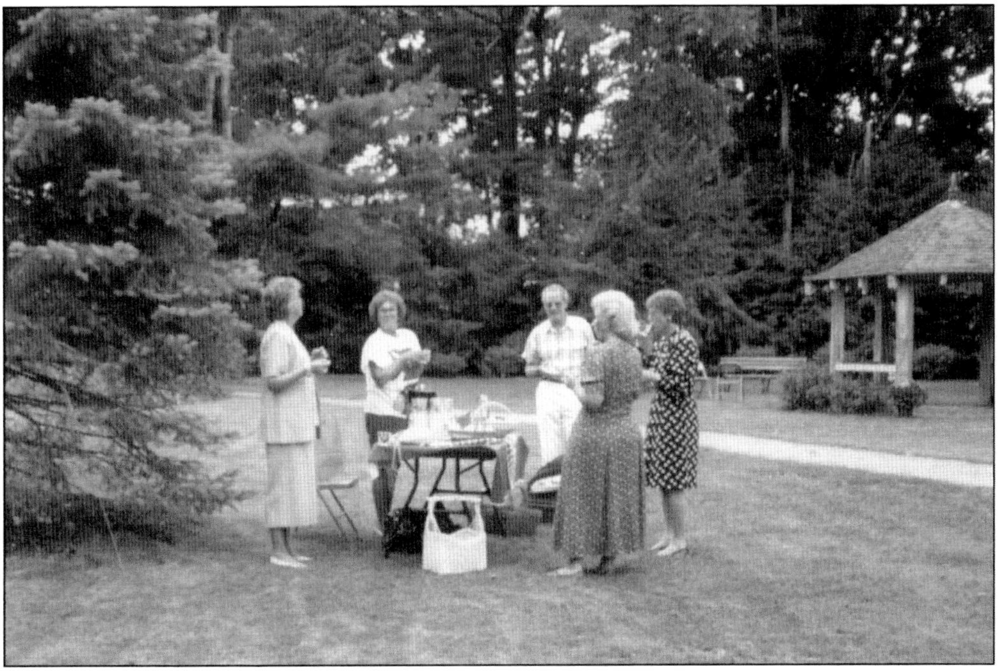

In 1992, the Marion Art Center encouraged people to enjoy catered picnics in the Bicentennial Park across from the art center preceding theater events (when weather permitted). Trudy Kingery, a former president of the Marion Art Center, is shown here greeting attendees.

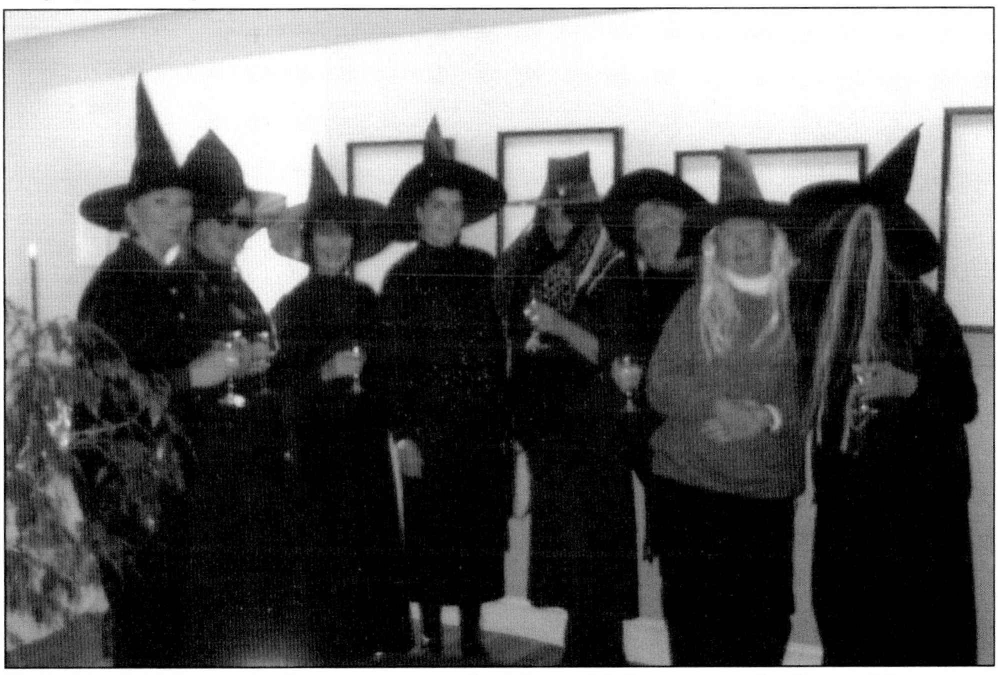

Each year, the Marion Art Center organizes the Marion Halloween parade. Some of the women members of the Marion Art Center dress up as witches and pass out treats to the little ones on Halloween. The event was planned by head witch Barbara Gee who is pictured here (on the left) with her witches in 1995.

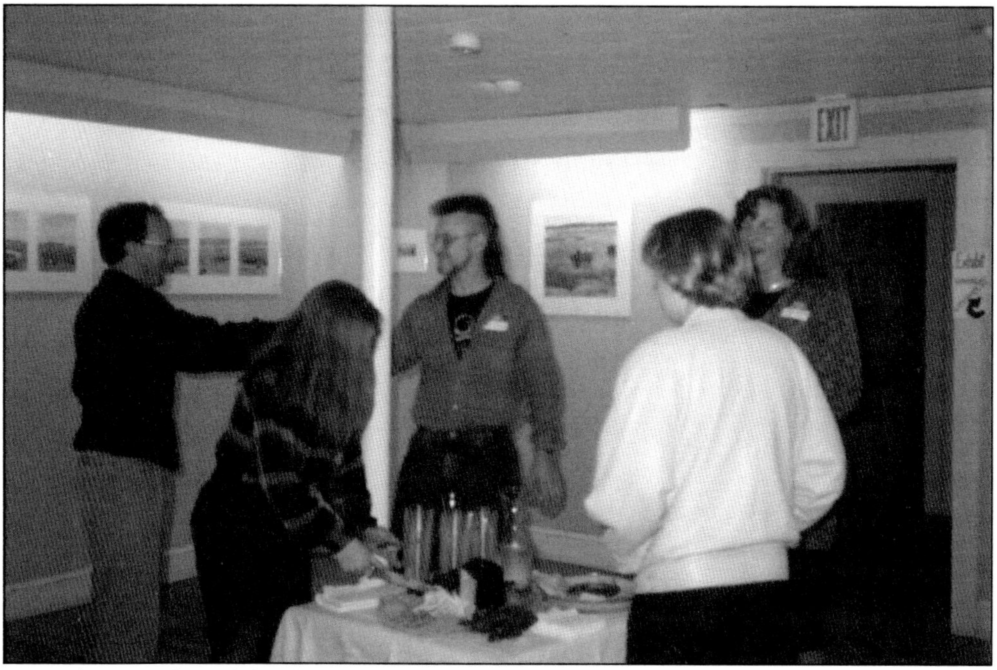

For each artist who exhibits his or her work at the Marion Art Center, the center plans a gallery opening with wine and cheese. This photograph was taken for artist Dave Baggerly's opening. He is shown at center.

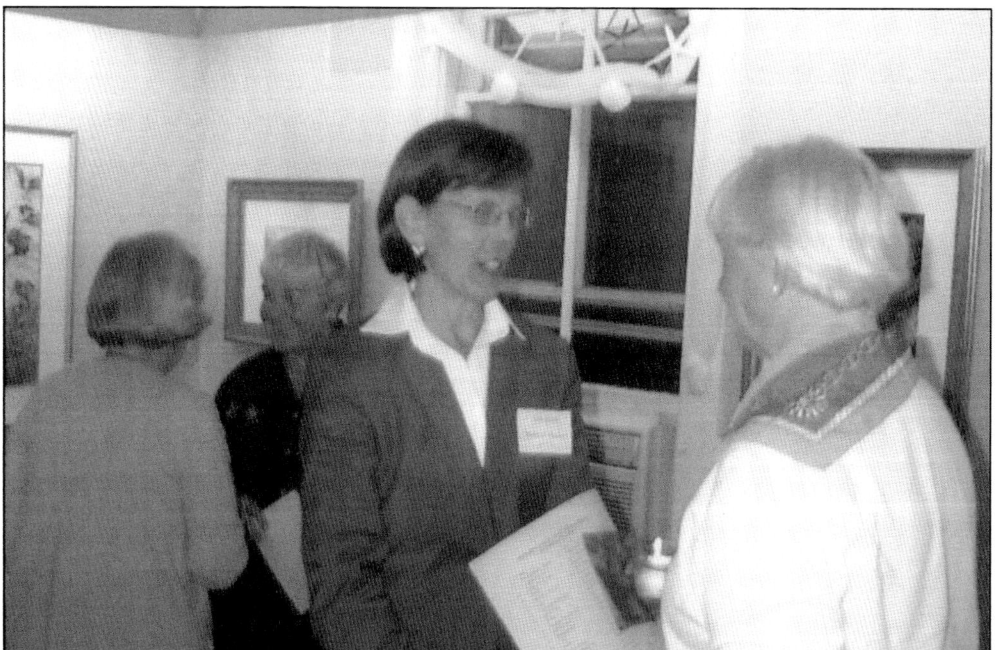

The Marion Art Center also sponsors members' shows where members of the Marion Art Center exhibit their work. Shown here at the opening of a members' show are, from left to right, Jane Ryder, Jeannie Lake, Judy Rosbe, and Nan Johnson.

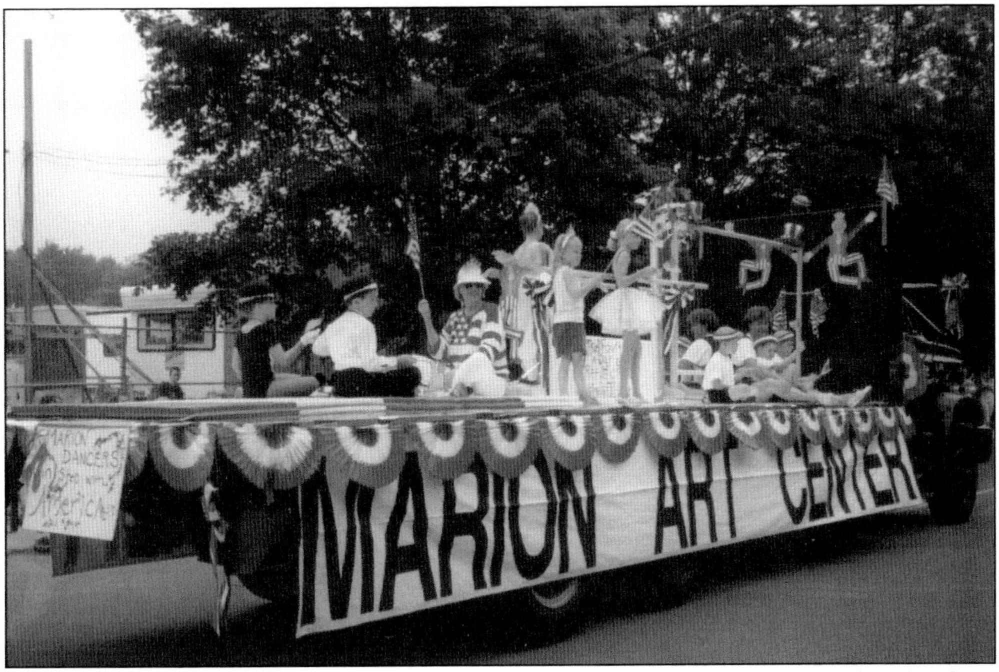

Each year, the Marion Art Center enters a float in Marion's Fourth of July parade. This float, which was organized by Barbara Gee, won first prize. Also shown is Wendy Bidstrup (below, center) playing the guitar.

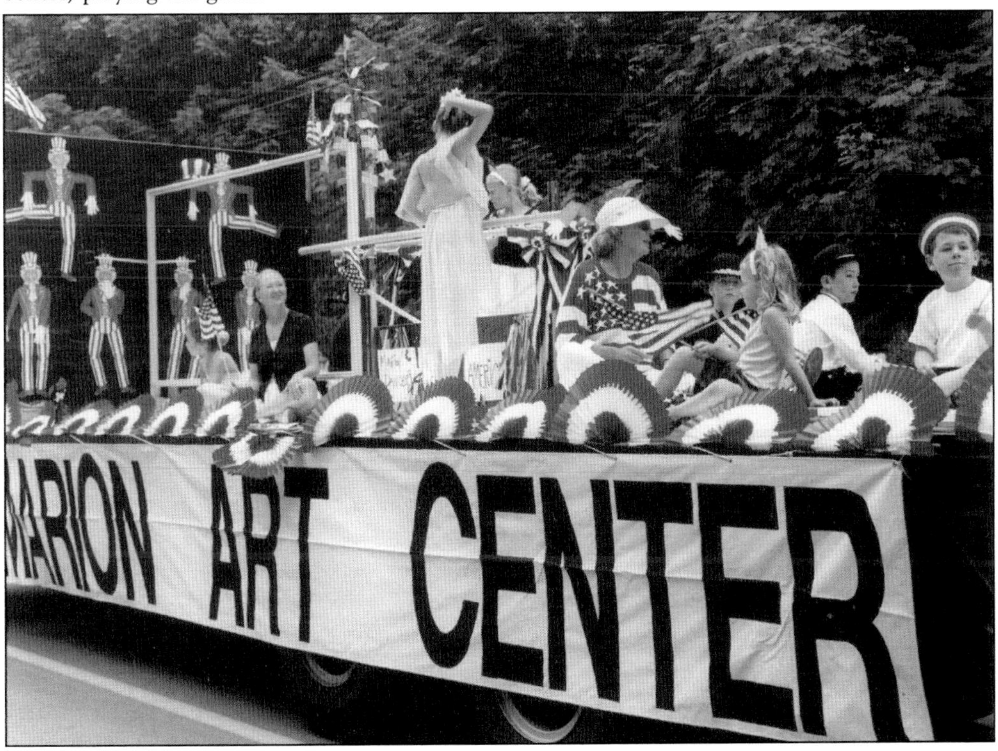

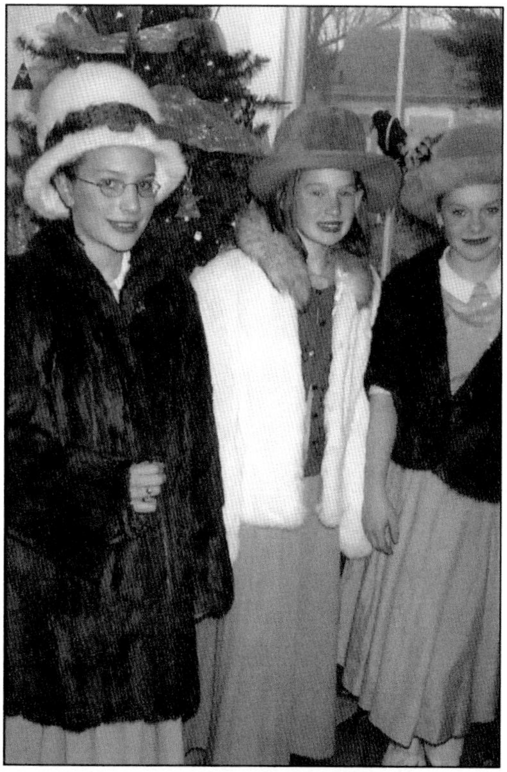

These photographs were taken of *The Best Christmas Pageant Ever*, sponsored by the art center.

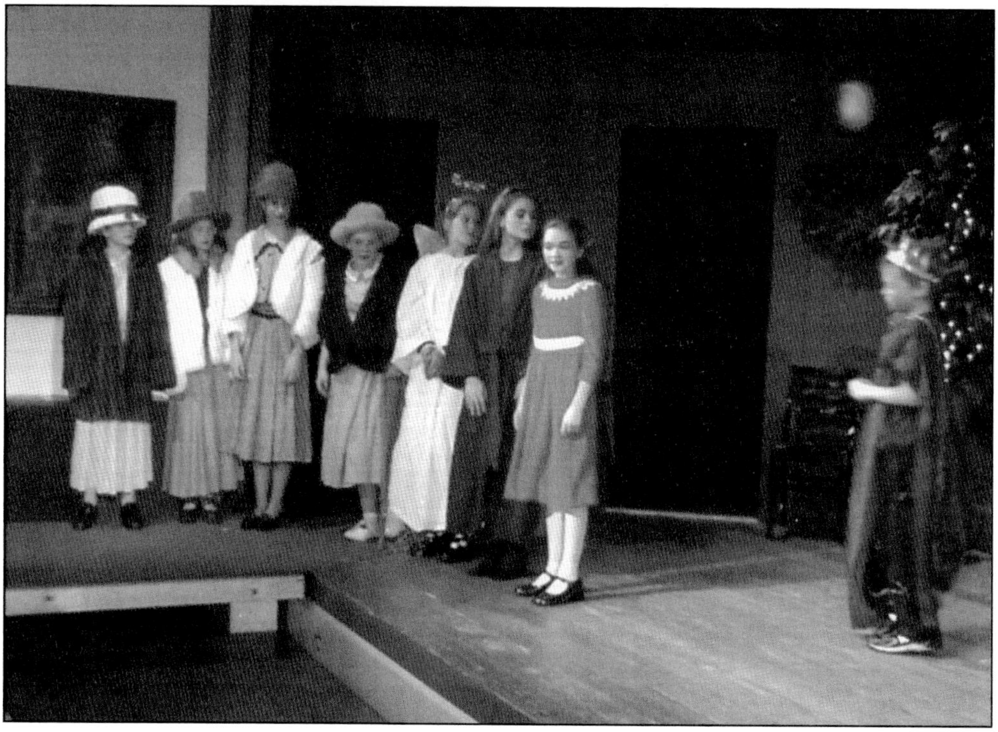

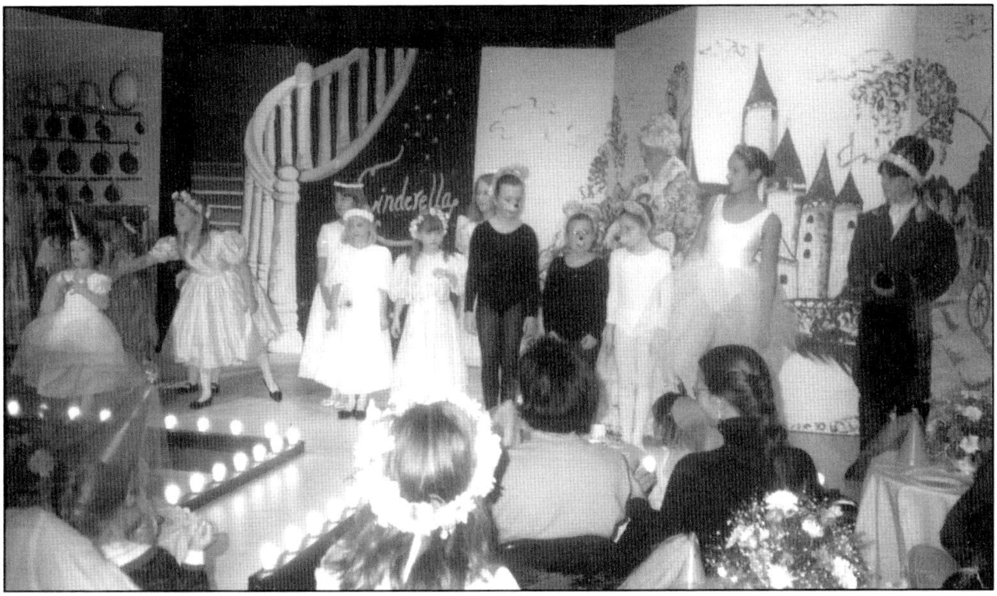

Barbara Gee also directed the Cinderella Tea Party and Fashion Show for the young members of the Marion Art Center. Gee is dressed up as the Fairy Godmother.

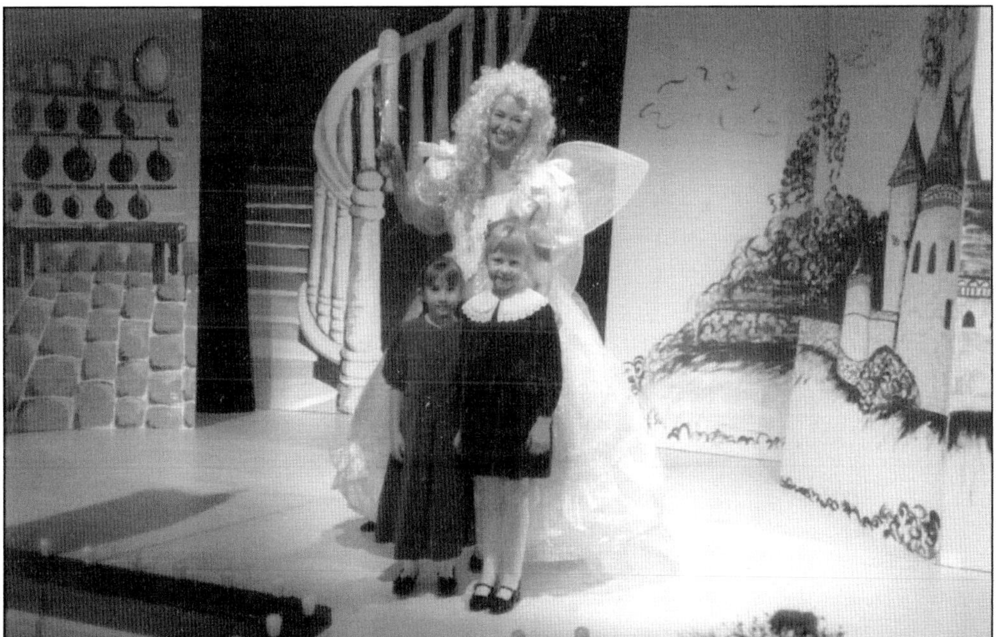

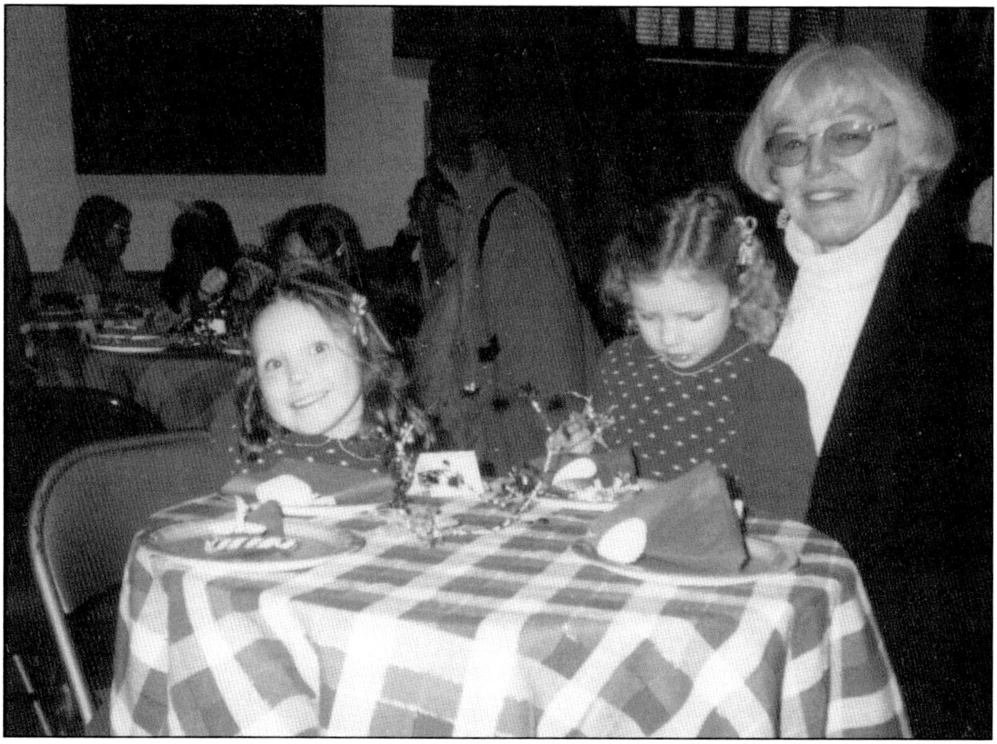

This photograph shows Nancy Mills and her two granddaughters at the Holiday Tea Party sponsored by the Marion Art Center in 1999.

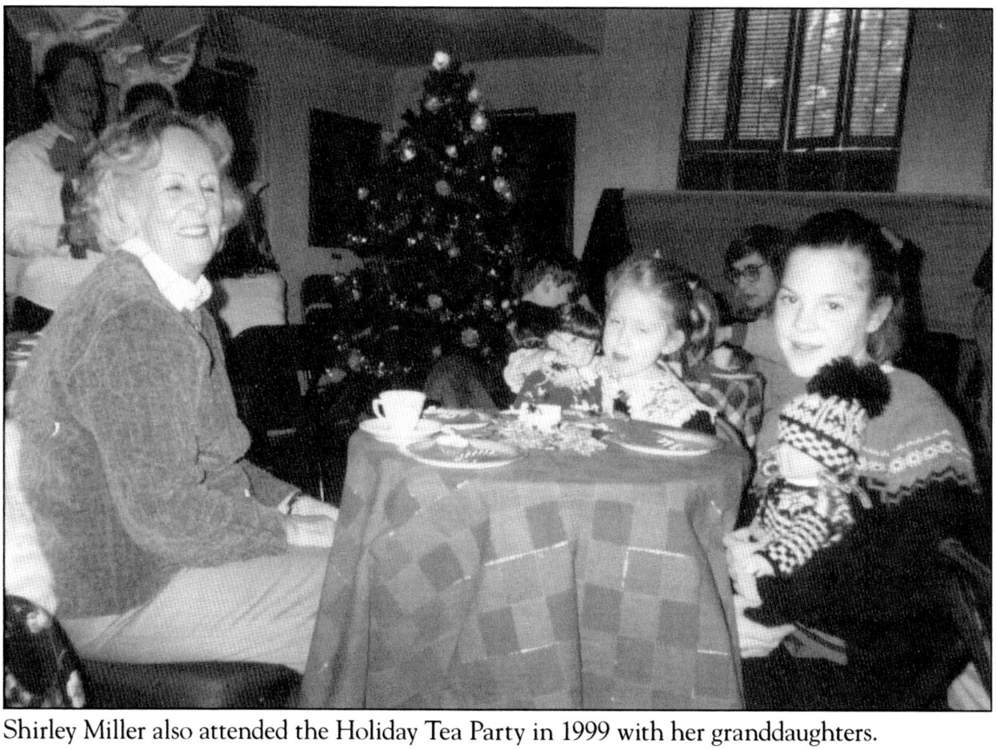

Shirley Miller also attended the Holiday Tea Party in 1999 with her granddaughters.

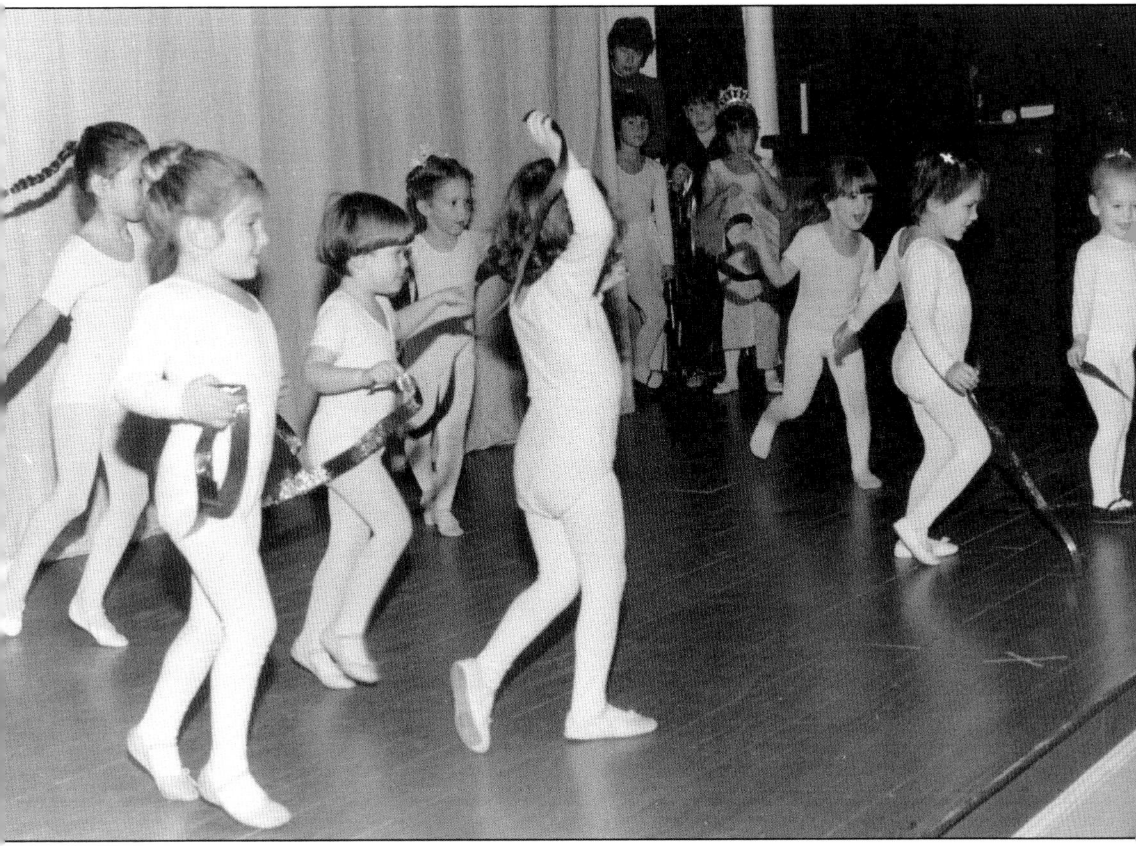

This photograph shows young dancers attending dancing school at the Marion Art Center in 1990. Kay Alden was the instructor.

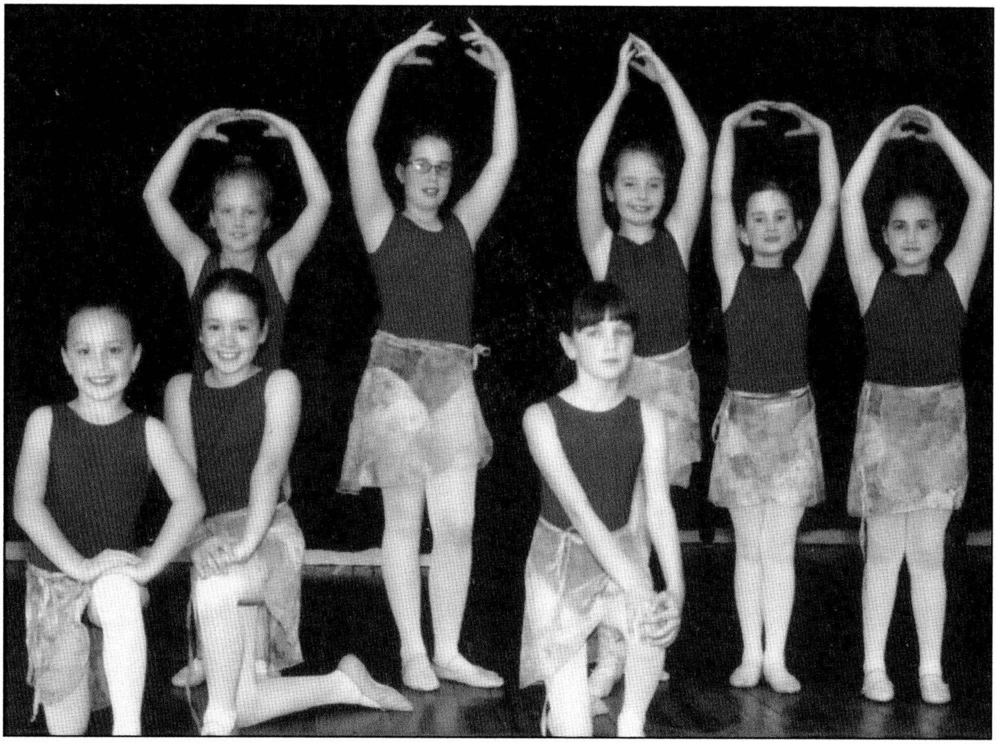

Young dancers in dancing school at the Marion Art Center in 1995 strike a pose.

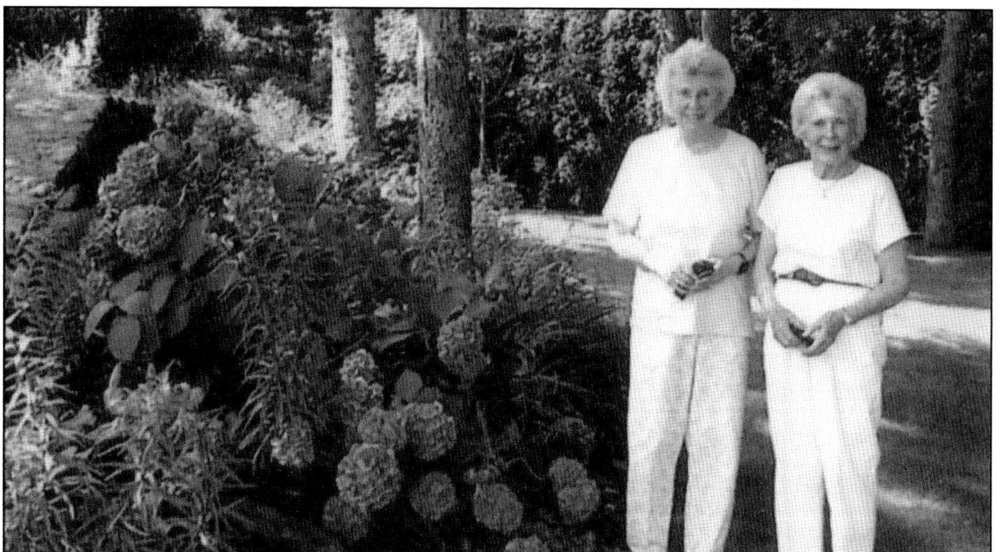

Lib Davis (left) and Betsy Arms have been benefactors of the Marion Art Center for many years. Because of their interest in art, and in particular Cecil Clark Davis, they have not only paid for the restoration and framing of most of the permanent collection of portraits by Davis at the Marion Art Center and the Sippican Historical Society, they have also provided lighting for the portraits and funded research and travel in connection with Marion's most cherished artist. Because of their generosity, the Marion Art Center also has in its possession most of the diaries, letters, and photographs as well as her guest book, address book, and other personal effects of Davis.

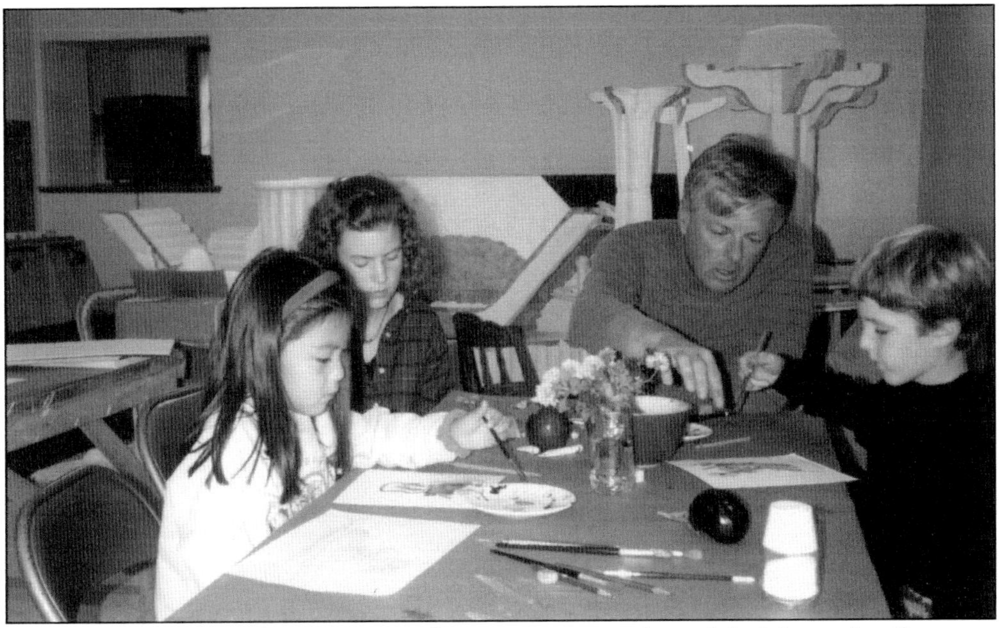

In 1989, artist Andy Anderson gave art classes to young members of the Marion Art Center.

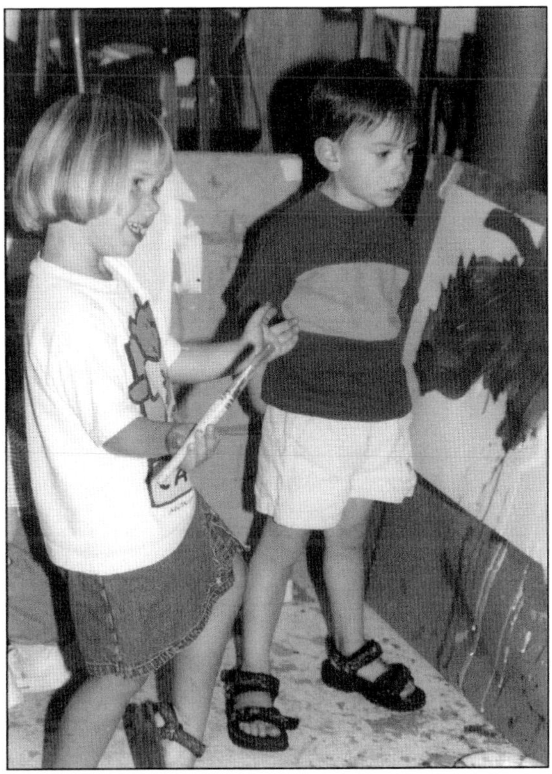

Maddy West and her cousin Connor West are shown in a children's painting class in 2001.

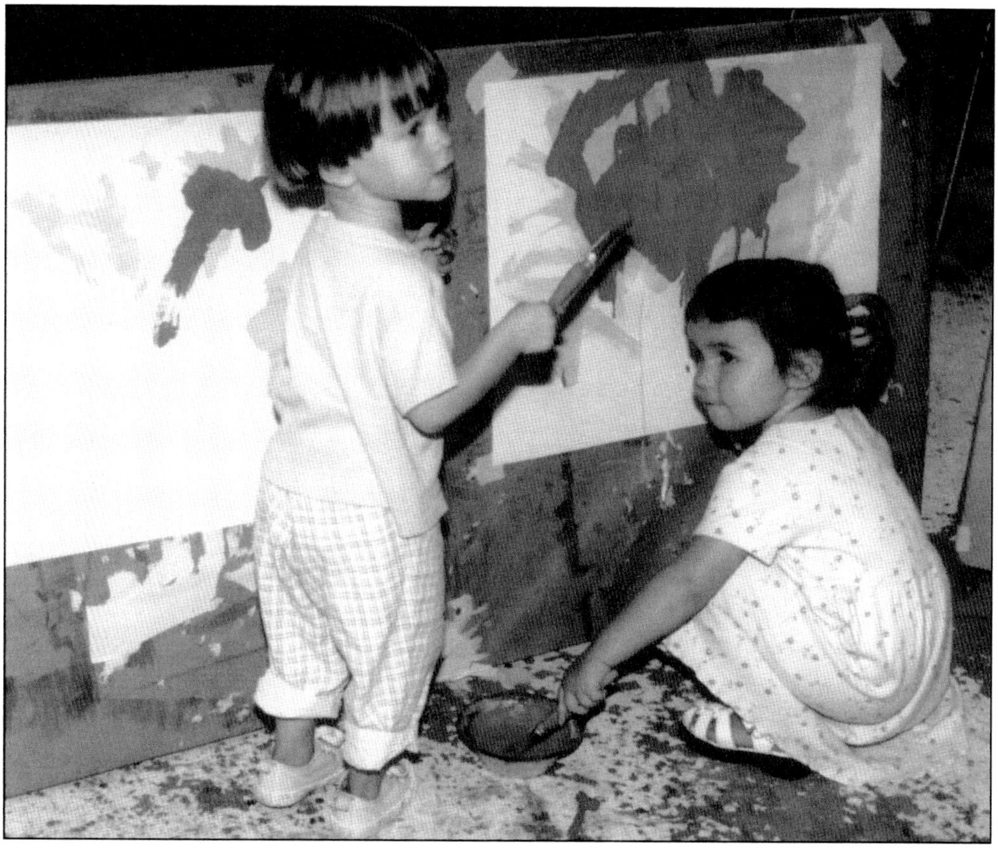

These young artists attended the Marion Art Center Art Camp.

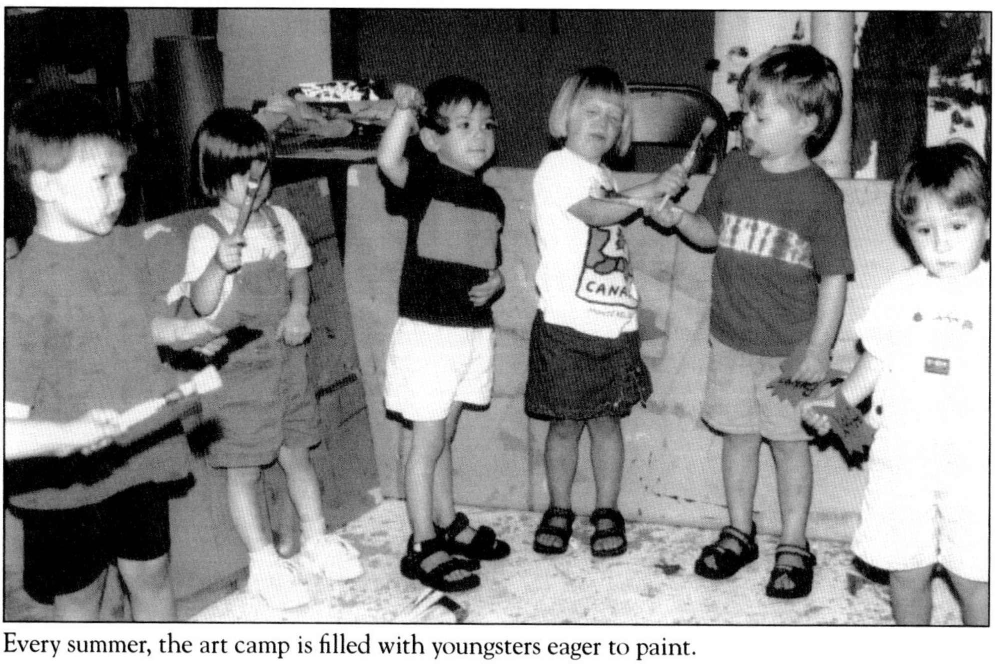

Every summer, the art camp is filled with youngsters eager to paint.

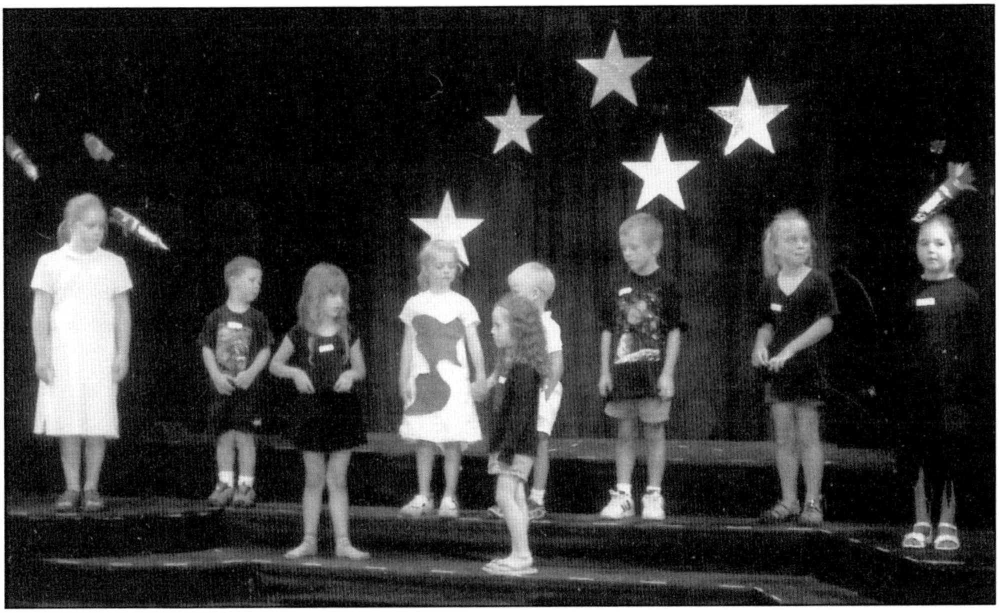

Art camp participants also participate in theater productions.

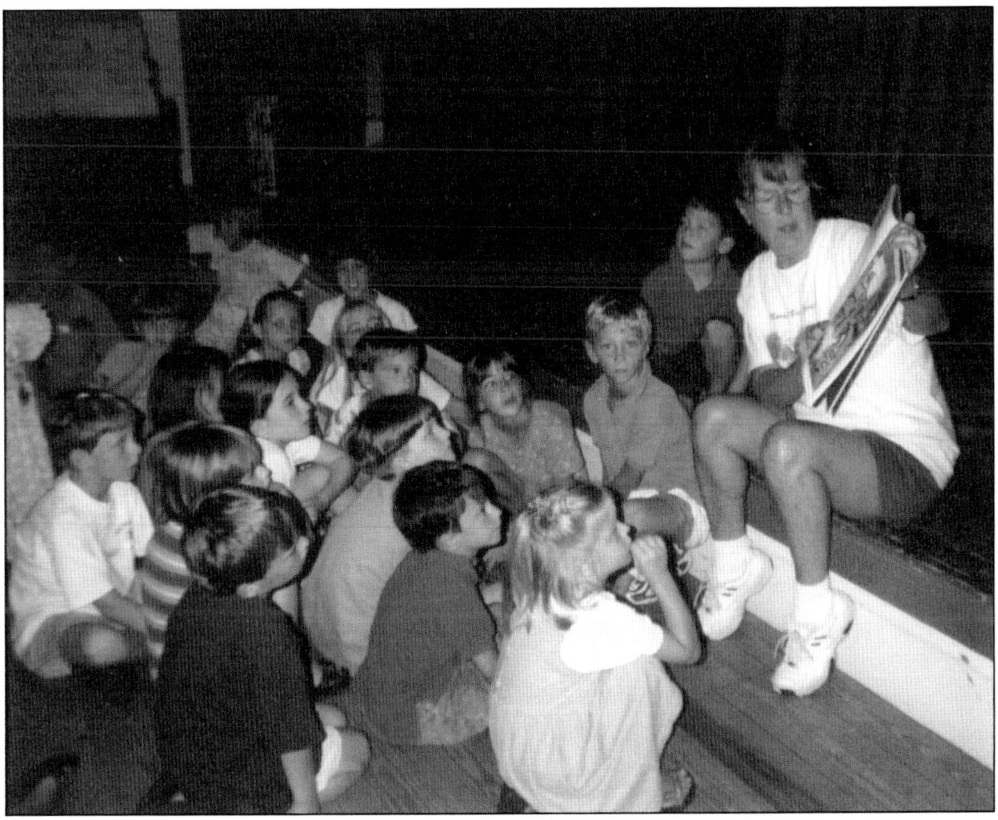

Wendy Bidstrup reads a story to art camp participants.

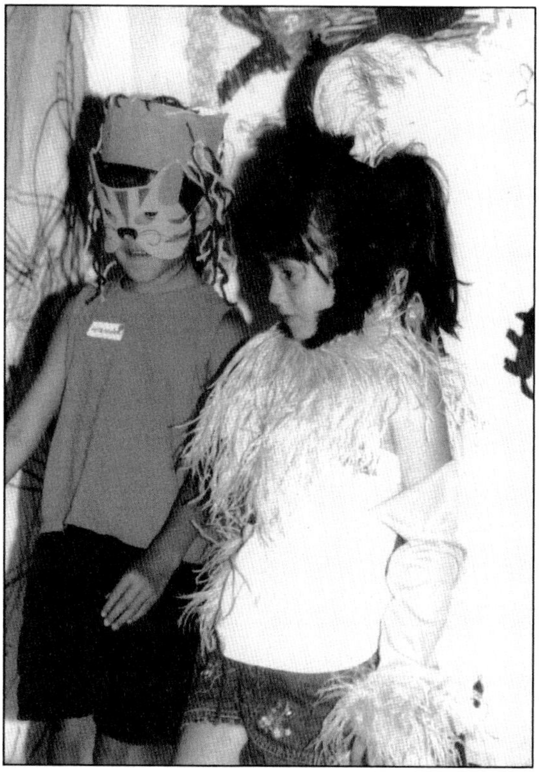

These photographs show a play being put on at art camp

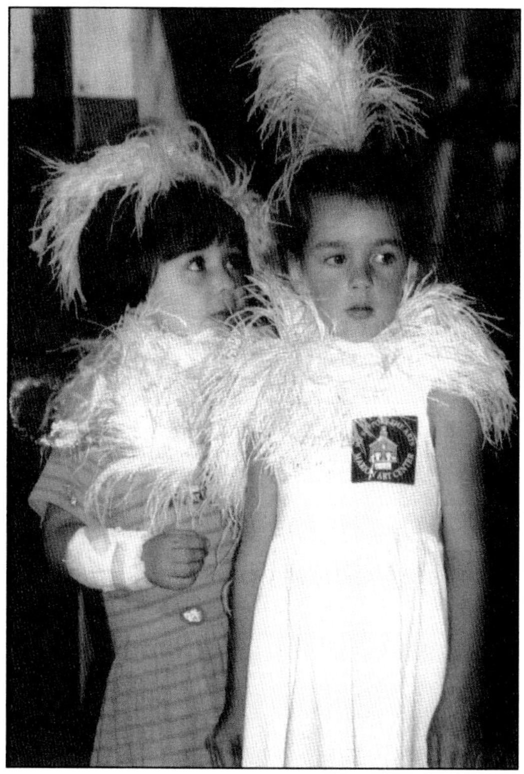

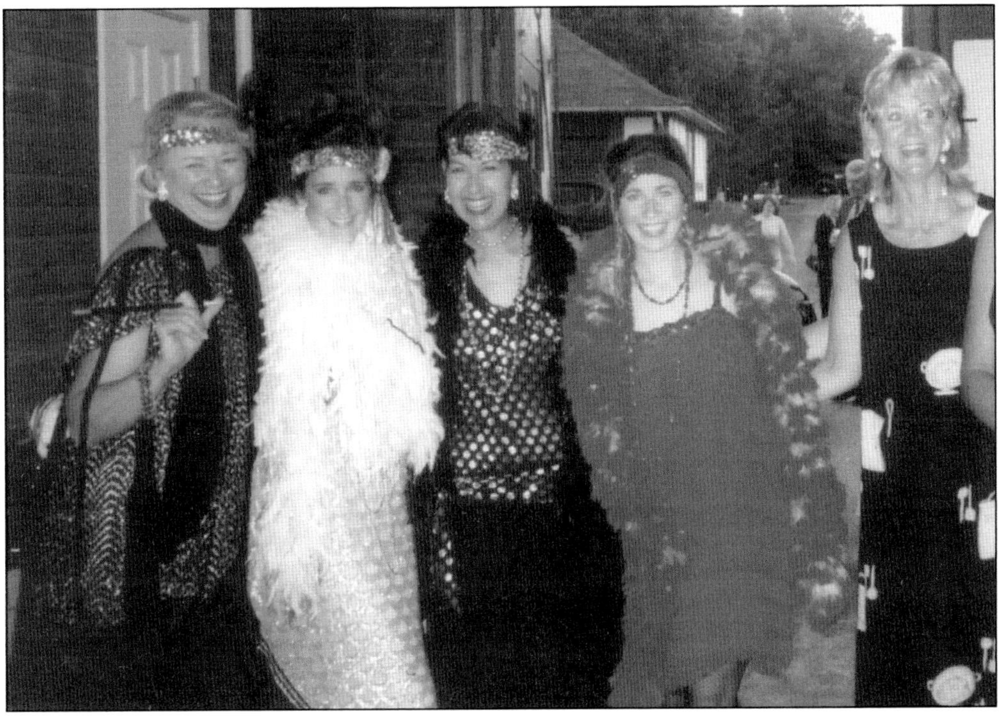

Each year, the Marion Art Center sponsors a summer fund-raiser. This photograph shows members enjoying the Bash at the Boathouse party in 1997 organized by Barbara Gee on the left.

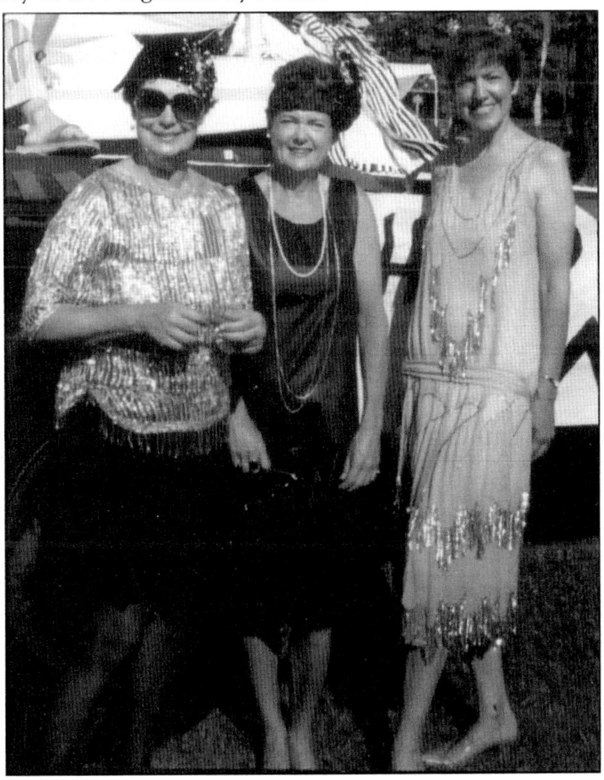

Other members enjoying the Bash at the Boathouse are, from left to right, Trudy Kingery, Bonnie Sorterup, and Joan De Rugeris.

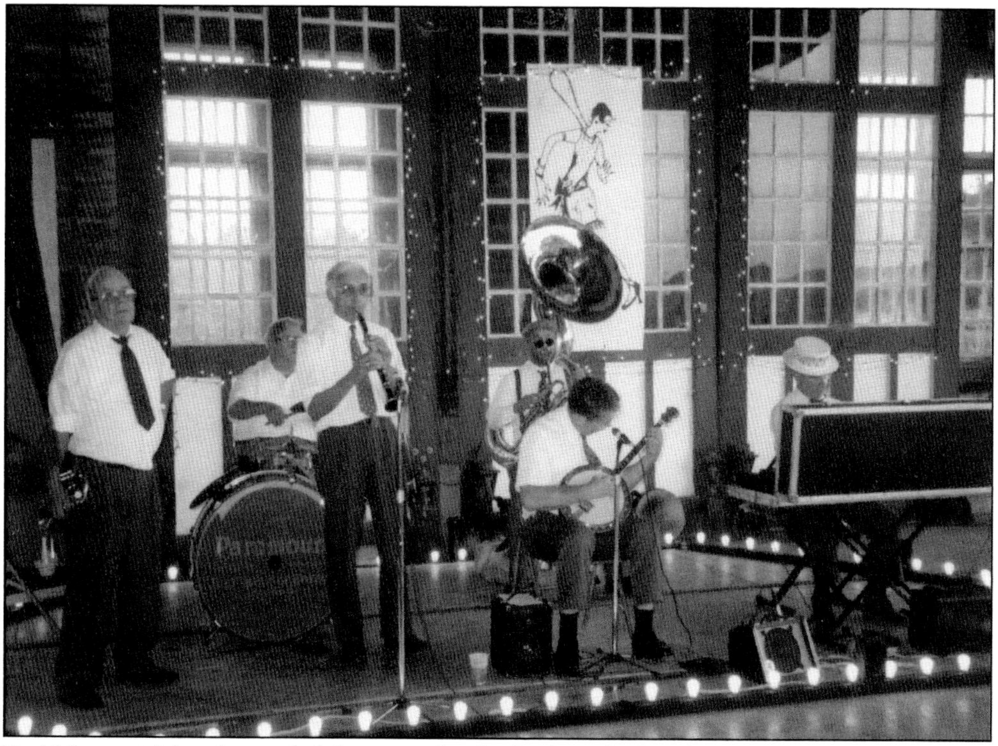

Paul Meymaris's band provided the music for the Bash at the Boathouse.

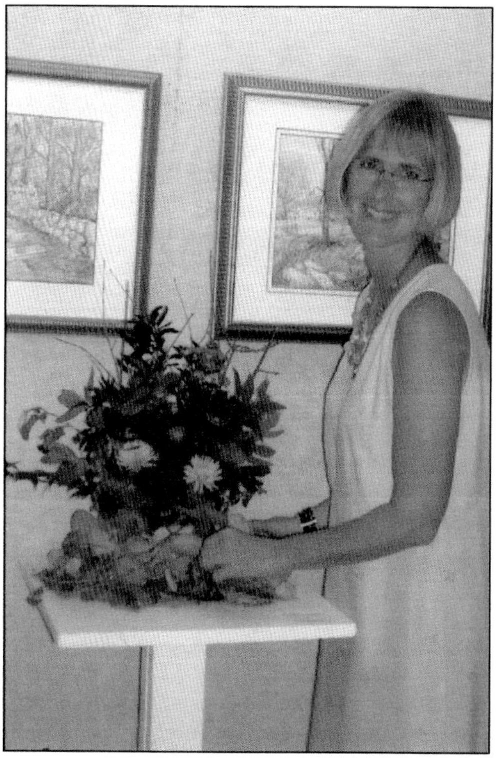

Lissa Magauren arranges flowers at the Art in Bloom exhibit at the Marion Art Center in 2000.

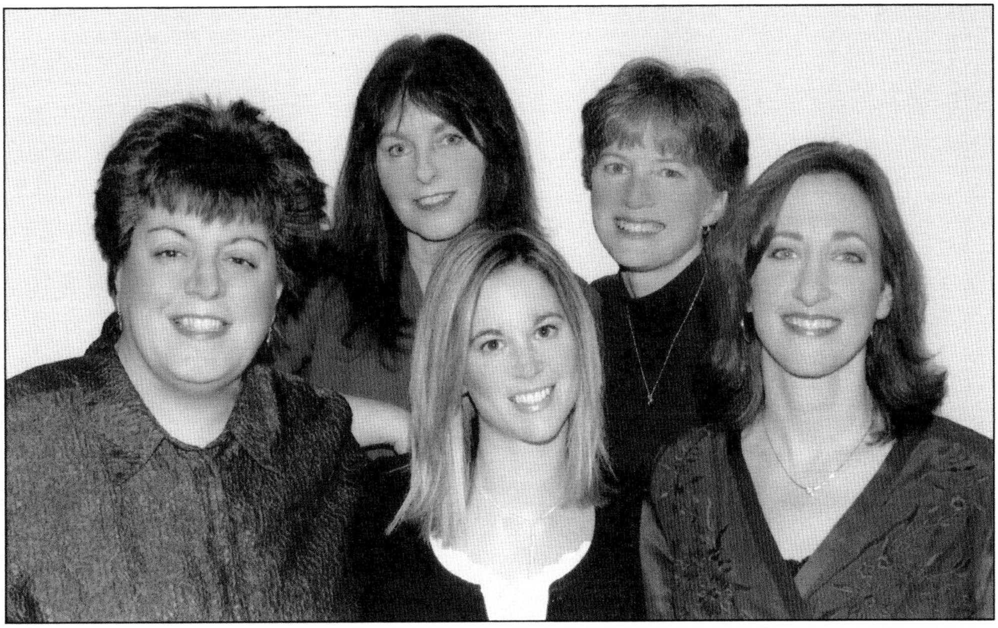

The popular That Chick Band entertains members and their guests at the Marion Art Center to standing-room-only crowds. From left to right, the members of the band are (first row) Sheila Furtado, Shelly D'Alia, and Nancy Sparklin; (second row) Beverly Hilliard and Karen Della Cioppa.

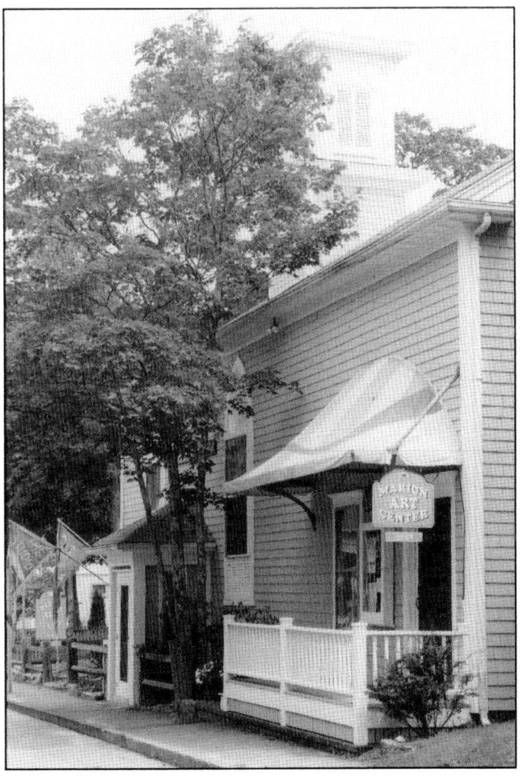

In 2007, the Marion Art Center celebrates its 50th anniversary. Since it began in August 1957, it has served the Marion community well.